MW01639631

The Factory of Dreams

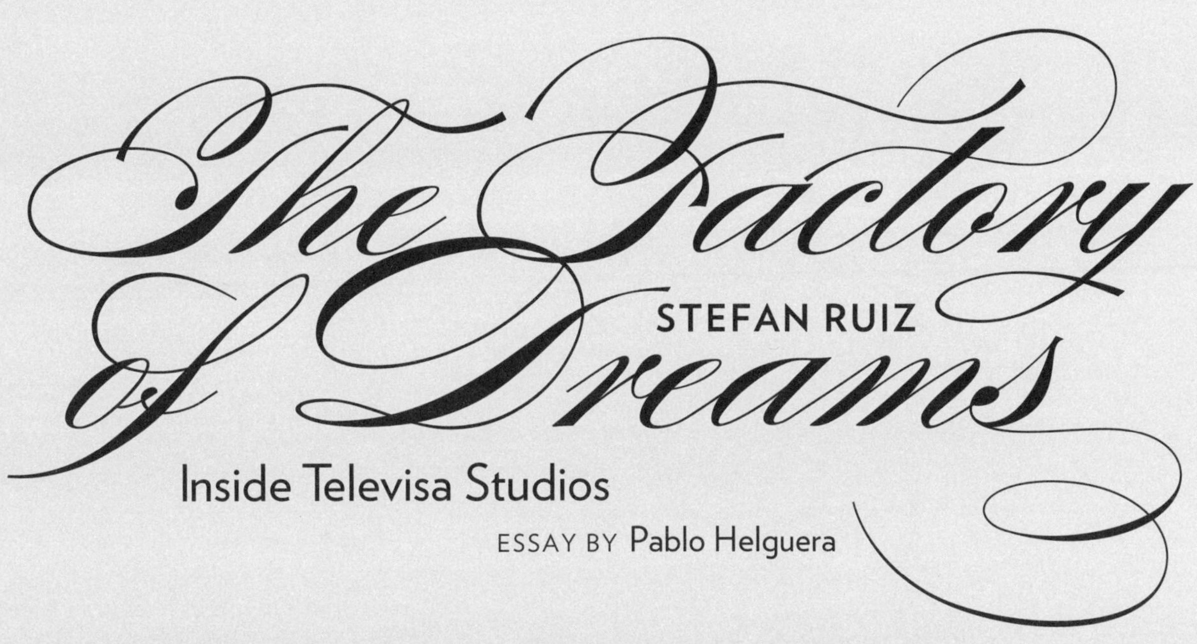

The Factory of Dreams

STEFAN RUIZ

Inside Televisa Studios

ESSAY BY Pablo Helguera

aperture

... the dream (author of representations),
in its theater, lifted on the wind,
and clothed in shadows of fair stuff.
—Luis de Góngora, "Poema a un Sueño"

THE FACTORY OF DREAMS
The Mexican Telenovela as Portrayed by Stefan Ruiz

Pablo Helguera

An attractive young man is reclining shirtless on the bed. Like a half-naked *majo*, he gazes at us seductively. The room might be in any upper-middle-class apartment, perhaps—judging from the nighttime skyline seen through the window—in Polanco, one of the commercial epicenters of Mexico City.

But there is something that doesn't accord with the apparent clarity of the scene: the Hitchcockian lighting, the extreme perfection of the furnishing and walls. The young man himself betrays a certain vulnerability: there is something in his gaze that suggests, more than seductive appeal, a yearning for approval. All this, of course, if we have not yet turned our attention to the darkened upper part of the image: an open ceiling of cables, screens, and theater lights. As in *The Truman Show*, a rift opens up to show us that the place where we are is a stage set, and that the real world is outside.

The subject of this particular photograph is a student from the CEA, or Centro de Educación Artística, the acting school of the Mexican television network Televisa, the largest Spanish-language broadcaster in the world, mainly because of its worldwide success at developing soap operas, or *telenovelas*, as an escapist product.

Founded in the 1950s, the Televisa emporium underwent a major global expansion in the 1990s, thanks in part to the international demand for its telenovelas, which began with the export of *Los Ricos También Lloran* (The Rich Also Cry, 1979) to the former Soviet Union. The melodramatic series provoked unprecedented fervor all over the country. It is estimated that, on average, some 200 million people, or 70 percent of the entire population of the former Soviet Union, regularly tuned in to the show, breaking the world ratings record for any television series.[1]

The global explosion of the telenovela in 1992 coincided with the international growth of Televisa, whose shares began to be traded on the Mexico City stock exchange in 1991, and the New York exchange in 1992. Televisa later acquired television channels in other parts of Latin America, and a satellite network that boosted the value of the company to U.S. $1.67 billion in 1993.[2] As professor John Sinclair has written: "Televisa was one of the first media corporations in the world to see the advantages of satellites for the distribution of programs to farflung and dispersed audiences, which were outside its borders, but which shared linguistic and cultural similarities with the programming's nation of origin."[3] The great discovery of television executives following the success of *The Rich Also Cry* (*Bogaty Tozhe Plachut*, in Russian) was that social-class dramas aimed at the Mexican lower middle-class would automatically strike a chord with hundreds of millions of people in countries with similar socioeconomic configurations of

1. Andrew Kopkind, "From Russia with Love and Squalor," *The Nation* (January 18, 1992), quoted in Kate Baldwin, "Montezuma's Revenge: Reading *Los Ricos También Lloran* in Russia," in *To Be Continued . . . Soap Operas around the World*, ed. Robert C. Allen (New York: Routledge, 1995), p. 286.
2. Data obtained from Televisa.com and Fundinguniverse.com.
3. John Sinclair, *Latin American Television: A Global View* (Oxford: Oxford University Press, 1999), p. 40.

racial and/or social inequality; so that a product originally conceived for one country could spread all around the world.

The central role of the telenovela in a powerful corporation's quest to achieve global hegemony —in the form of a genuine factory of dreams, as revealed by the images in this book—calls for a brief account of the socioeconomic phenomenon of this television genre.

The Latin American telenovela has its roots in the Cuban radio dramas of the 1940s. Writers such as Félix B. Caignet developed a kind of serial melodrama based on the models of late-nineteenth-century Spanish and Latin American realist, naturalist, and *costumbrista* novels, with complicated plots, dozens of characters, and themes of social class. The story of one of Caignet's melodramas, *El Derecho de Nacer* (The Right to Be Born), became a prototype of the telenovela. Retold dozens of times over the decades, the story combines social and racial drama with a love story in a way that would come to define the Mexican telenovela.

The telenovela is historically distinct from the American soap opera, owing partly to its central place in programming (the daytime audience for the waning "soap" is relatively marginal, whereas the telenovela occupies prime time and is seen by millions of viewers), but above all to its format: while a soap opera tends to go on indefinitely, its Latin American counterpart has a closed format, which eventually arrives at a dénouement, even if it takes one hundred or two hundred episodes. The dénouement is significant because of the expectations it awakens in the television audience. The telenovela promises a conclusion, which consists almost inevitably of the triumph of love over apparently insurmountable obstacles. The virtual certainty of this positive outcome generates a sense of complicity and identification in the viewer, who seeks the gratification of a happy ending after months of witnessing the various emotional ups and downs of the actors and the plot.

Another peculiarity of the Latin American televised melodrama, and the artificial setting it constructs, is the indirect relationship it establishes with reality: the outside world is there, but only in an abstract way, simplified by the forces of good and evil, which only operate within the confines of the fairy tale. As Tomás López-Pumarejo has shrewdly observed, one of the characteristics of the telenovela is that it deals "more with consequences than with actions, and more with the family circle than with the public world. As in the naturalist drama of Ibsen and Chekhov, the characters experience the outside world in the domestic sphere."[4]

4. Tomás López-Pumarejo, "Soap Opera, Globalization, and National Culture" in *Assaph Studies in Cinema and Television*. (Tel Aviv: Tel Aviv University, 2001), p. 143.

But as in Plato's cave, the shadows projected are instinctively recognized by the viewer: that is, the fiction presented by the telenovela alludes to all kinds of desires, fantasies, and anxieties of an entire social class, selling dreams of self-help and offering a collective catharsis for those class issues never confronted in real life. This is how telenovelas have had concrete social effects around the world. The transmission of *Simplemente María* (Simply Maria), originally broadcast in Argentina in 1967, the story of a poor campesino woman who takes night classes in sewing in order to triumph in the big city as a fashion designer, boosted both enrollments at night schools and the sales of sewing machines. The Venezuelan production *Cristal* (1985), in which one of the characters has breast cancer, led to a considerable increase in breast exams in Spain and Venezuela. The successful Colombian telenovela, *Yo Soy Betty la Fea* (I Am Ugly Betty, 1999–2000), which told the story of a secretary working in the fashion business, provoked nationwide debates on the economic state of the country, in which even the minister of finance and the attorney general took part.

This subtle ability of telenovelas to influence social trends, and to maintain the interest of viewers over long periods of time, has been developed and refined by writers and producers. Over the years, certain infallible formulas have been achieved. Although Televisa briefly tried out a sort of "edutainment" telenovela (promoted by the writer and producer Miguel Sabido in the

1980s), such experiments did not prosper. In the end, a telenovela is a commercial product and the object of a telecommunications company is to use entertainment as a source of revenue. More altruistic aims, therefore, tend never to free themselves of the idea, whether innocent or perverse, that television in a country like Mexico can do no more than serve as opium for the masses. As Emilio Azcárraga Milmo himself (then president of Televisa) famously pointed out in an interview in 1993: "We are in the entertainment business, the information business, and we can educate, but fundamentally entertain . . . Mexico is a country with a very screwed-up poorer class that is not going to stop being screwed up. It is an obligation of television to bring entertainment to these people and to take them out of their sad reality and difficult future."[5]

Few would call it a coincidence that the empire of the telenovela has emerged from a country like Mexico, whose deep social inequalities, combined with the alliance between television and a single political party, offered the ideal conditions in which to fill the spiritual void of a nation with stories of triumph, social ascent, and the attainment of impossible love. In any case, it is through this philosophy of entertainment that the dream factory of the telenovela generates, intentionally at times, at times unwittingly, the circumstances in which only the dichotomy of escapism and solitude can be conceived, a climate described by Carlos Monsiváis as the "dictatorship of taste": "a new social identity sustained by the values of consumption," in which "censorship, contempt for the audience, and artistic degradation get their own way: the people are transformed into a market, just as in other countries."[6]

5. Interview with Emilio Azcárraga Milmo, *Proceso* (February 15, 1993).

6. Carlos Monsiváis, "Lo entretenido y lo aburrido: La televisión y las tablas de la ley," in *Aires de Familia: Cultura y sociedad en América Latina* (Mexico City: Anagrama, 2000), pp. 211–45.

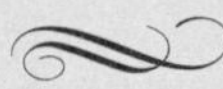

The telenovela industry does not consist only of the presentation of stories on the screen, or of actors whose workday is over when each episode is completed. The "private" lives of the stars, and the gossip that circulates around them, constitute a second narrative that their fans follow faithfully in magazines, generally managed by the same company that produces the telenovelas and functioning as a promotional strategy for the series. The actors continue to be engaged in the construction of their real-life persona, as a counterpart or complement to their television character. The dynamic is not so different from that of the glossy magazines that serve as accessories to television and the movies in the United States; but in the case of Televisa, thanks to its television and publishing monopoly, the choreography of this dynamic is controlled almost hermetically. The supposed glimpses into the "real lives" of the actors are only another story within a story, fitting seamlessly into reality.

Where the seams begin to show, however, is precisely in the photographs taken by Stefan Ruiz since 2003, the year he traveled to Mexico for the first time to do an article on telenovelas, for which he was given special access to the television studios. The portraits in this book show the actors posing during the brief limbo between playing their role and being "themselves," photographic sessions without guidelines that place the subjects in a kind of existential uncertainty, stripped of their officials roles both as characters and as actors. Ruiz's work enters into dialogue with the work of other contemporary photographers who expose the seams between fiction and reality; as in the figures in Madame Tussauds wax museum photographed by Hiroshi Sugimoto. Like the subjects of the early photos of Katy Grannan, who made portraits of people who answered classified ads for models, Ruiz's actors occupy the frame uncomfortably, as if aware that the photo is scrutinizing their psychology in ways a moving image does not permit. As in some of the work of Rineke Dijkstra, the photos of acting students reveal a certain fragility in these aspiring individuals. In the Mexican context, the most relevant reference is the well known series *Ricas y Famosas* (Rich and Famous, 1998–2002), in which Daniela Rossell portrayed various young women of her own generation, the daughters of Mexican millionaires showing off their wealth in narcissistic poses, surrounded by servants in interiors cluttered with extreme kitsch, all unaware that they were parodying their own pretentiousness and vulgarity. Ruiz, given access to another kind of interior never seen by ordinary people, shows us the prototypes of these empty models to which we all aspire, both rich and poor, embodied by actors professionally committed to such representations.

In this series of images we are offered a brief history of the Mexican telenovela, showing its thematic development over the last decade (with the incorporation, for example, in Plate 60 of the theme of drug-trafficking in recent productions), and includes both legendary actors, such as Fernando Allende and Rogelio Guerra (the protagonist of *The Rich Also Cry*) in Plates 42 and 76, and more recent stars, such as Fernando Colunga and Leticia Calderón (from the internationally successful *Esmeralda*) in Plates 13 and 68. A particularly important photograph in this group is the portrait of the late Ernesto Alonso in Plate 75, who was known as "Mr. Telenovela" for having produced, directed, and acted in dozens of telenovelas, and for having been one of the principal generators of the narrative model employed in them. In contrast to the other subjects of these photographs, the hieratic image of Alonso confronts our gaze steadily from a chair that resembles a throne, lending the subject an air of Raphael's Pope Julius II. Stefan Ruiz, who studied painting and sculpture in Venice before taking up photography, turns naturally to classical composition in framing his images. This strategy, which formalizes—and to some extent monumentalizes—the image, tends to accentuate the very artificiality of the setting. In other cases, as in the portrait of actresses Azucena Preciado Hernández and Claudia Janet Prado Terrazas, who appear in their roles as servants on the set of *Amarte es mi Pecado* (Loving You Is My Sin) in Plate 14, the image recalls the portraits of Hermenegildo Bustos, a self-taught Mexican painter of the nineteenth century who captured the psychological depths of the members of the provincial society he portrayed.

Even as he intertwines these historical references and deals with the specificity of each setting and character, Ruiz also shows us how this world is not much more than a great catalog of mannequins in action; of idealized prototypes of the same characters and stories, slightly modified in each successive program, revolving around the elemental polarizations of good and evil, sin and virtue, crime and punishment. The prototypes reside in stereotypical settings—whether hacienda, office, or luxury apartment in Mexico City—and within a highly conservative and restrictive view of what is feminine (differing degrees of sexualization, from virginity to promiscuity) and masculine (differing degrees of virility, from the hero to the macho). In other words, we are viewers of the same story, represented over and over, with slight variations each time—updates made in accord with the historical moment—and with a continuous flow of younger actors issuing from the acting school to replace characters who grow older, and assume in turn the roles of parents and, still later on, of grandparents. An endless human comedy with a tangled, but at the same time elemental, story of love and hate, for a public that, as Monsiváis points out, "never grows up." "If we don't do it this way, my maid won't understand," said Valentín Pimstein, another of the progenitors of the Mexican telenovela.

But the sophistication and to a certain extent the genius of the telenovela resides precisely in its ability to offer the lowest common denominator in the emotional narrative of a people. "Give me a telenovela and I'll give you a nation," the Canadian writer and journalist Denise Bombardier has said. Paraphrasing her, it might be said that every nation gets the telenovela it deserves. Because telenovelas, however shallow they may seem and however much we seek to minimize their importance, are an indirect reflection of our complexes, our desires, our stereotypes and fears. Stefan Ruiz instinctively understands the subliminal context of this world, and in his photographs he shows us the psychological rifts—in the face of the defiant, yet vaguely improbable, northern Mexican villain; in that of the stunningly beautiful domestic servant; in the cable hanging from the ceiling; in the false wall half-hidden in the corner—that reveal the fragility of this universe of shadows transmitted on the air. Behind this universe there is only the blackness of the studio, which might also be the existential darkness awaiting the country that should choose to reject escapism. To recall the phrase of the poet Xavier Villaurrutia: "To wake up is to die. Don't awake me."

Plates

René Casados as Juan Carlos
1 *Amarte es mi Pecado* (Loving You Is My Sin), 2003

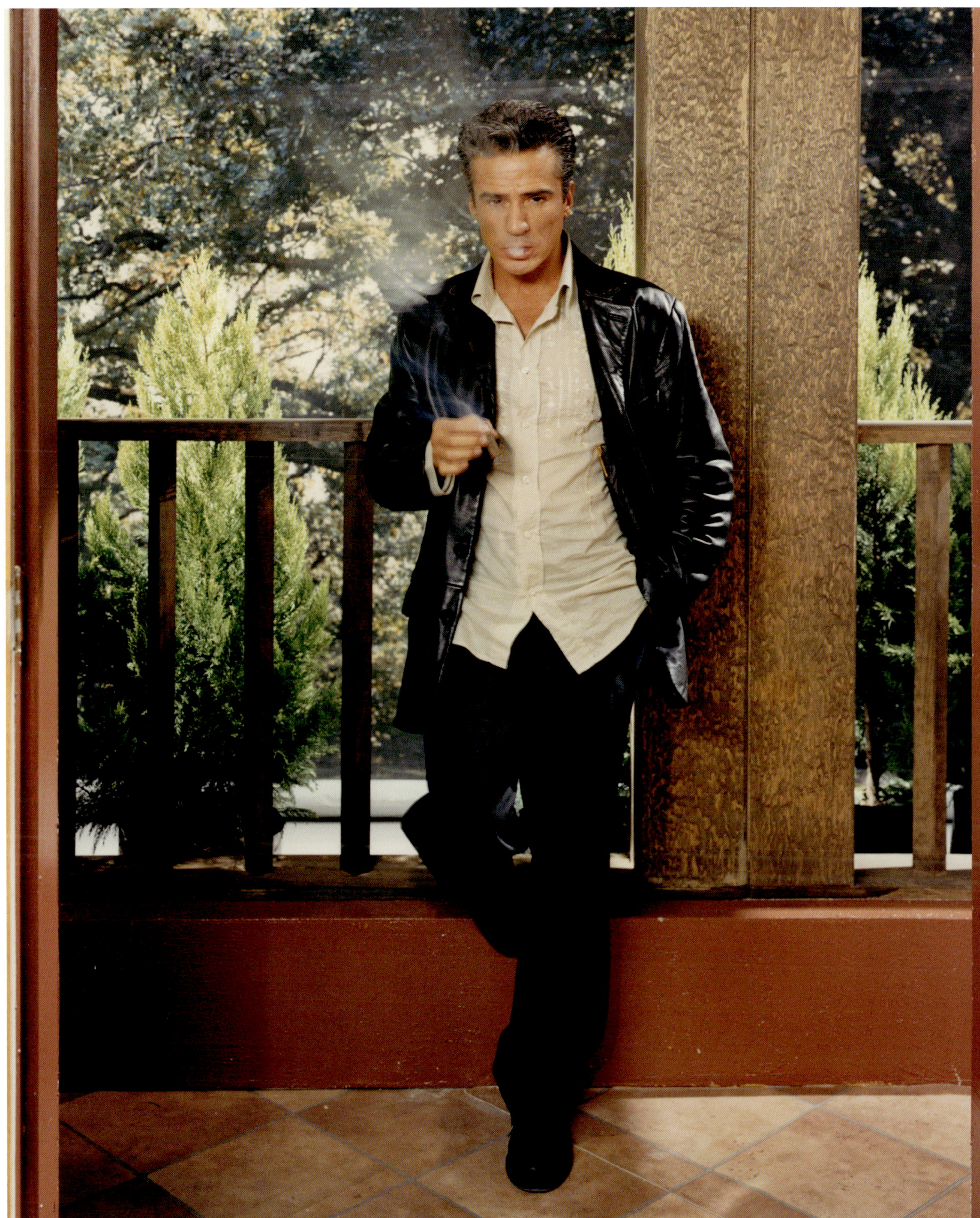

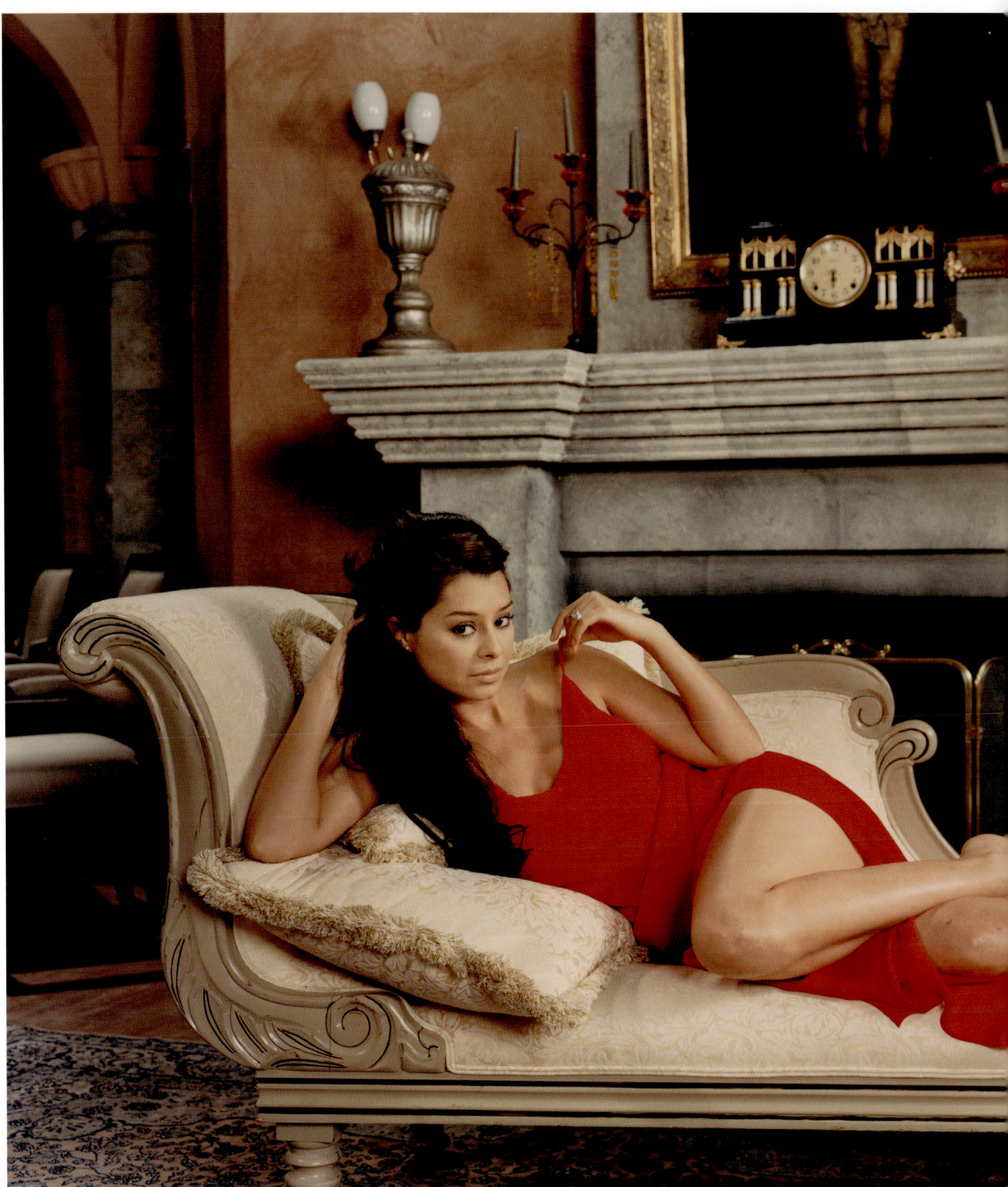

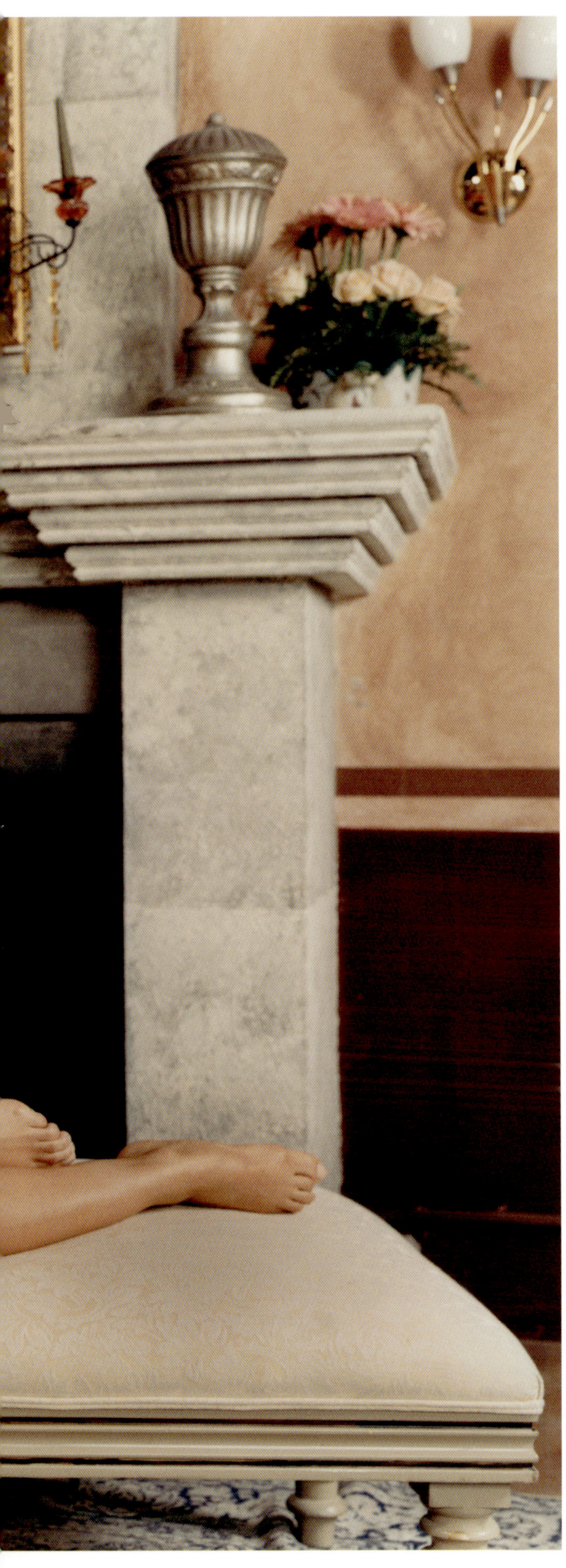

Yadhira Carrillo as Leonora "Nora"
Guzmán Madrigal de Orta de Palacios-García
Amarte es mi Pecado (Loving You Is My Sin), 2003

SONIA

Young, pretty, polite, well spoken, and highly qualified, Sonia has a flair for business and public relations. She speaks fluent English and French and dresses with style. She has become Yago's right-hand woman, and is also the favorite among his lovers. In business dealings, she is cold and calculating; but she has a good heart and is full of tenderness.

She is a woman who has had to disguise her romantic side and hide her love, so that Yago doesn't feel harassed or trapped, because she knows this is the only way to hold on to him. In the eyes of society, she is his "official" girlfriend, but everyone knows what a ladies' man Yago is, and feels sorry for her, because if there is one thing that can't truly be concealed, it is love. They have an open relationship, which she has accepted because she genuinely loves him and there is no other way to remain so close to him. Sonia suffers because she would really like to be his wife, to be the only woman in his life.

Just when she is about to achieve her objective, Rubí appears, a woman for whom Yago would do anything. Sonia can't endure it and hates Rubí. Her jealousy causes tension with Yago. It turns into a love/hate relationship, and she even considers taking terrible revenge.

Marlene Favela as Sonia
Rubí, 2004

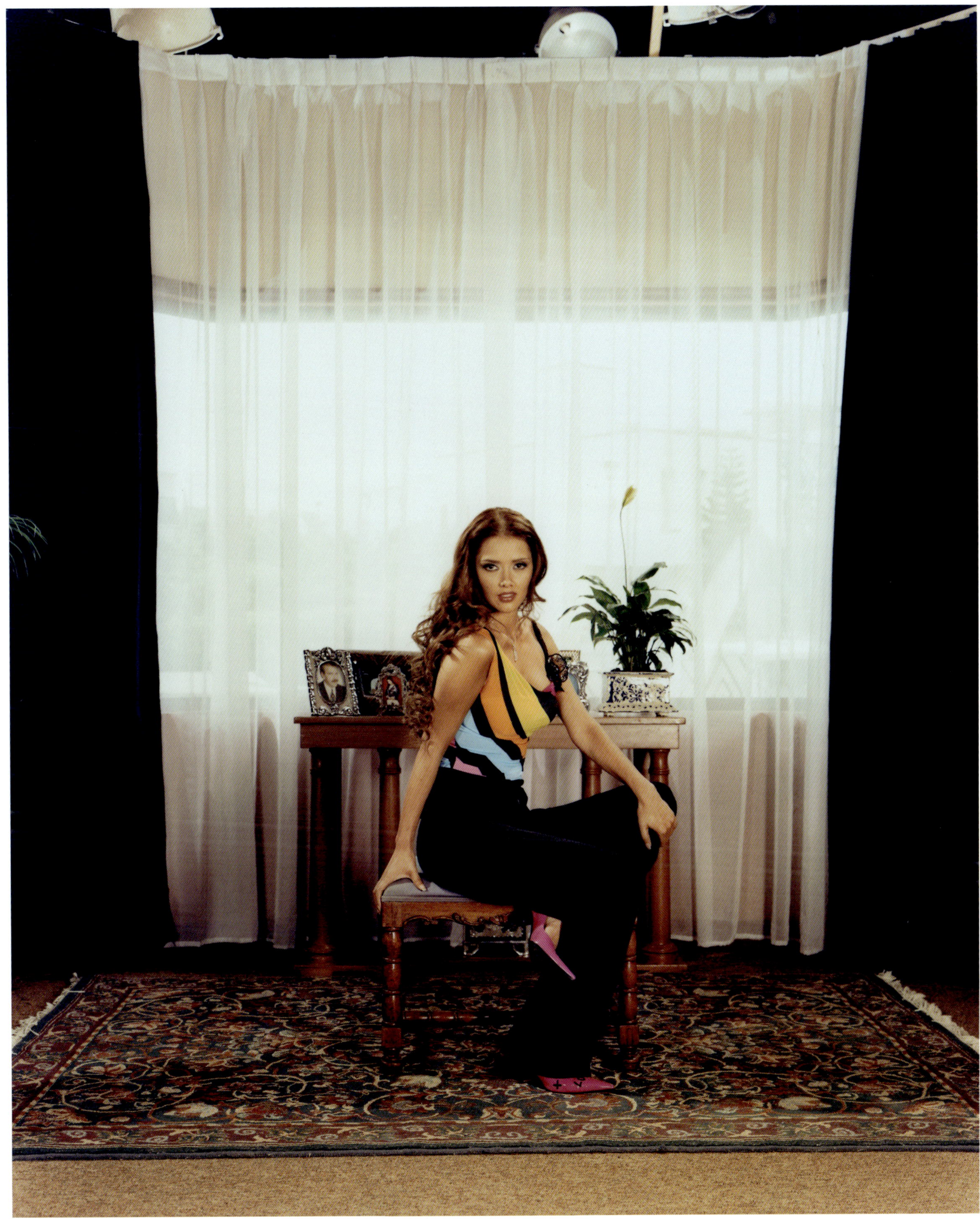

Roberto Palazuelos as Camilo Elizalde Rivera
Mañana es para Siempre (Tomorrow Is Forever), 2009

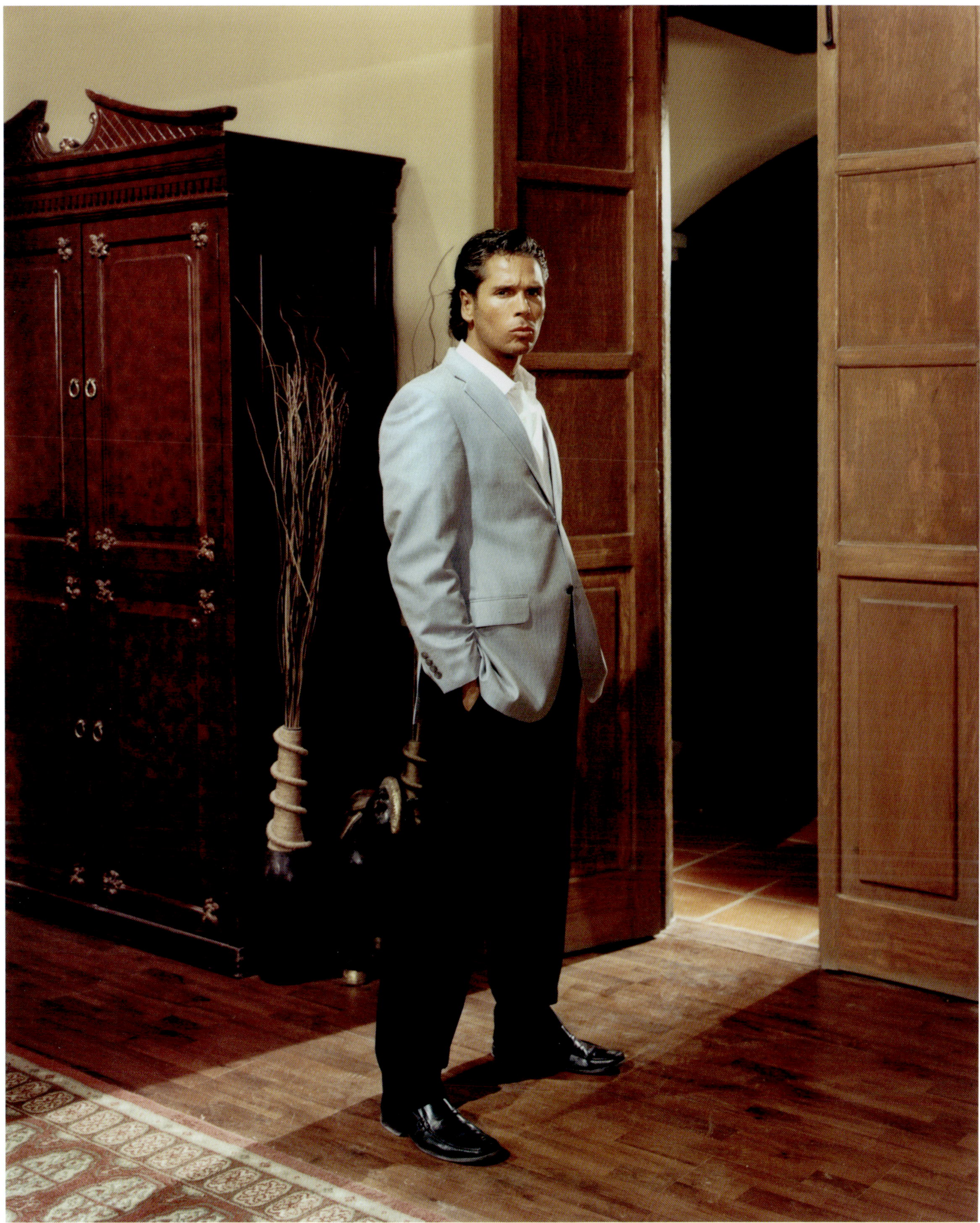

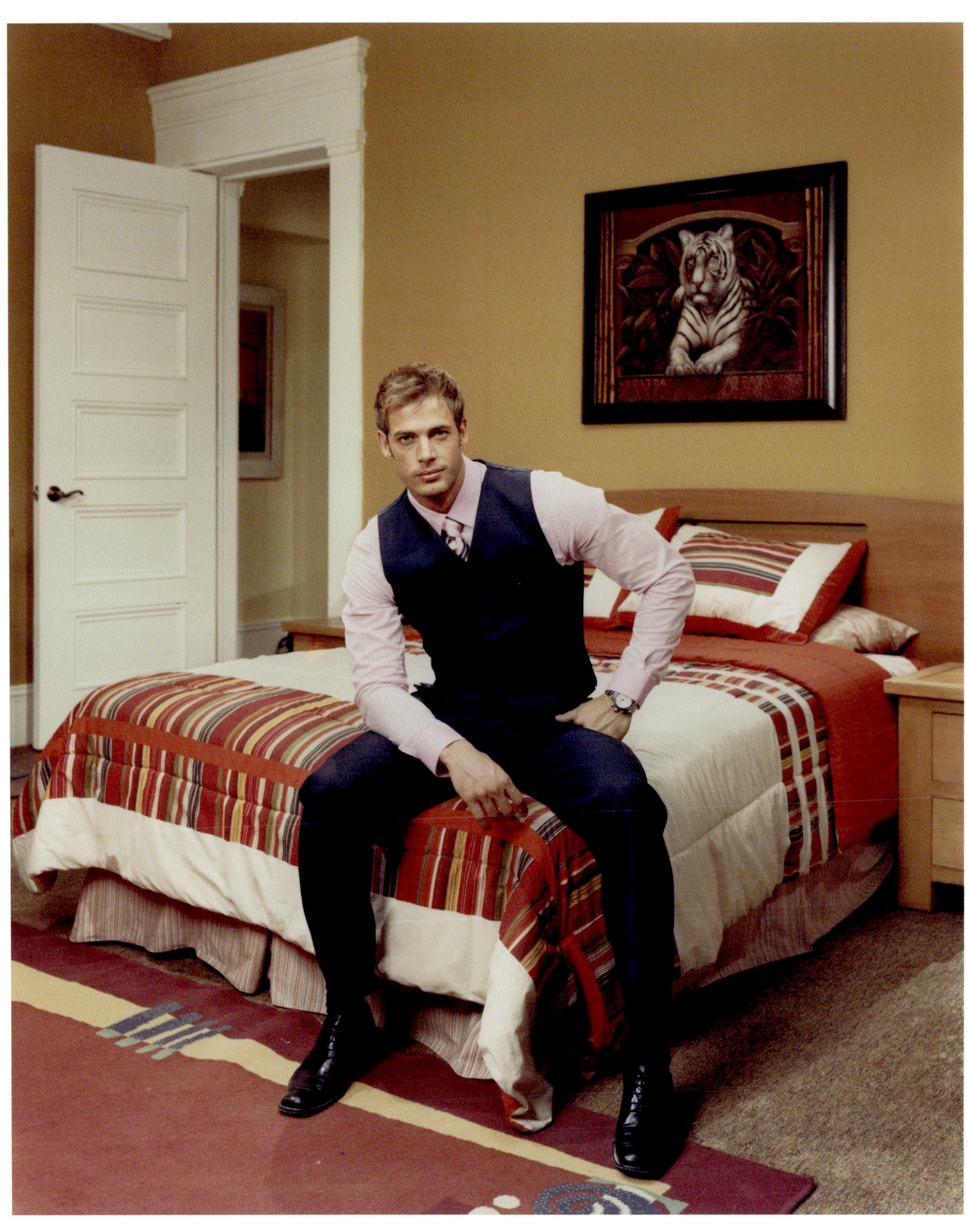

William Levy as Alejandro Lombardo
Sortilegio (Love Spell), 2009

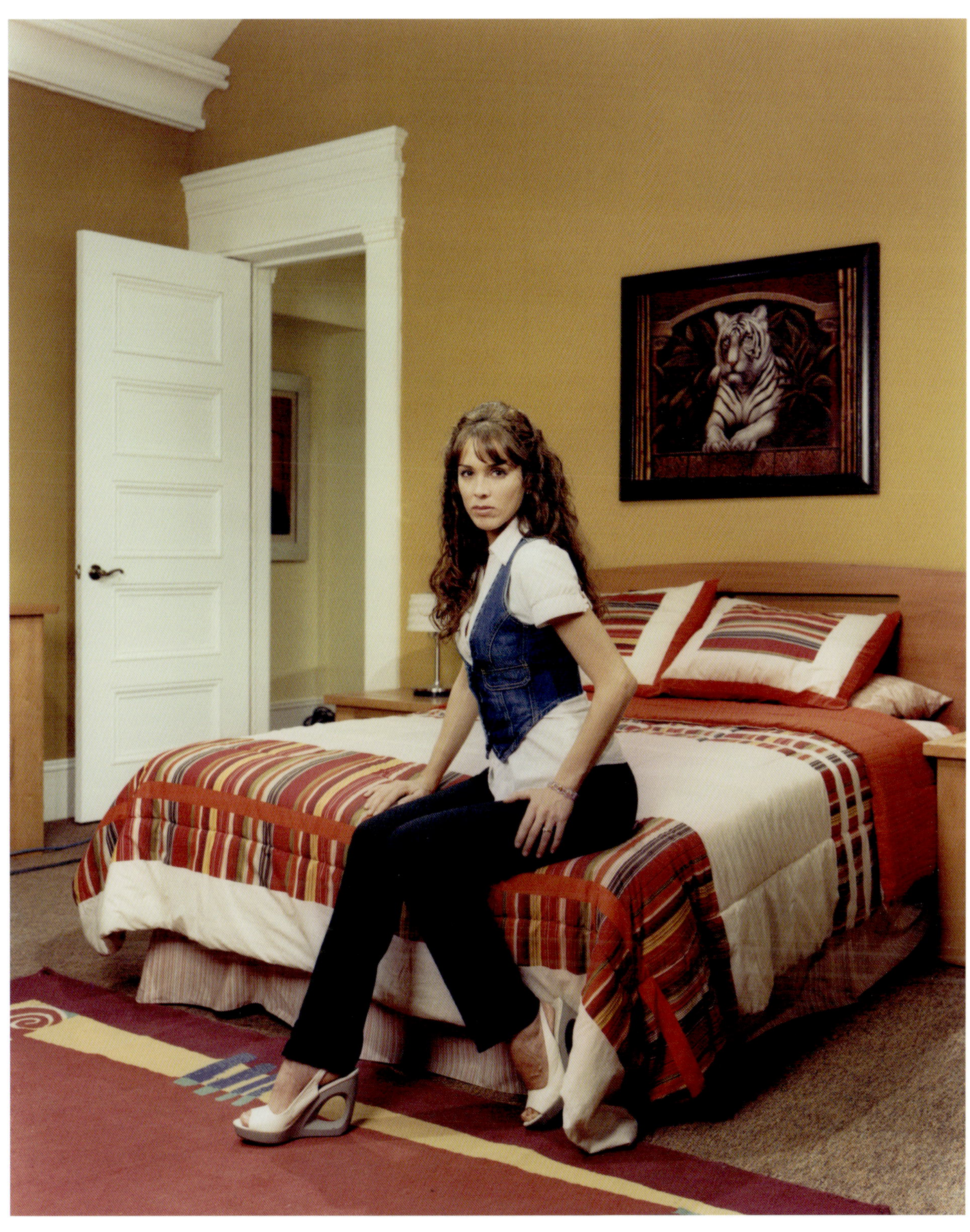

Jacqueline Bracamontes as María José Samaniego Miranda
Sortilegio (Love Spell), 2009

Synopsis of *Amarte es mi Pecado* (Loving You Is My Sin)

In the city of Patzcuaro lives Nora, a beautiful woman full of illusions. She is envied by the women and admired by the men, but she only has eyes for Alfredo, a young and daring man with no resources. Her father, Jacobo, insists continuously that she should marry a rich and important man. Nora, so as to not to upset him due to his ill health, keeps her relationship with Alfredo a secret. But after the death of Jacobo, Nora suffers a great disappointment—when her stepmother Isaura sells her to the richest man in town, Heriberto.

In defense of her honor, Nora wounds Heriberto, but he does not press charges against her, to avoid any scandal. But due to the pressure of the gossip among the neighbors, she moves to Morelia with her aunt Alejandra. In Morelia, Nora meets Arturo, and the two surrender themselves to each other in body and soul. Arturo loves her, but he has to go to a foreign country where they are offering him the job he dreamed of: pilot for a commercial airline. Arturo promises that he will come back and marry Nora, which makes Nora happy, so she prepares the wedding behind the back of her aunt Alejandra.

Meanwhile, Arturo meets Paulina, a journalist. They become good friends, but one night, after much drinking, they wake up to discover that they had slept together. They quickly say goodbye, as they have important things to do. Upon her return to Mexico, Paulina tells her fiancé, Juan Carlos, what happened. He is very understanding, and insists that they should go on with the plans for their wedding. But Paulina now has doubts about it, since she realizes she has fallen in love with Arturo.

Nora discovers she is pregnant with Arturo's child, but before she can tell him, Arturo gets a call from Paulina informing him that she is also pregnant. The feeling of responsibility obliges Arturo to tell Nora what happened. Feeling betrayed, she does not tell Arturo about her pregnancy, deciding to raise her child alone and dedicate herself completely to it. But when the baby is born, Nora's stepmother Isaura switches the baby with that of Casilda, Nora's ugly cousin, (who later turns out to be her half-sister), whose child Nora believes she is only the godmother to. Destiny has taught her how cruel it can be.

Completely destroyed, Nora swears she will never fall in love again, and remakes her life with one objective: to use her beauty to take revenge and exploit men. Now a hard and coldhearted woman, she is determined to make a fortune from whoever; and to find a way, at whatever cost, to take revenge on Arturo, the one she wants to hate with all her soul, but cannot stop loving, because loving him will be her sin.

Margarita Isabel as Alejandra Madrigal de Horta
Amarte es mi Pecado (Loving You Is My Sin), 2003

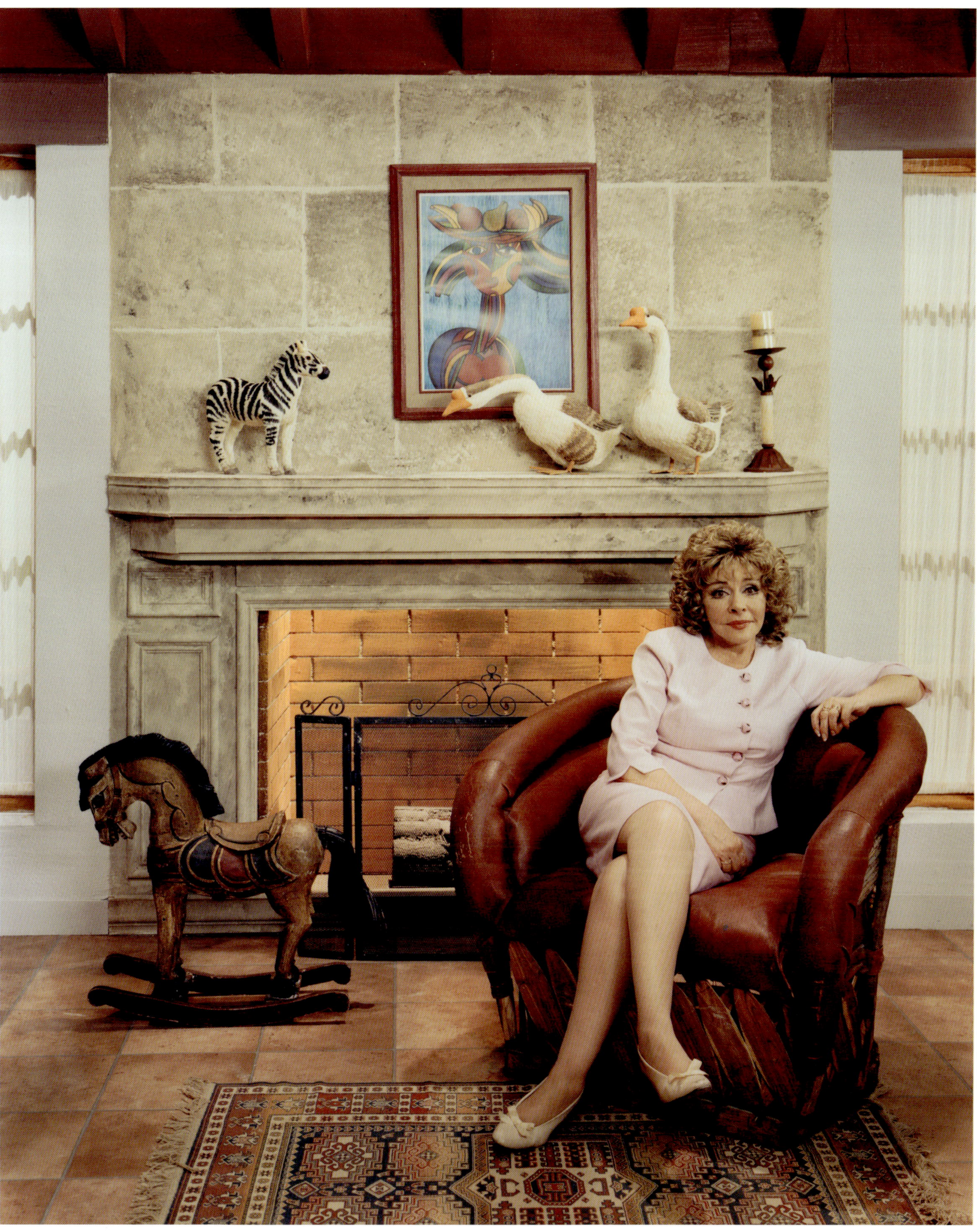

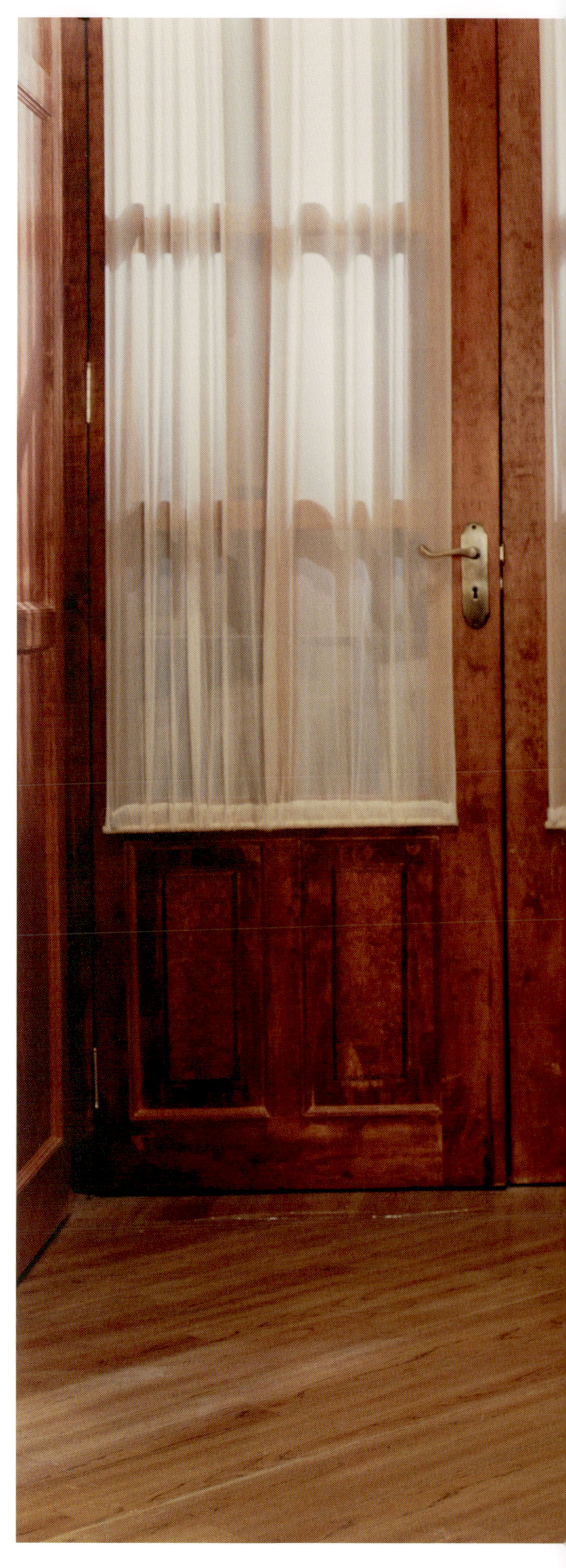

Tiaré Scanda as Casilda Gómez
Amarte es mi Pecado (Loving You Is My Sin), 2003

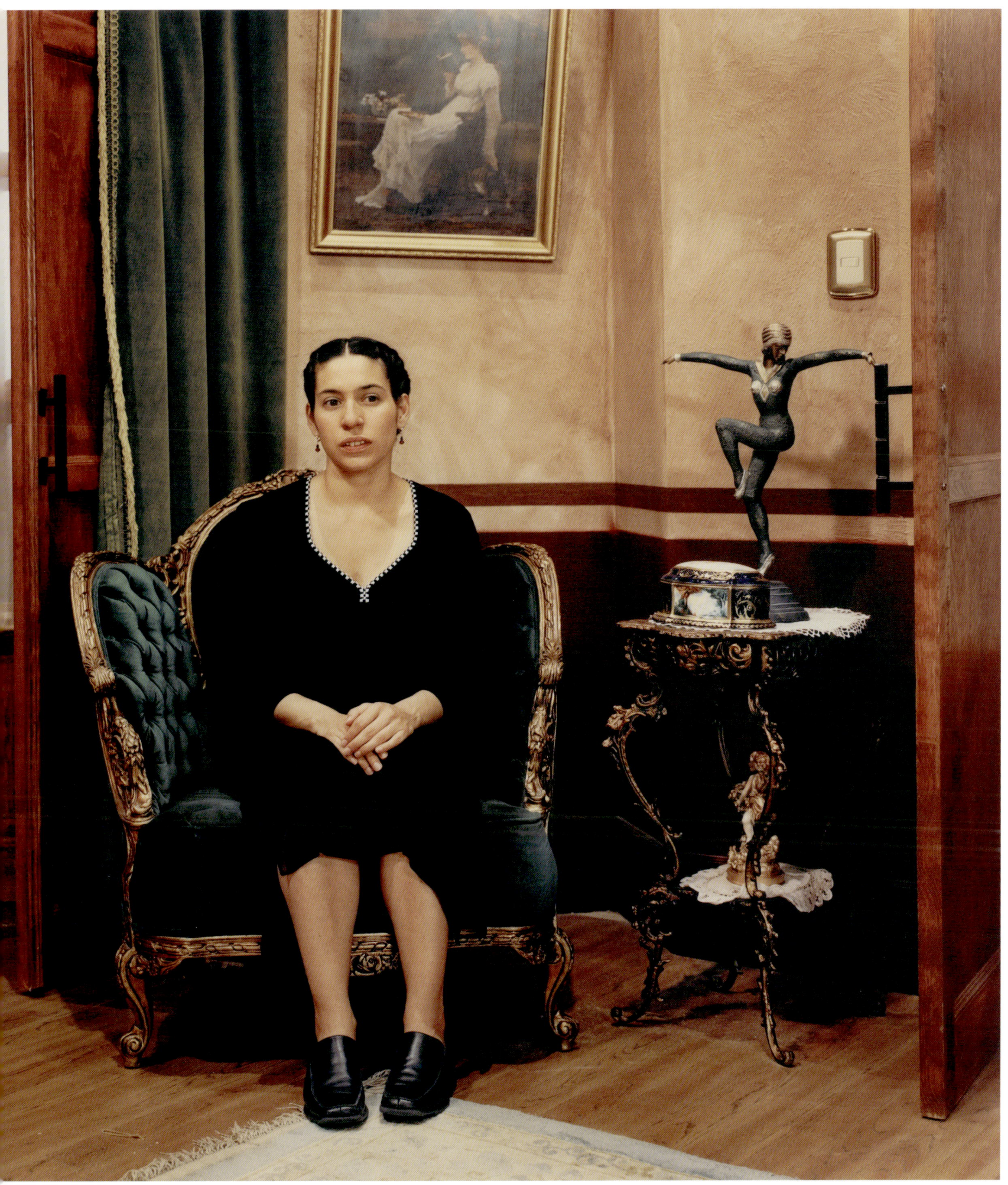

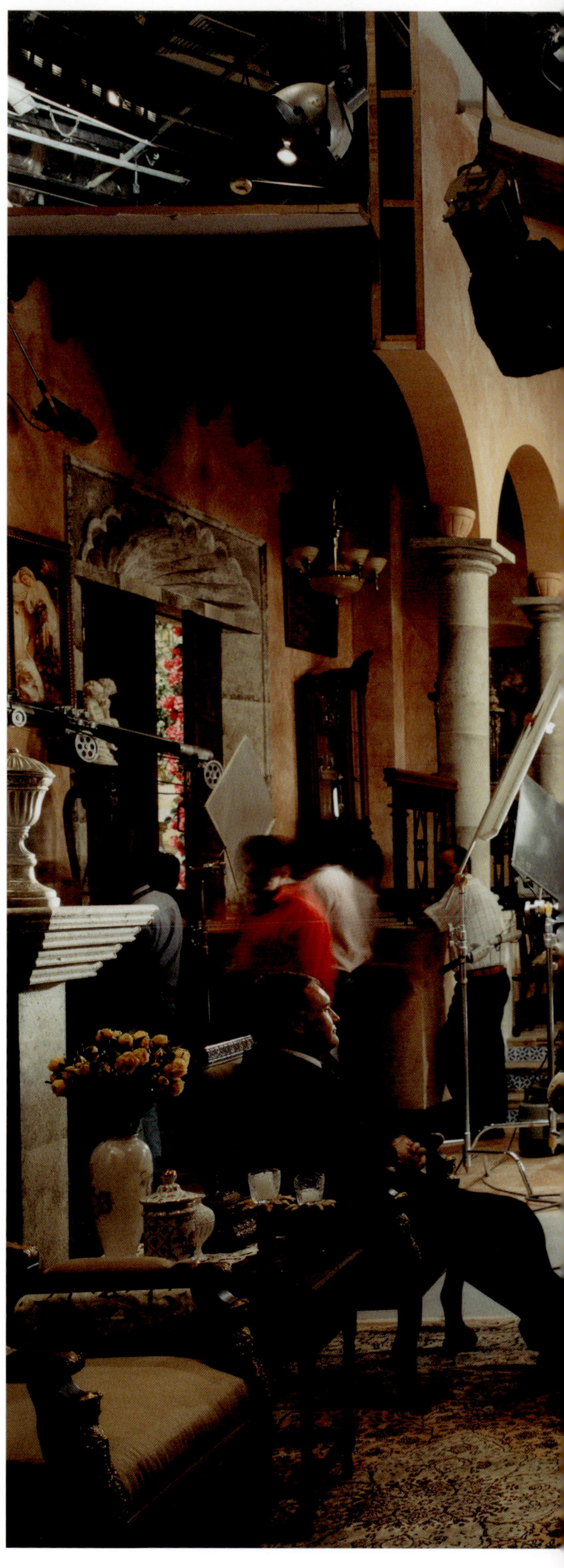

9 *Amarte es mi Pecado* (Loving You Is My Sin), 2003

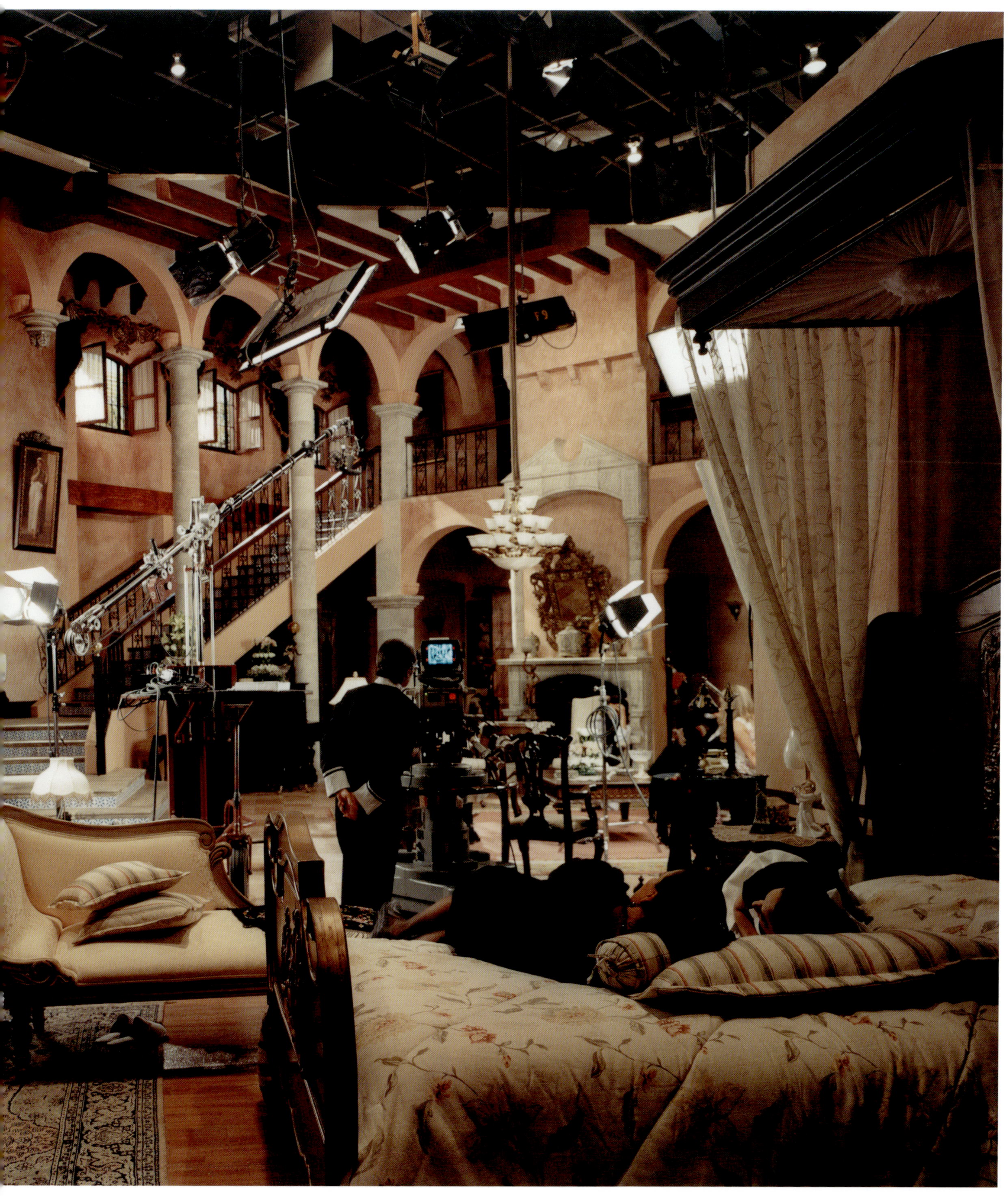

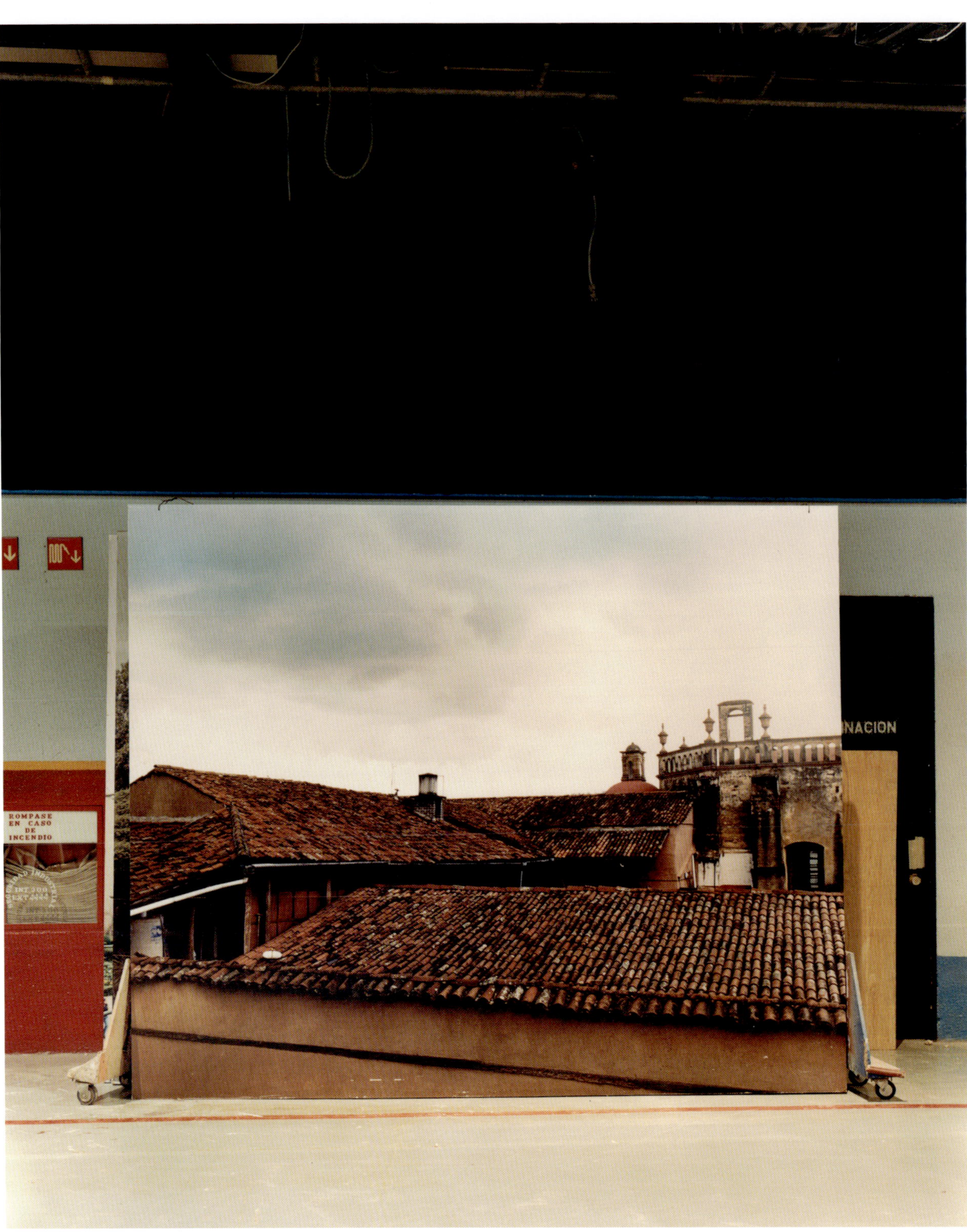

 Amarte es mi Pecado (Loving You Is My Sin), 2003

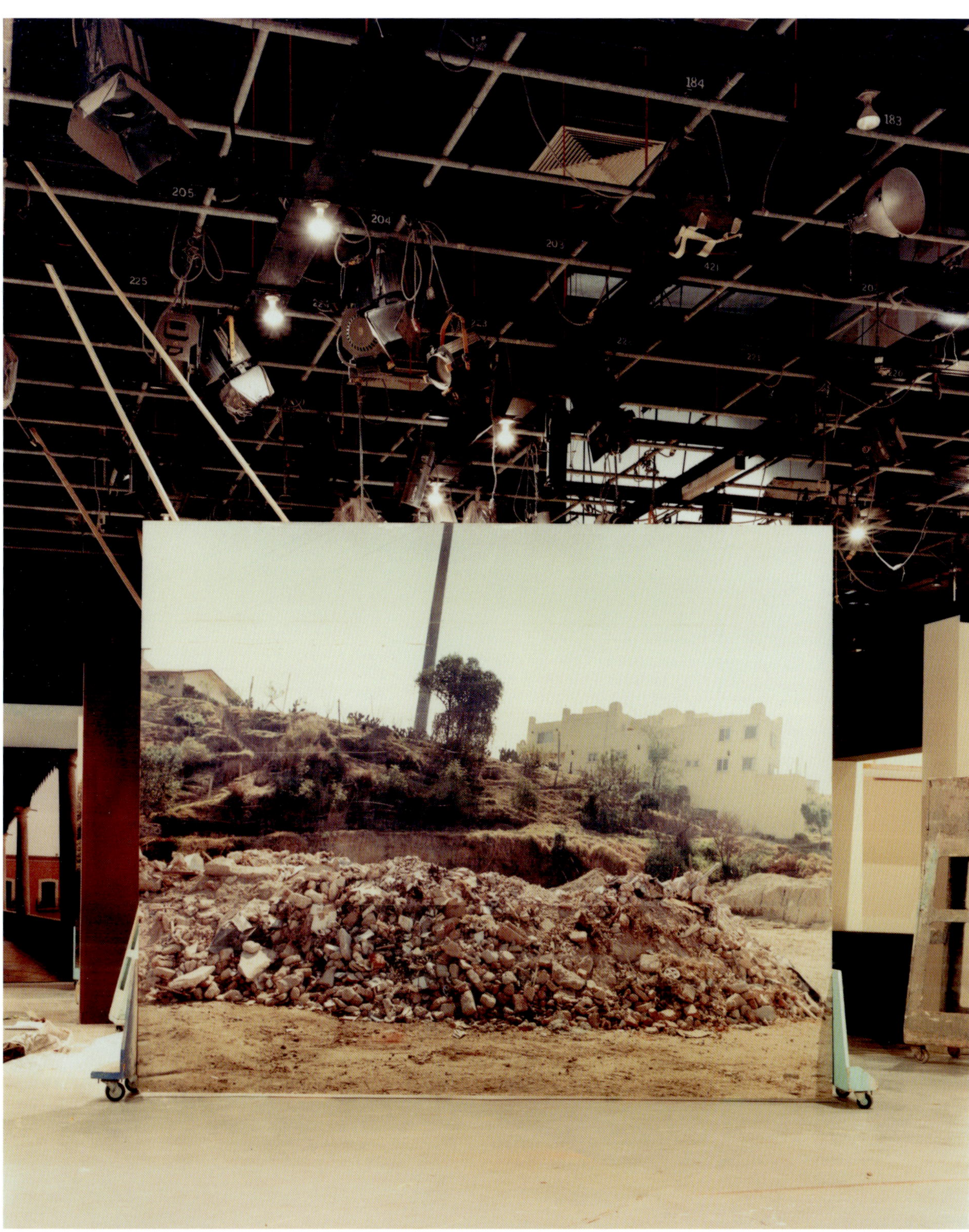

11 *Amarte es mi Pecado* (Loving You Is My Sin), 2003

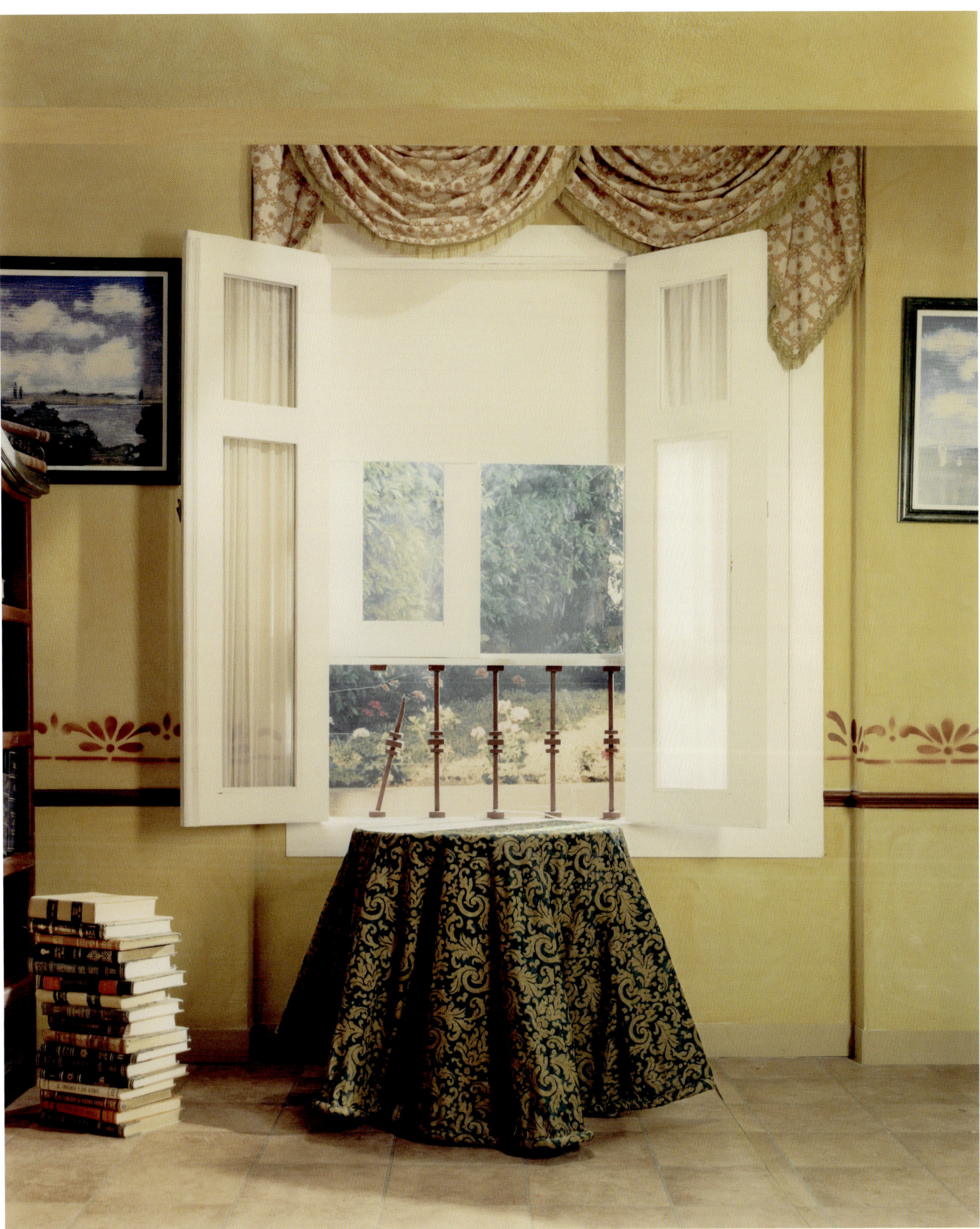

FRANCO SANTORO

Franco is a cheerful, upright young man with deep feelings, who adores his mother. From his father, who died when he was six years old, he has inherited his love of animals and respect for nature. He is a dreamer, but his love for Fernanda is as solid as a rock. Although Bárbara's malevolence keeps them apart for years, on his return, Franco realizes that his love is intact and that he is prepared to fight for Fernanda and to put things right.

Fernando Colunga as Franco Santoro
Mañana es para Siempre (Tomorrow Is Forever), 2009

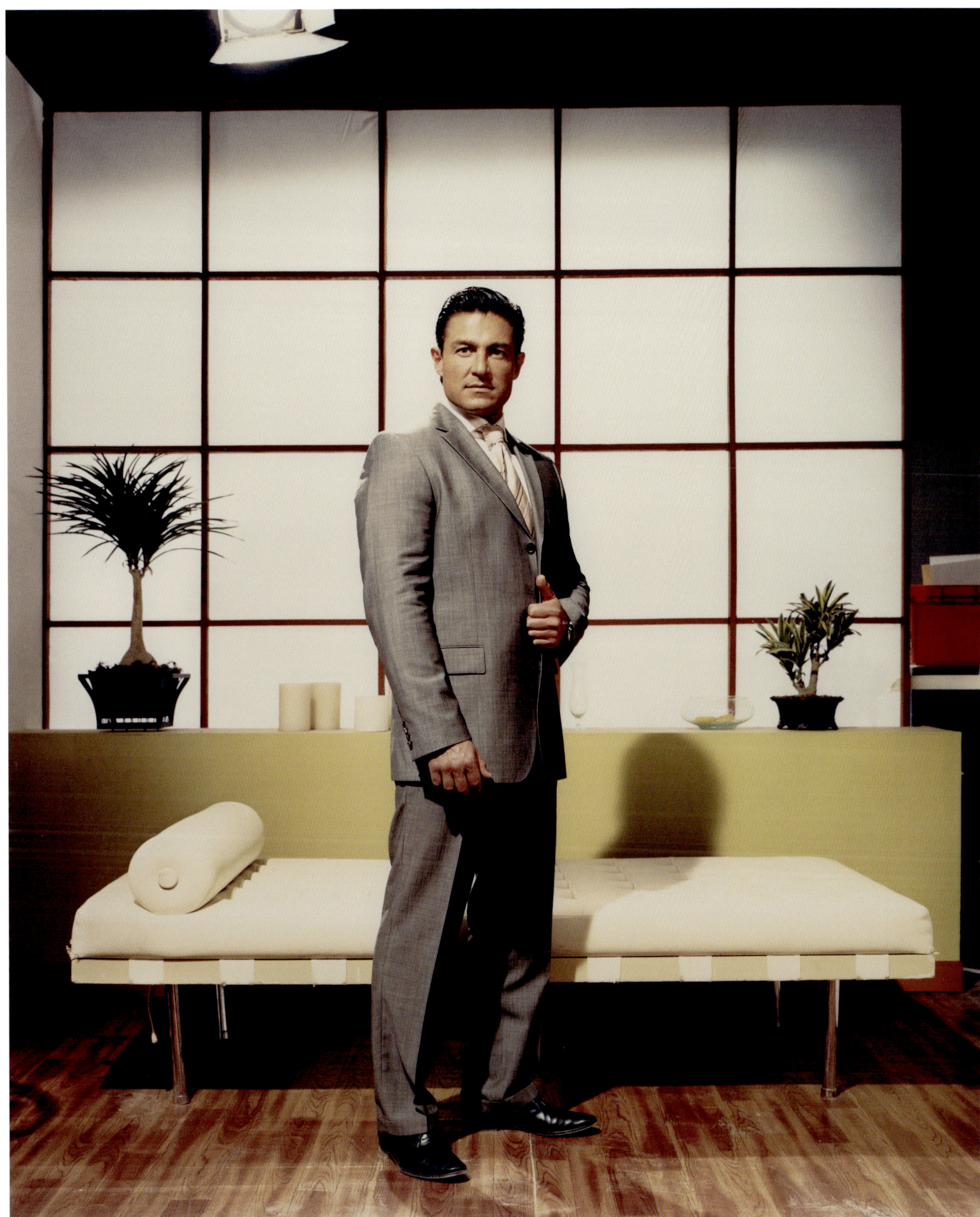

Azucena Preciado Hernández and Claudia Janet Prado Terrazas
Amarte es mi Pecado (Loving You Is My Sin), 2003

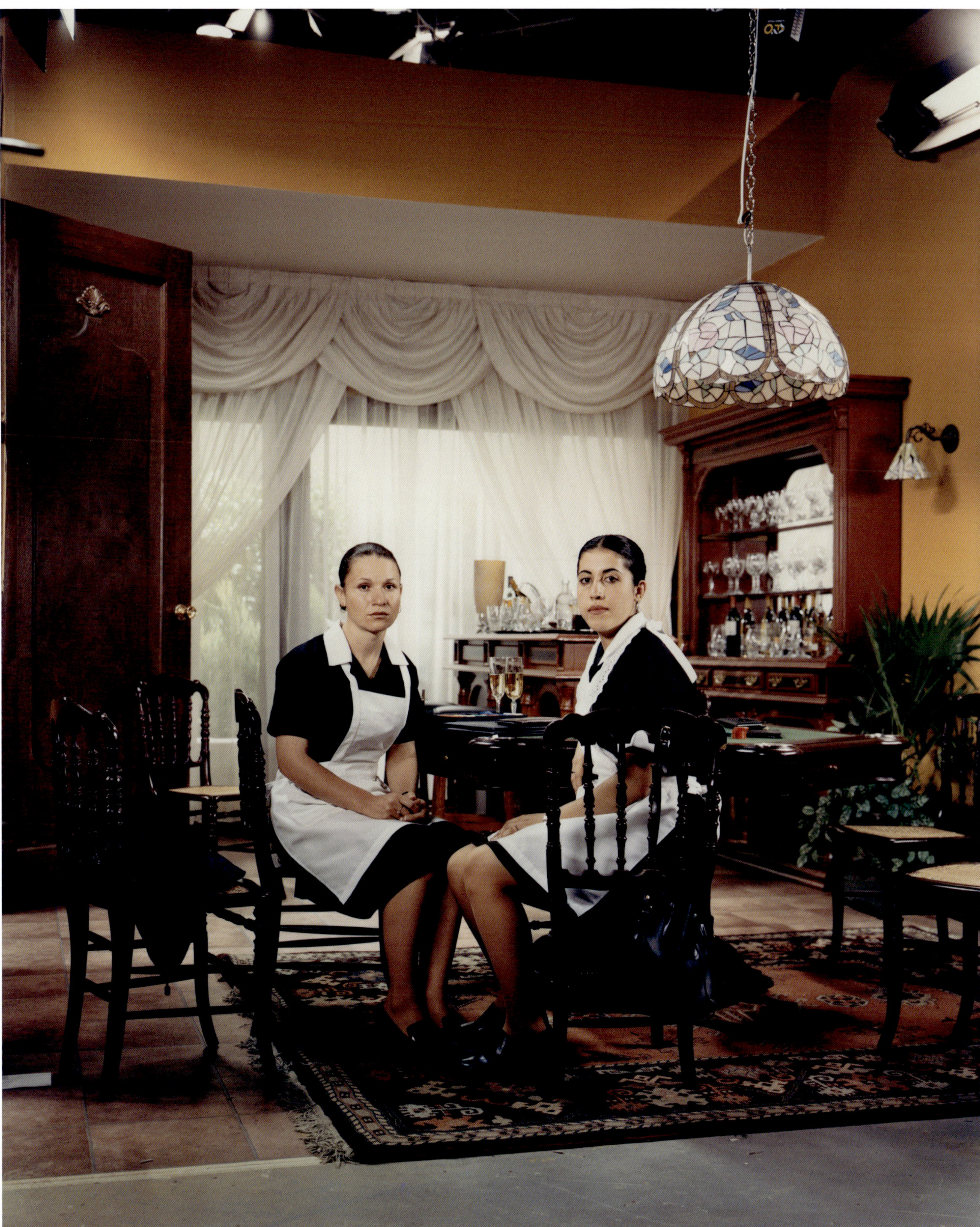

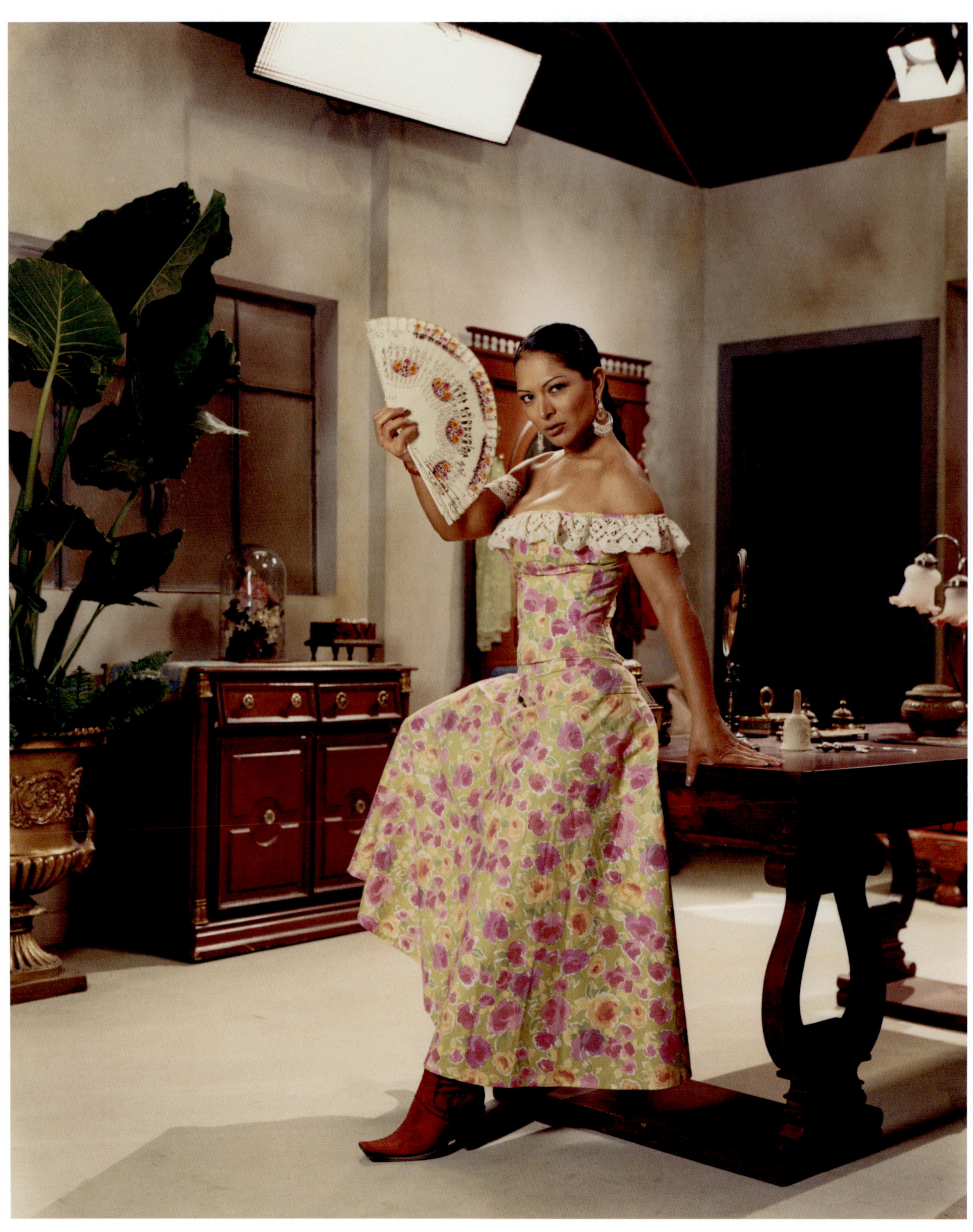

Siena Perezcano as Alfonsina Ríos
Duelo De Pasiones II (Duel of Passions), 2006

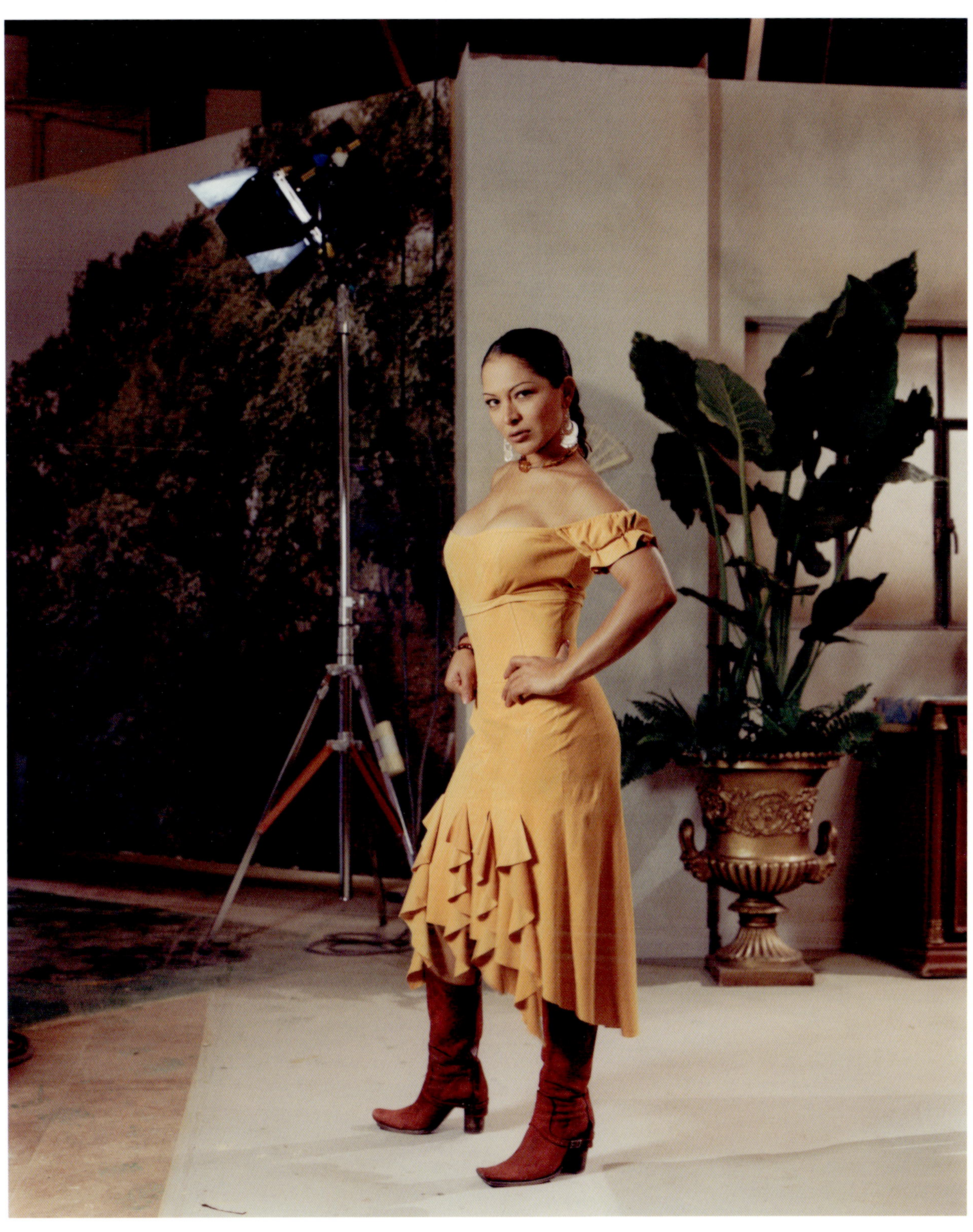

Siena Perezcano as Alfonsina Ríos
Duelo De Pasiones II (Duel of Passions), 2006

Arath de la Torre as Pancho López
Una Familia Con Suerte (One Family with Luck), 2011

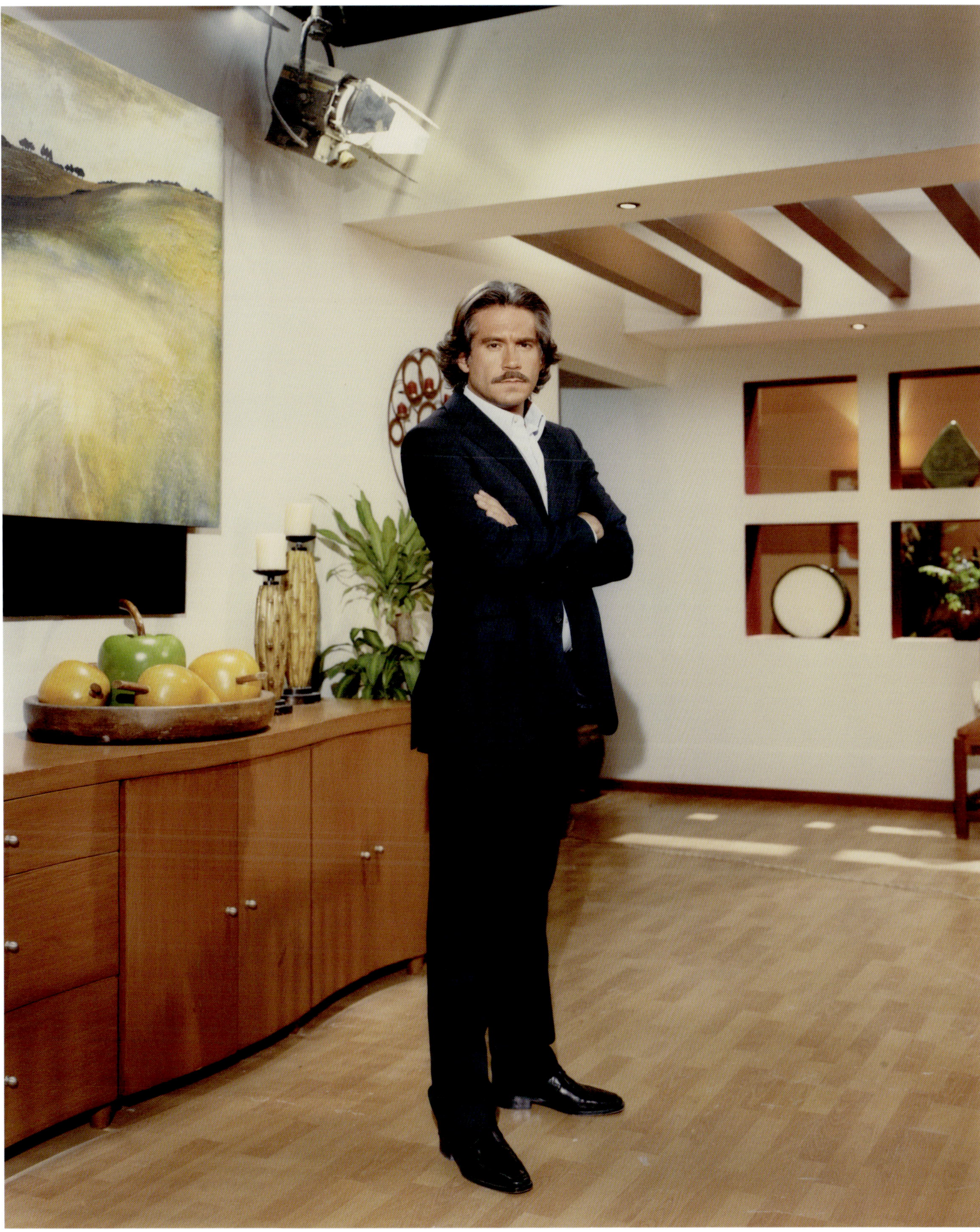

Sergio Sendel as Arturo Sandoval de Anda
Amarte es mi Pecado (Loving You Is My Sin), 2003

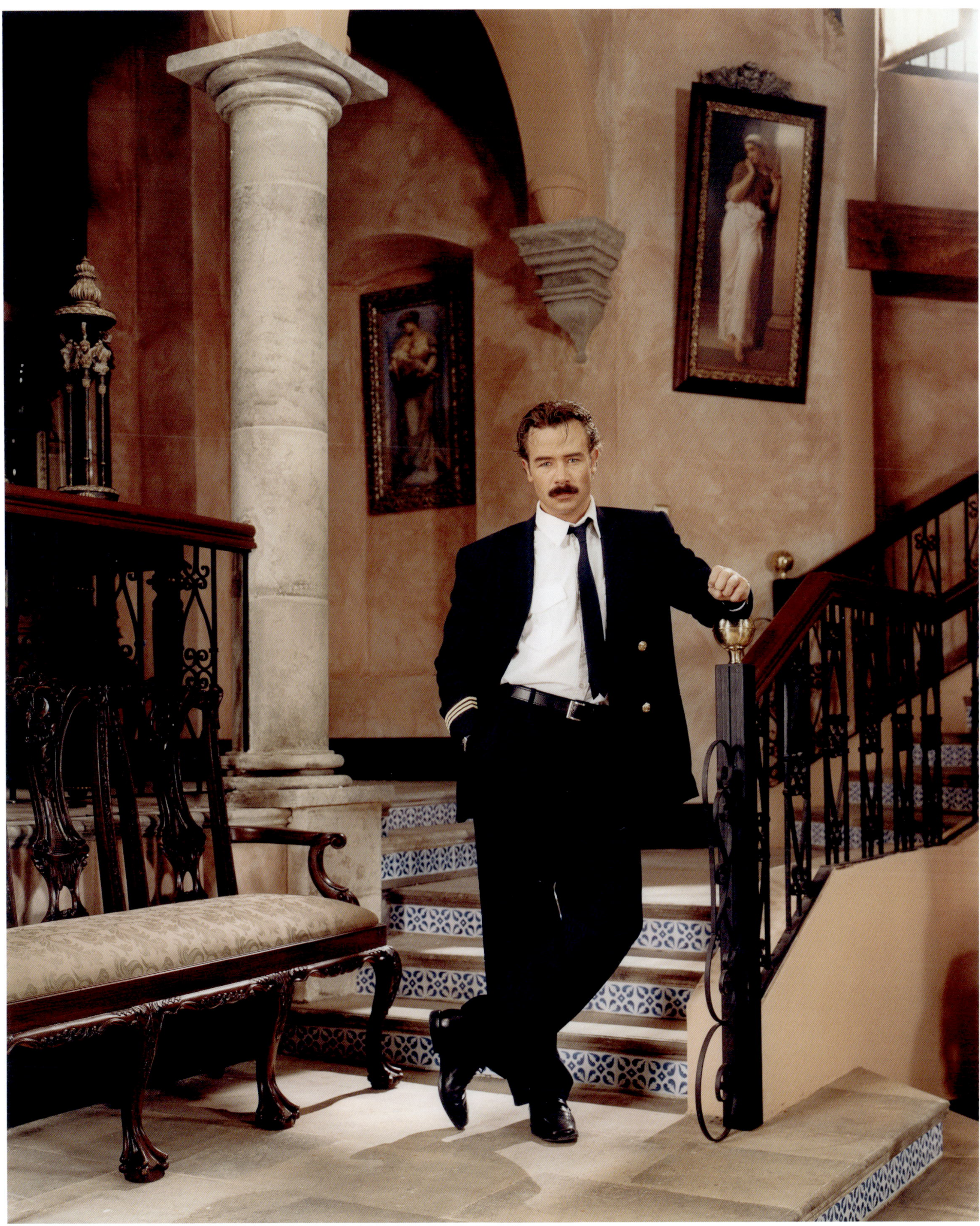

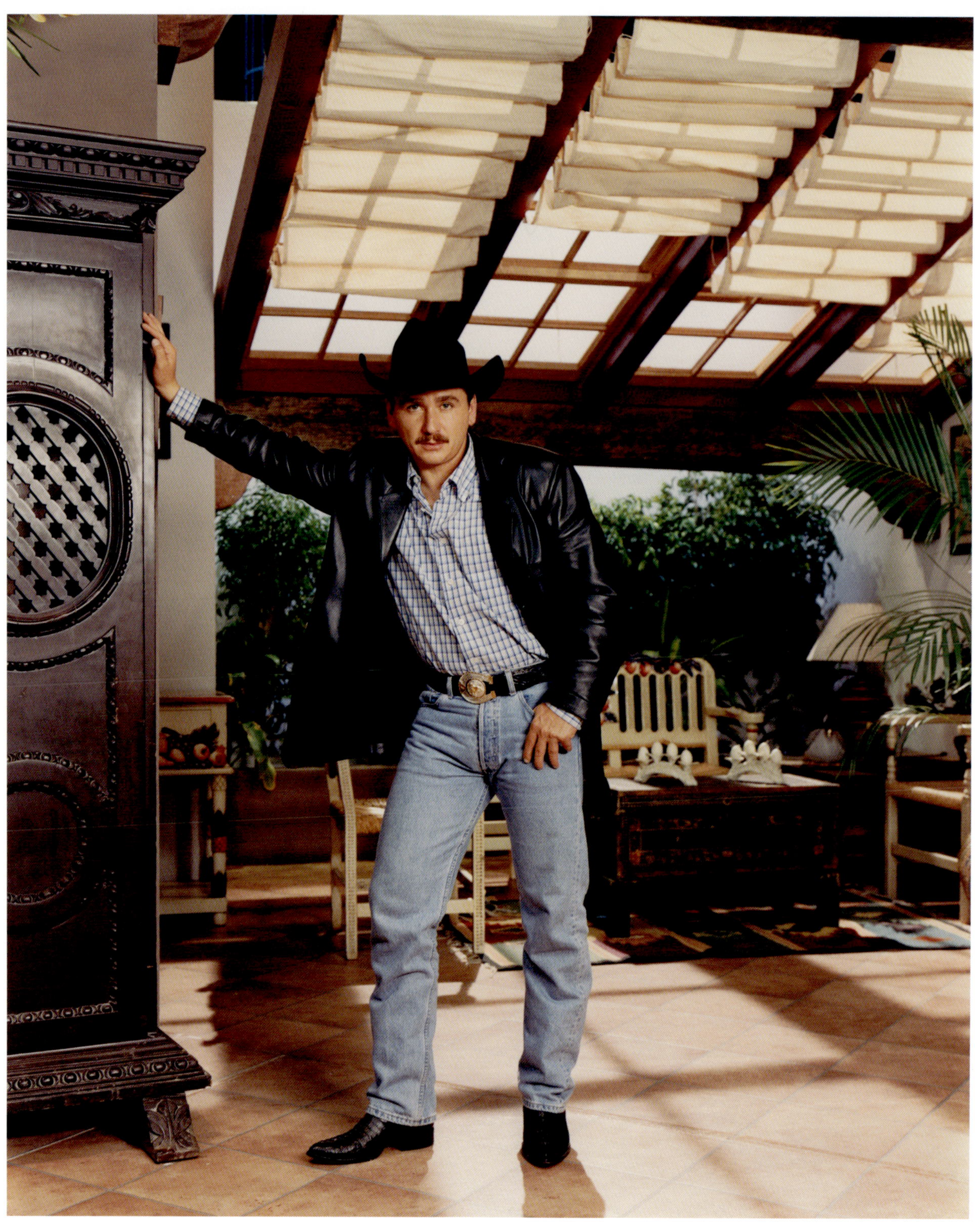

Germán Gutiérrez as Osvaldo Quintero
Amarte es mi Pecado (Loving You Is My Sin), 2003

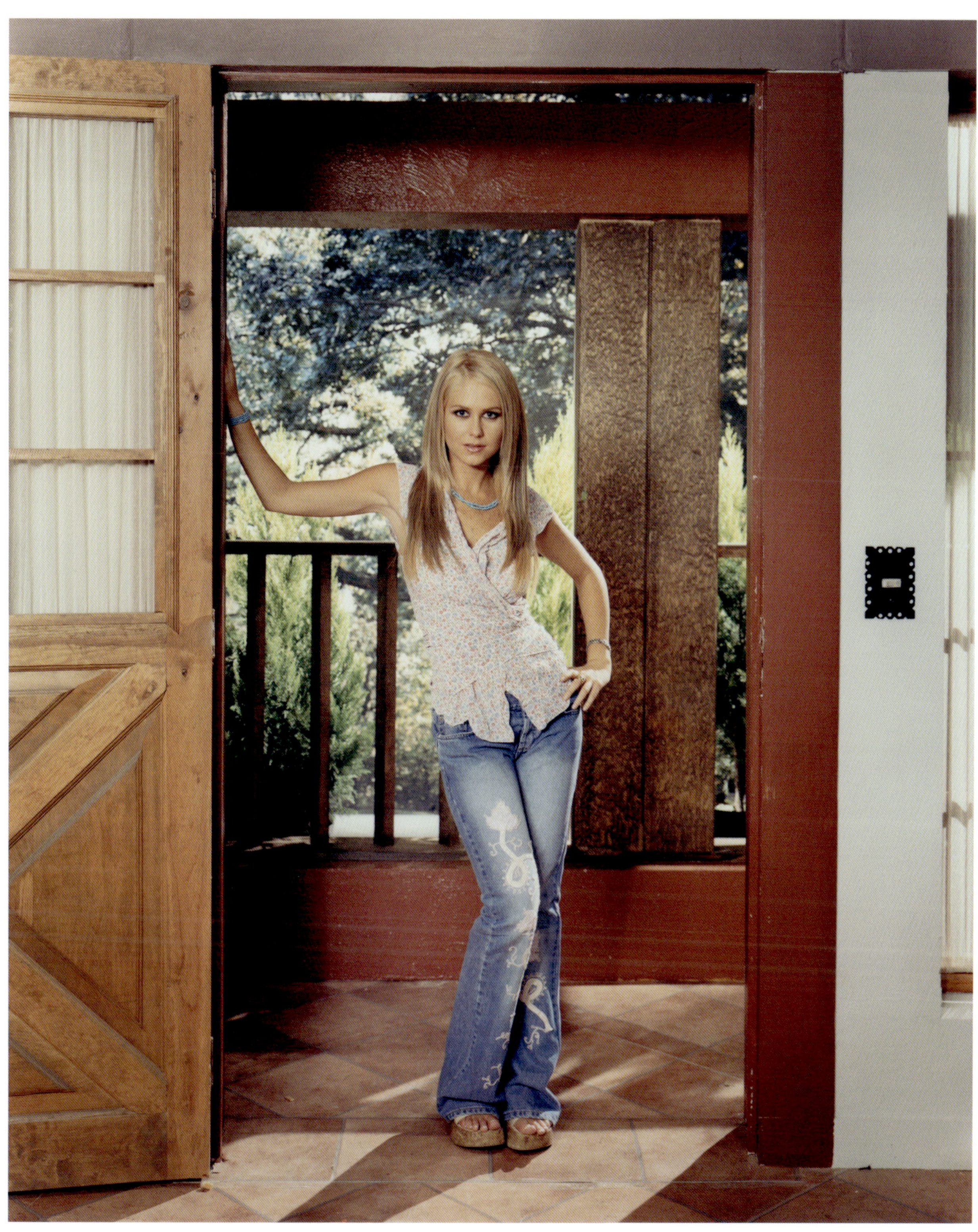

Ingrid Martz as Renata Quiroga
Amarte es mi Pecado (Loving You Is My Sin), 2003

Xavier Marc as Don Heriberto

Amarte es mi Pecado (Loving You Is My Sin), 2003

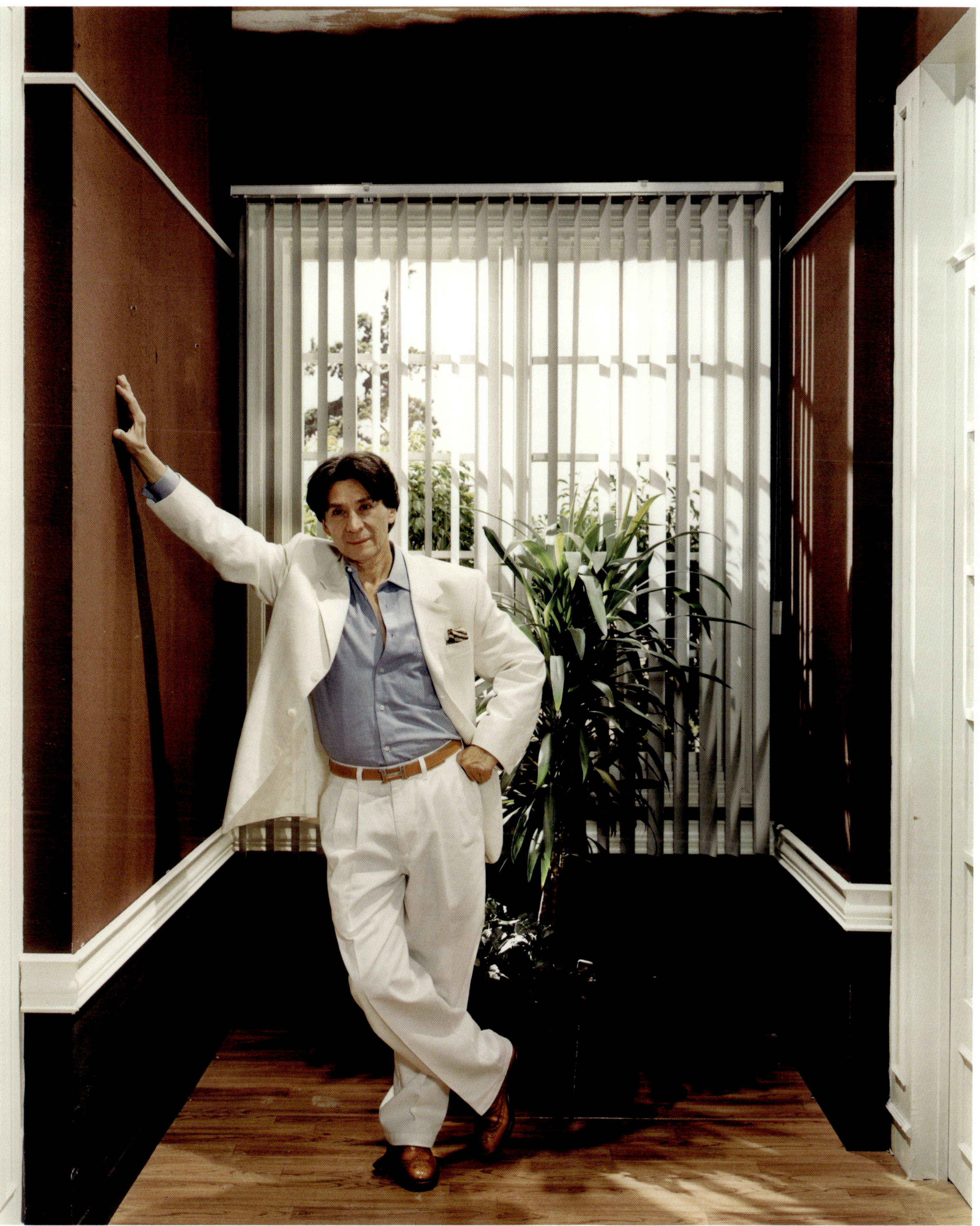

Synopsis of *Sortilegio* (Love Spell)

Antonio Lombardo, a successful building contractor, falls in love in spite of himself with Victoria, the wife of his best friend, Samuel. A set of twins, Bruno and Raquel, are born of the relationship, but Antonio never gets to know them, because Samuel takes Victoria to Europe before she gives birth.

Years later, Victoria and Antonio meet again, as widow and widower. They decide to join their lives together, along with their children Bruno and Raquel; and Alex, Antonio's son by his late wife Adriana. The children grow up without knowing the truth about their biological father. Bruno wholeheartedly rejects Alex, treating him with rudeness and hostility as the years go by.

Antonio, disappointed by Bruno's rebellious and irresponsible behavior and by Raquel's frivolity, designates Alex his sole heir. When Antonio tells Victoria what he has decided, they have a heated argument. Antonio dies unexpectedly, and Alex takes his place at the head of the family and of the Lombardo business. Bruno's hatred of Alex deepens.

Bruno meets a simple, beautiful provincial girl named María José and proposes marriage to her, passing himself off as his younger brother, Alex, and contriving a twisted plan to get rid of him and take over the management of the Lombardo companies. Bruno makes an attempt on the life of his brother, who is declared dead following a terrible accident. In fact, he is only badly injured, and reappears a few days later, to everyone's surprise, especially Bruno's. His alleged widow becomes unwittingly entangled in complications and blackmail from which she struggles to free herself. At stake is her own freedom and that of her father and sister. Meanwhile, her husband (Alex), suffering from memory lapses after the accident, is greatly surprised to find himself with a wife. He cannot remember having gotten married, but he is not insensible to the beauty of the girl.

The love between the hero and heroine is clouded by the scheming of their enemies Bruno and Maura, who will stop at nothing in order to separate them.

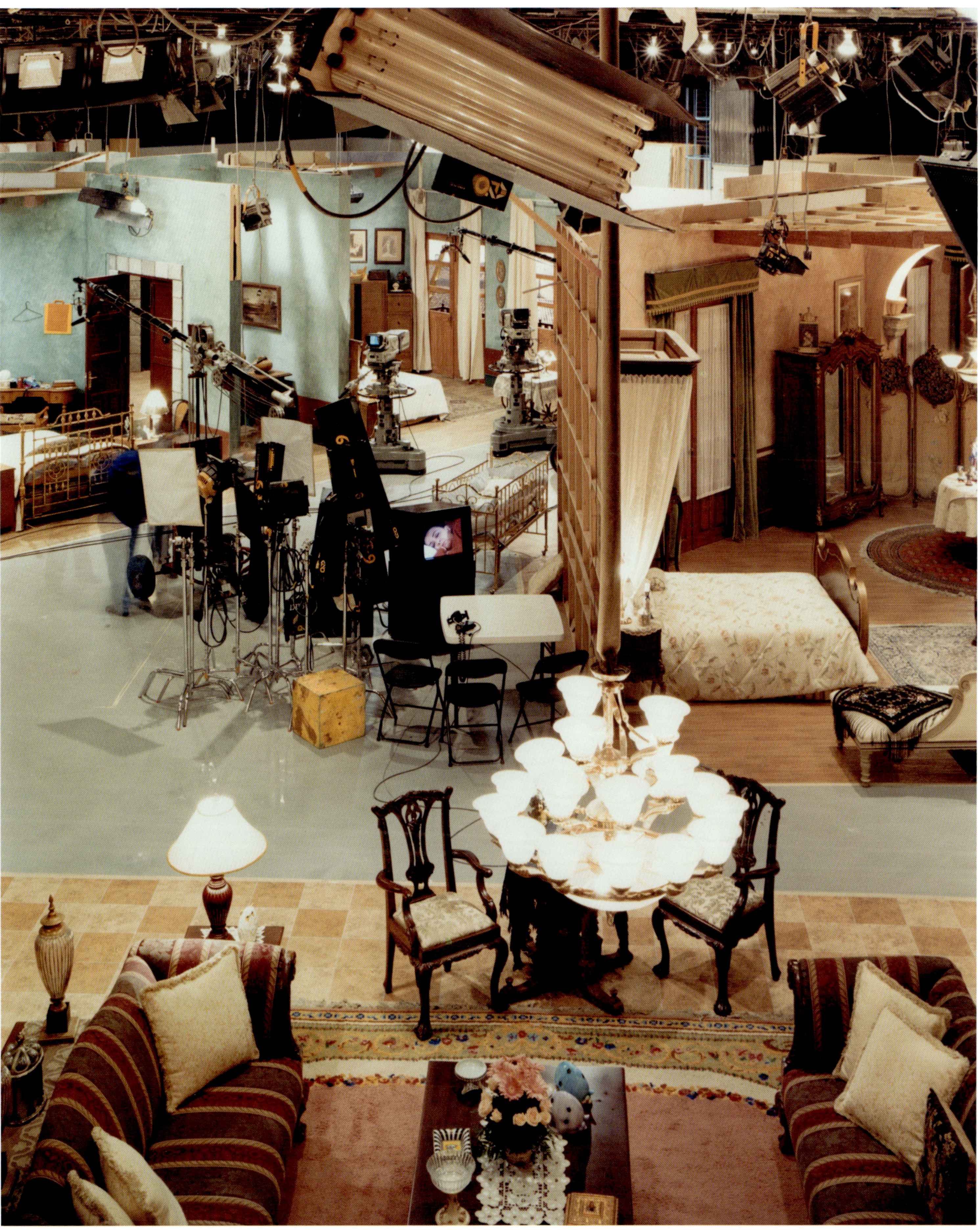

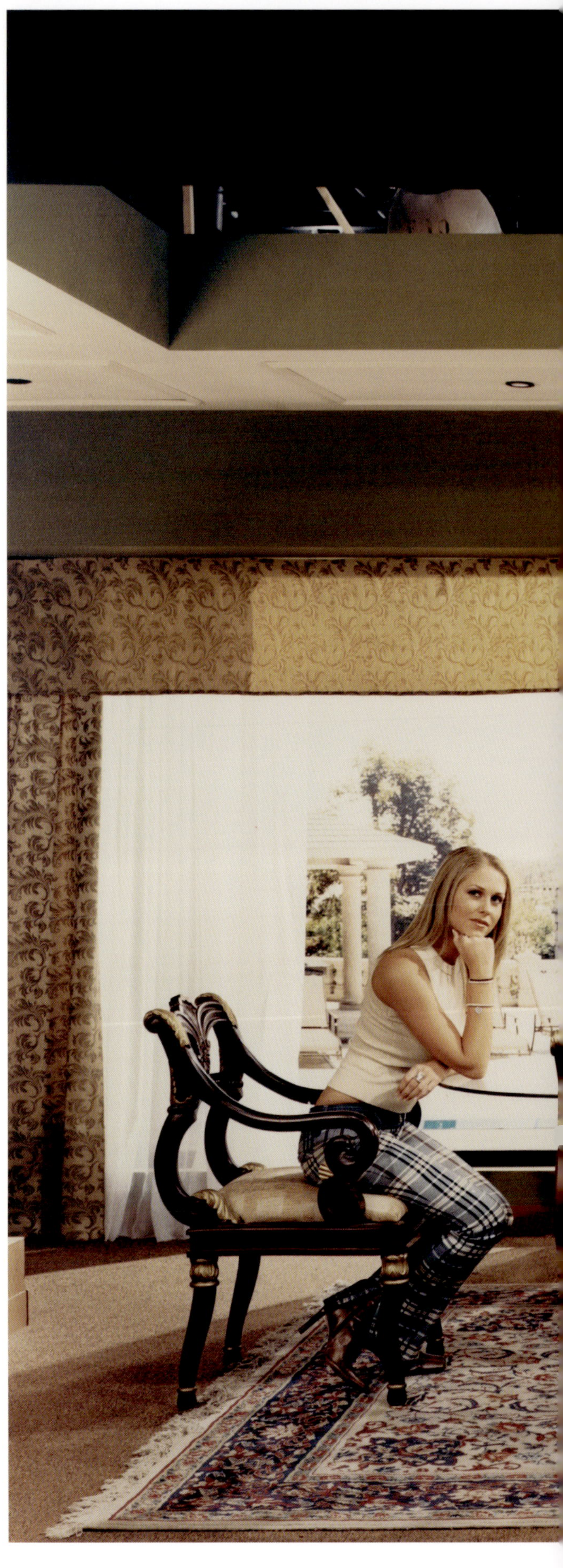

Ingrid Martz and Alejandro Ruiz
as Renata Quiroga and Diego Fernández del Ara
Rubí, 2004

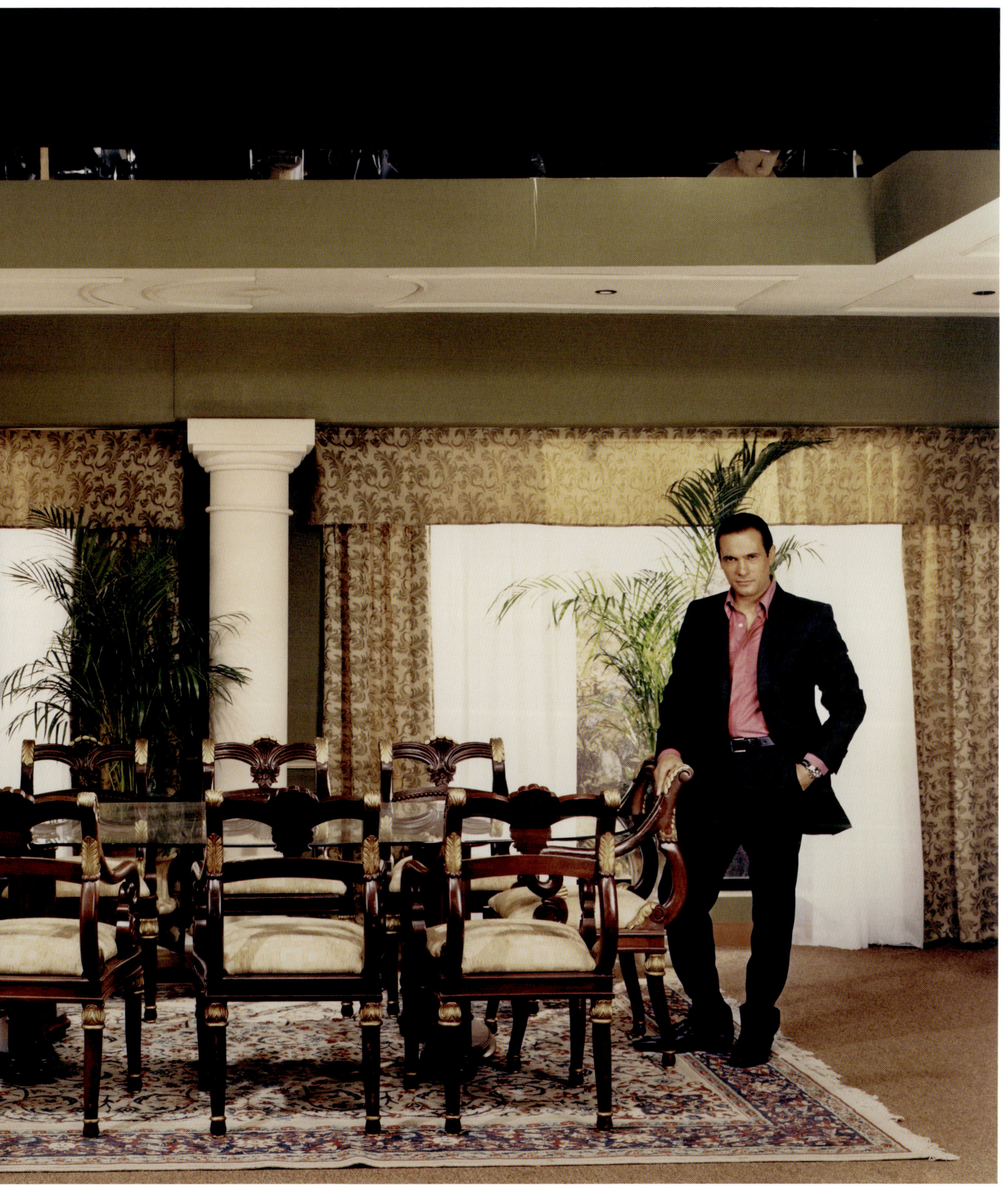

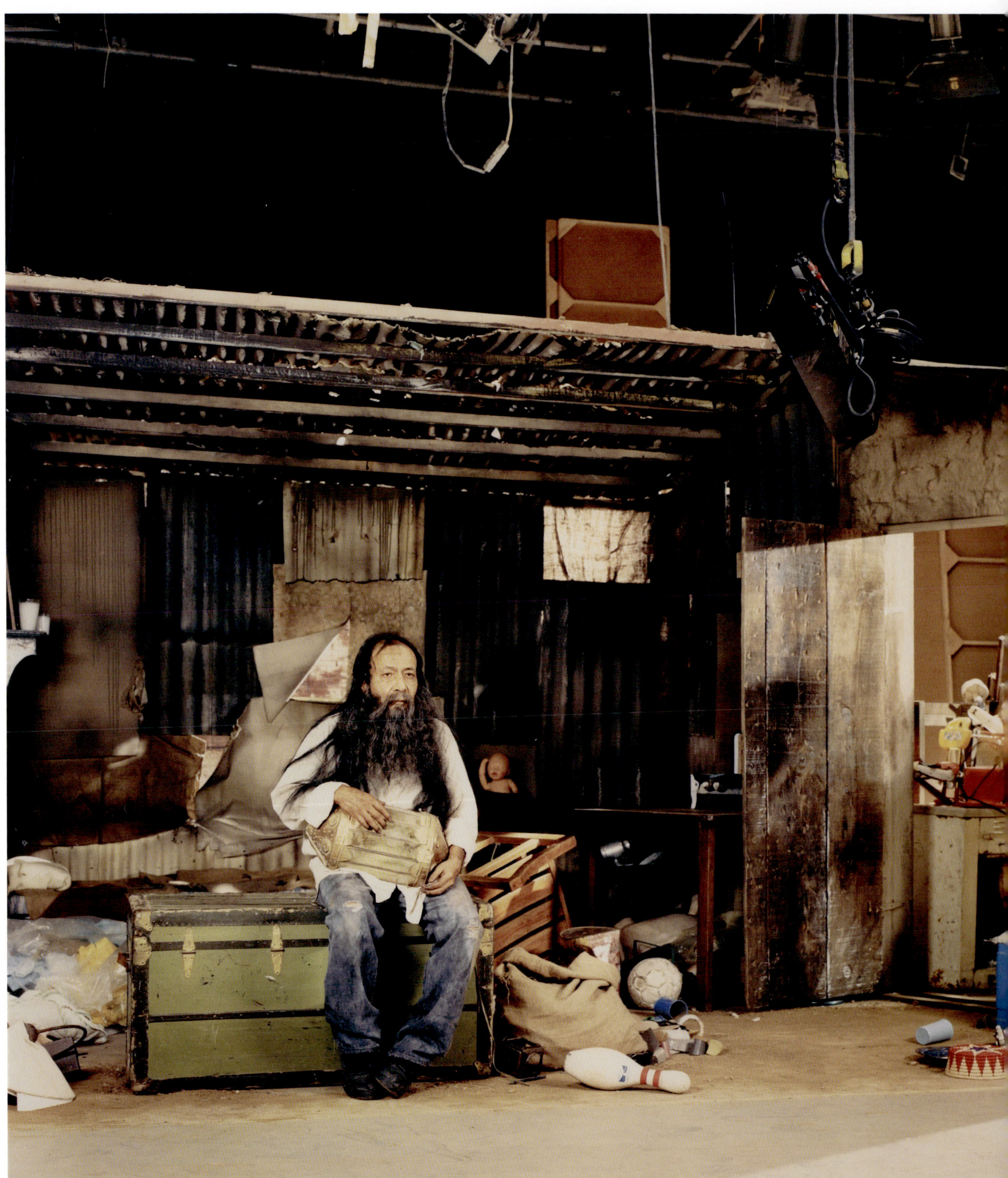

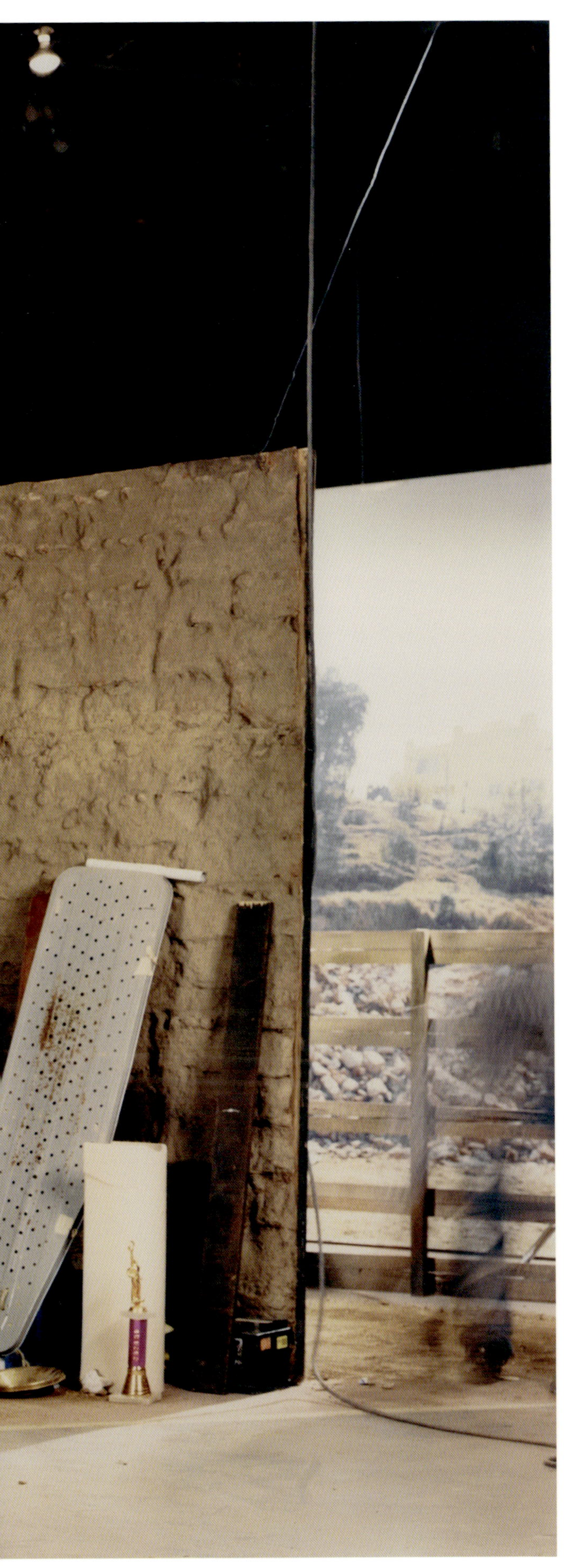

Baltazar Oviedo as Juan Salvador
Amarte es mi Pecado (Loving You Is My Sin), 2003

25 *Amarte es mi Pecado* (Loving You Is My Sin), 2003

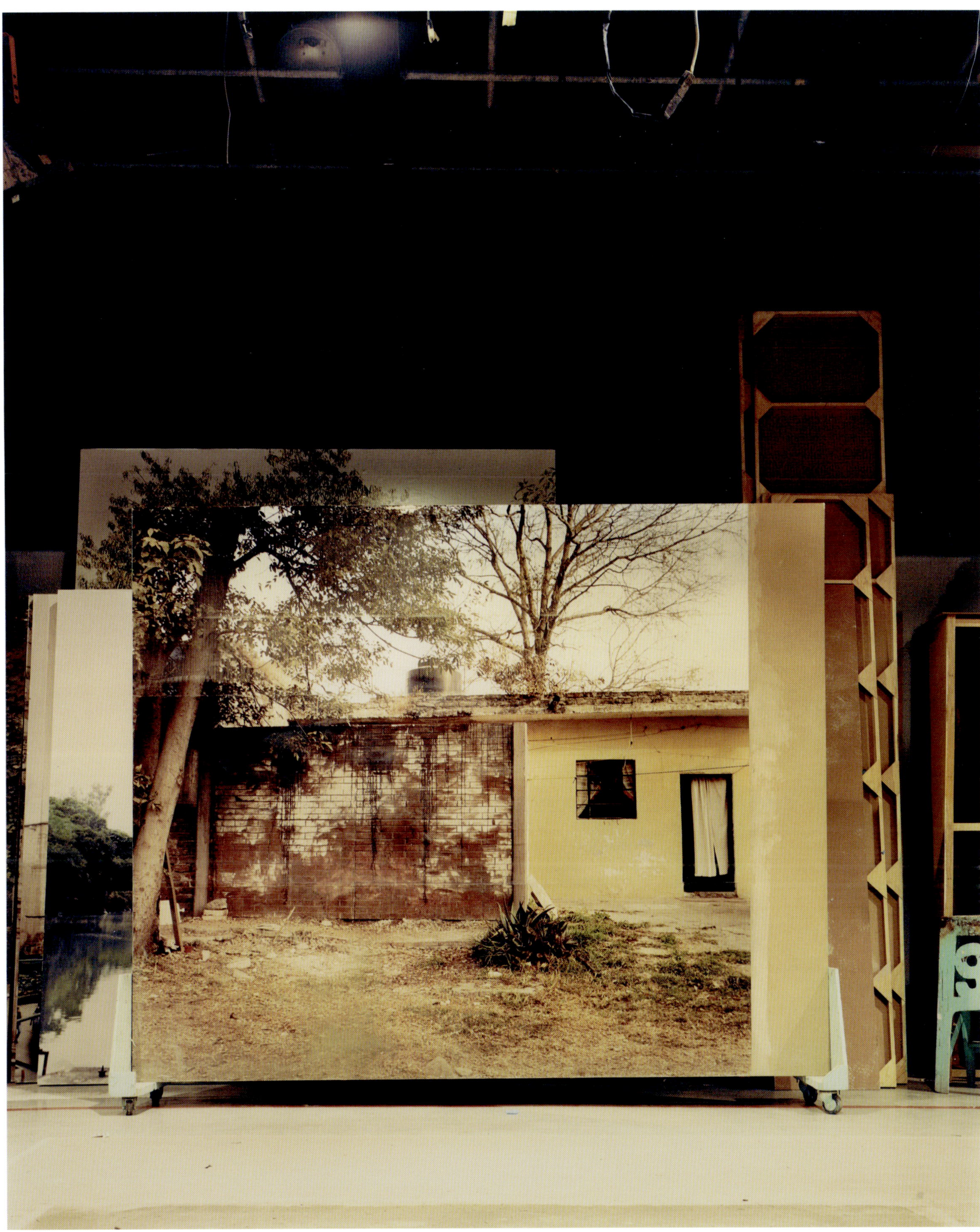

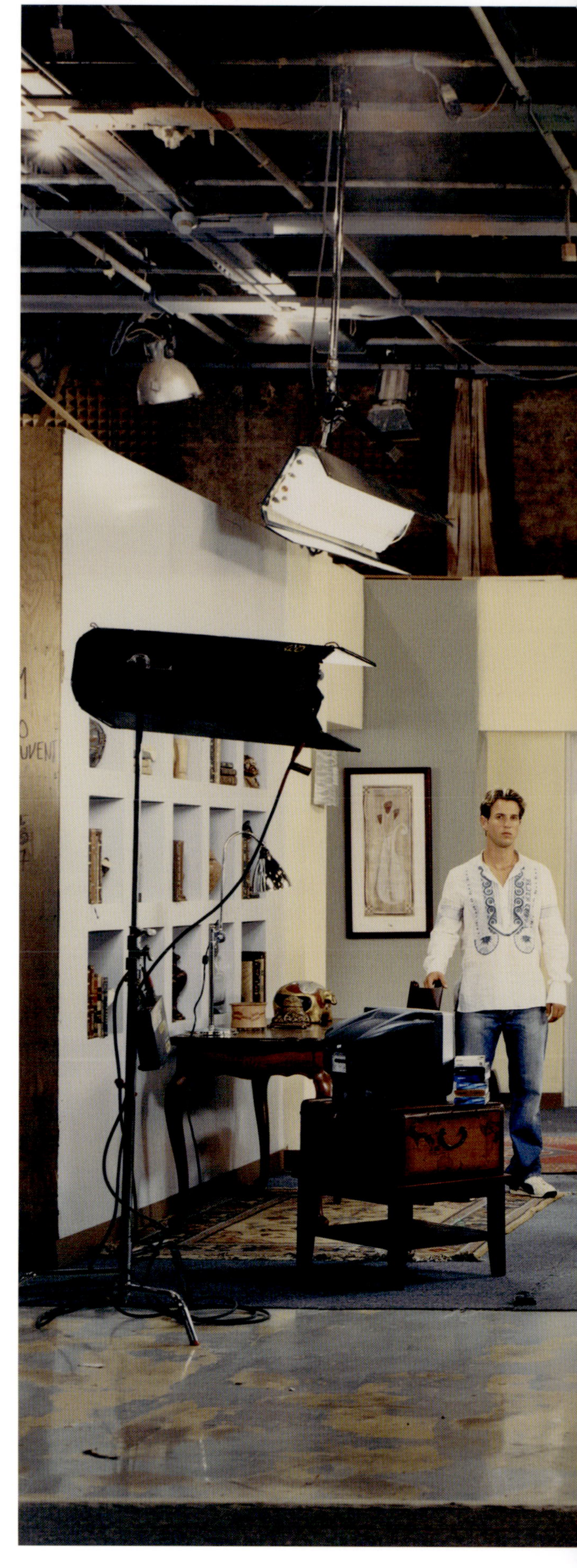

Daniel Berlanga, Miguel Ángel Biagio, Sherlyn, and Daniel Habif as Damián, Samuel Cisneros Castro, "Conny" Concepción Pérez Ávila, and Alberto
Corazones al Límite (Hearts to the Limit), 2004

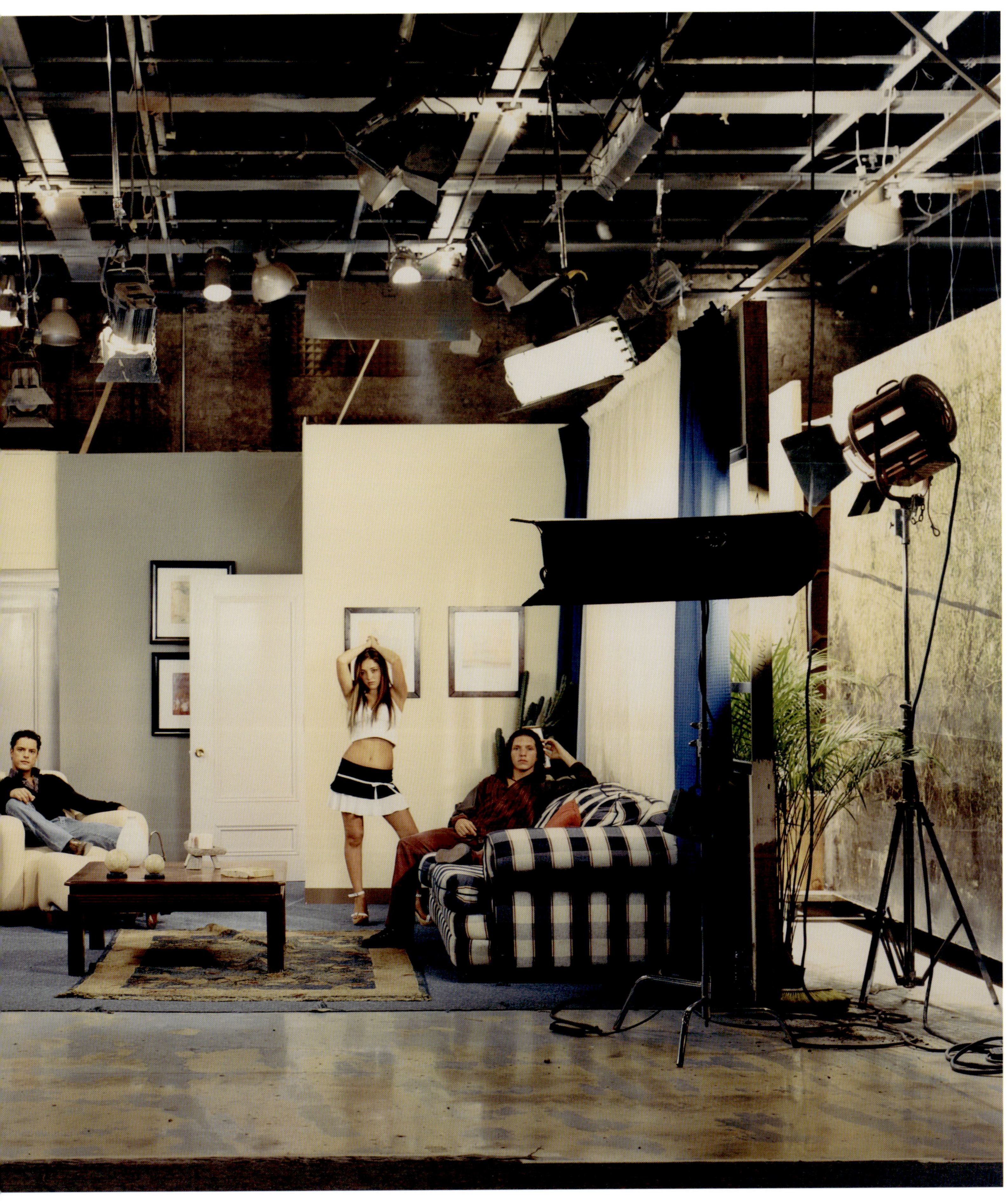

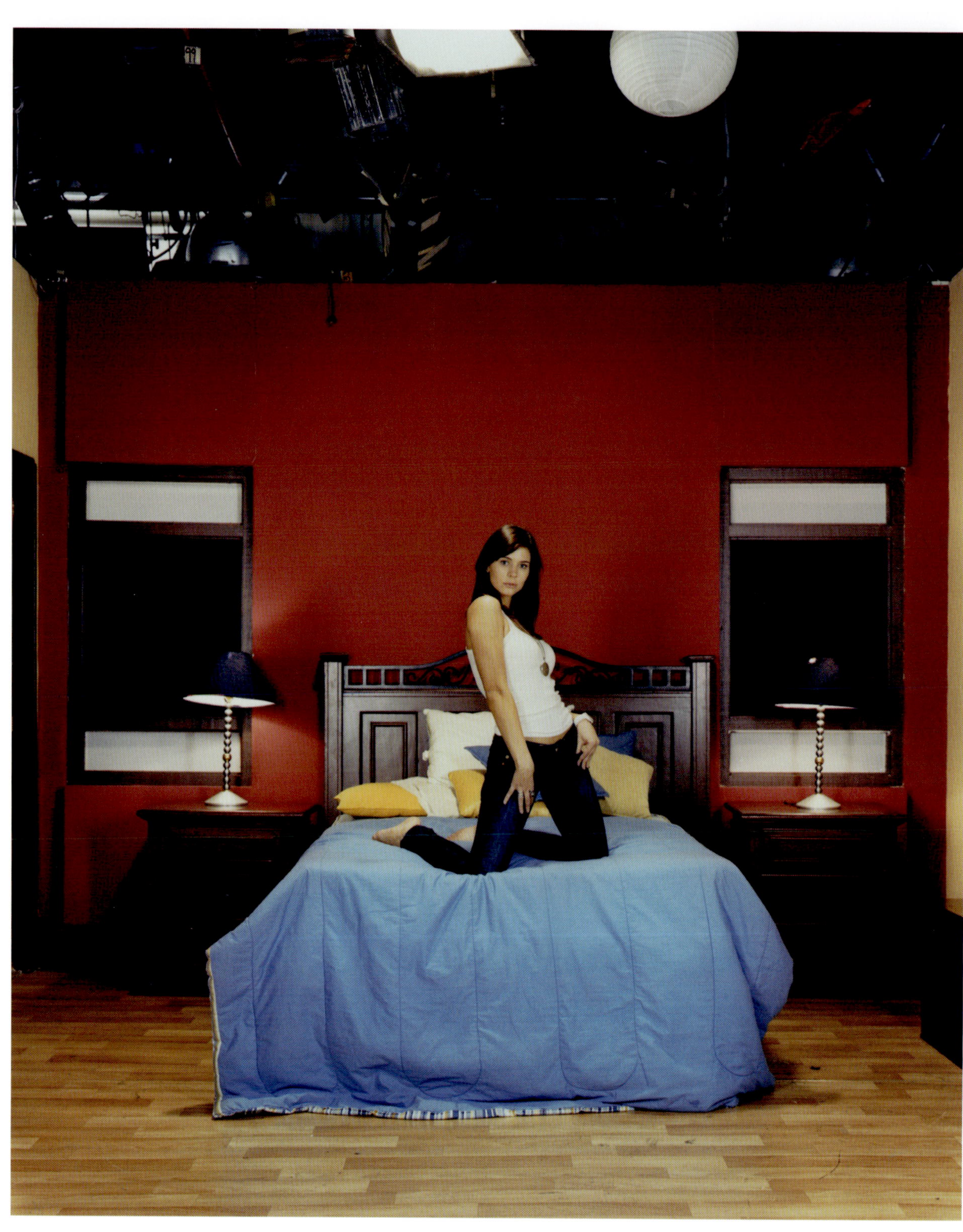

Mariángela Meotti
CEA, Televisa Acting School, 2009

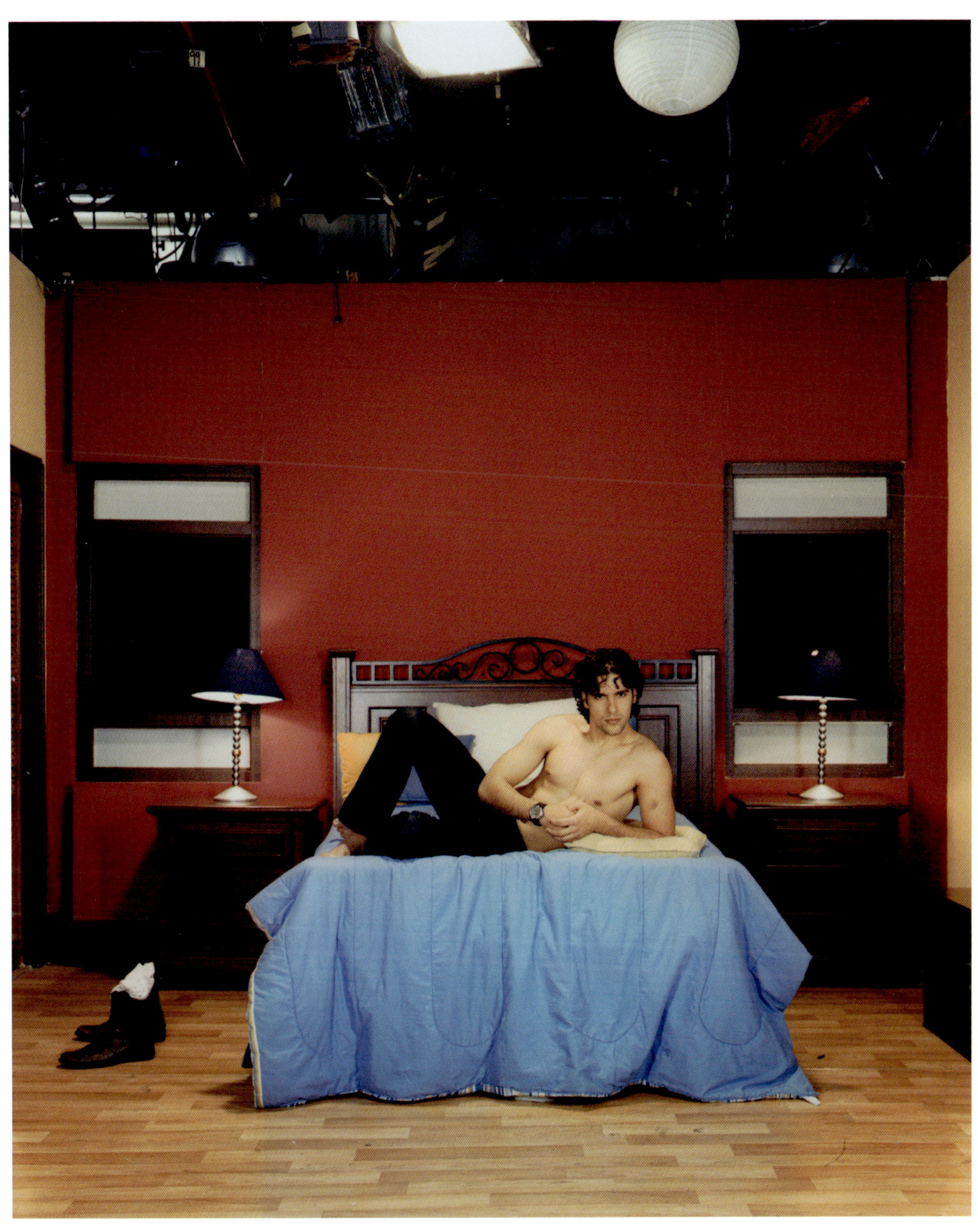

Lenny de la Rosa
CEA, Televisa Acting School, 2009

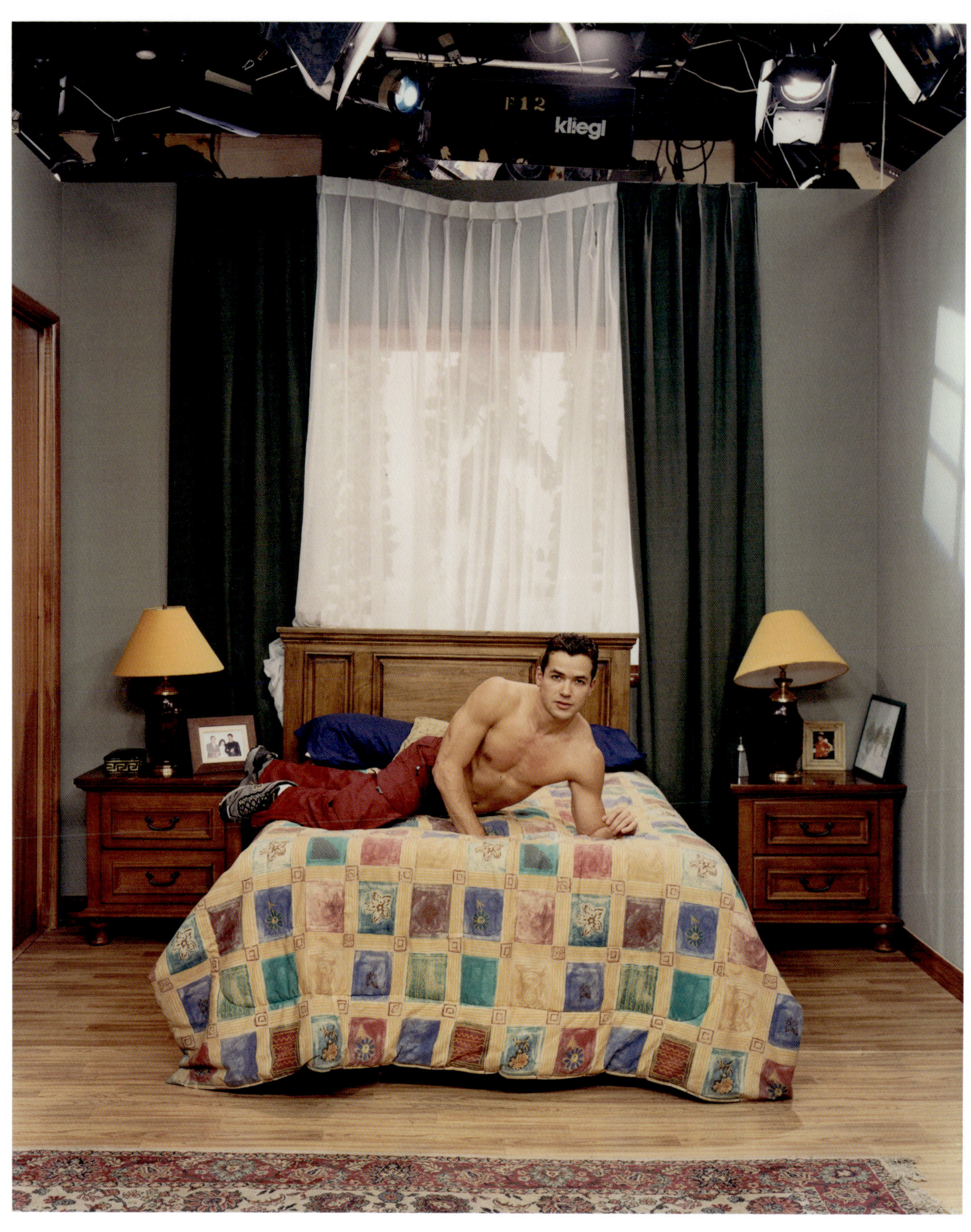

Israel Garduño
CEA, Televisa Acting School, 2003

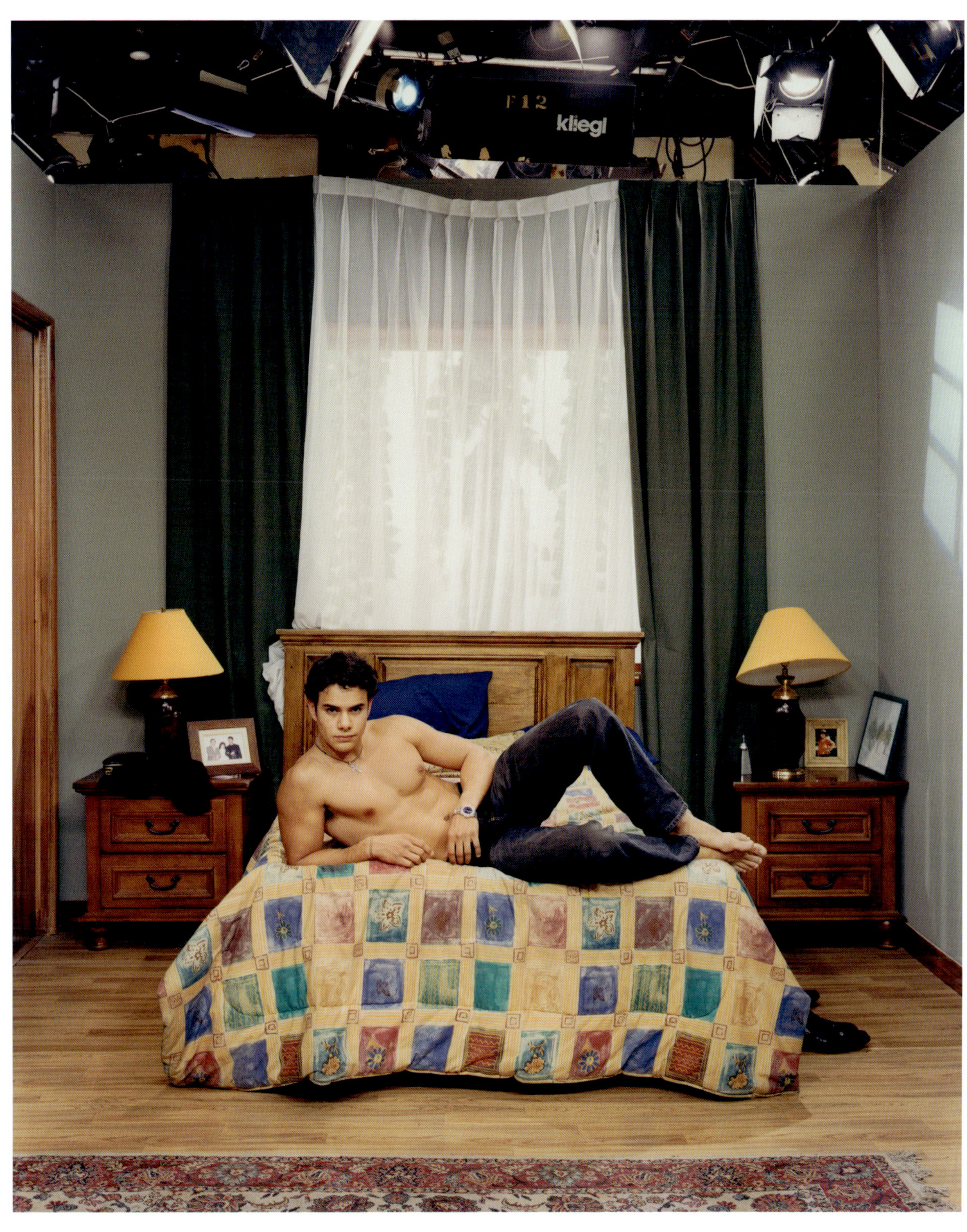

Daniel Cortés
 CEA, Televisa Acting School, 2003

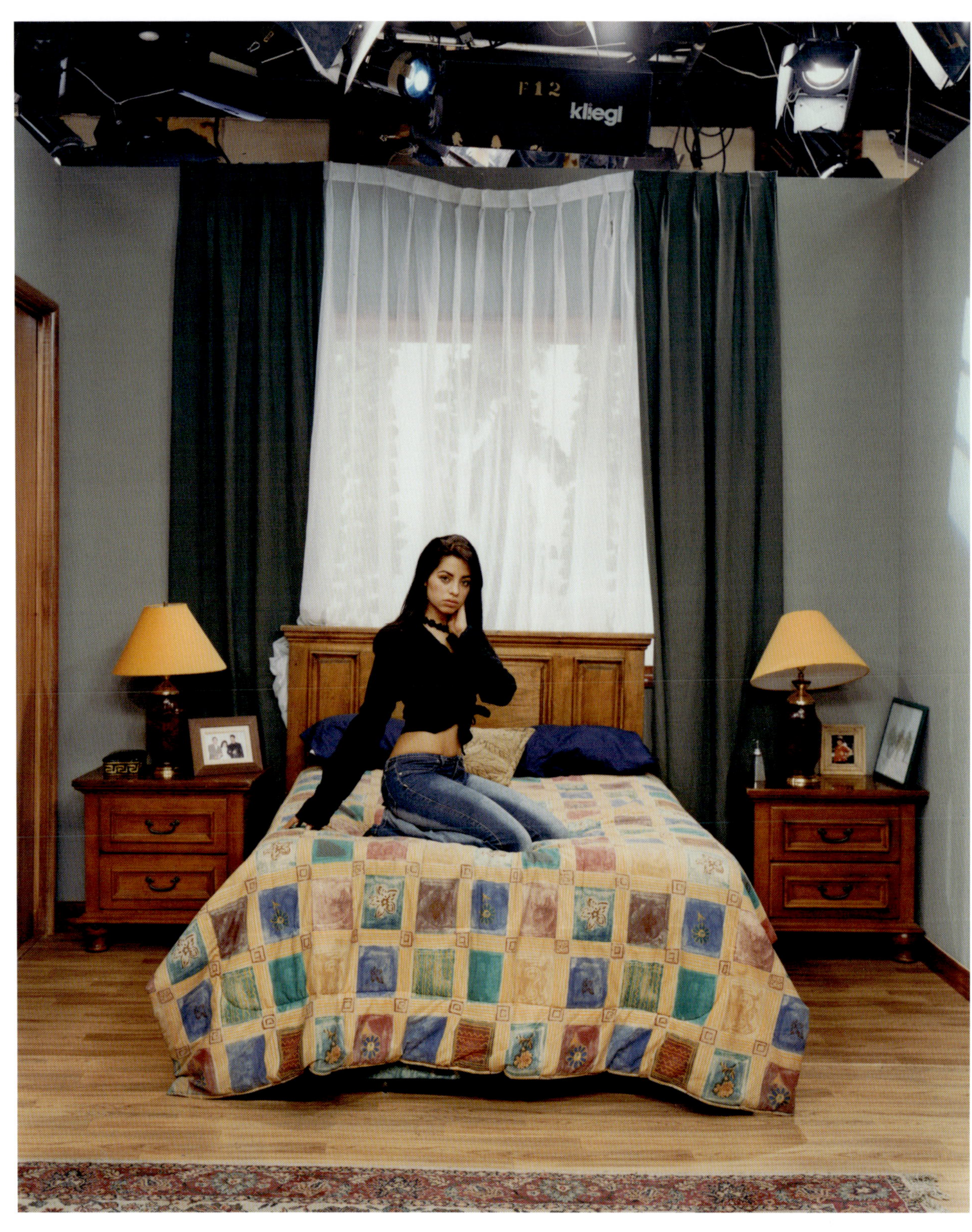

Mariana Morones
 CEA, Televisa Acting School, 2003

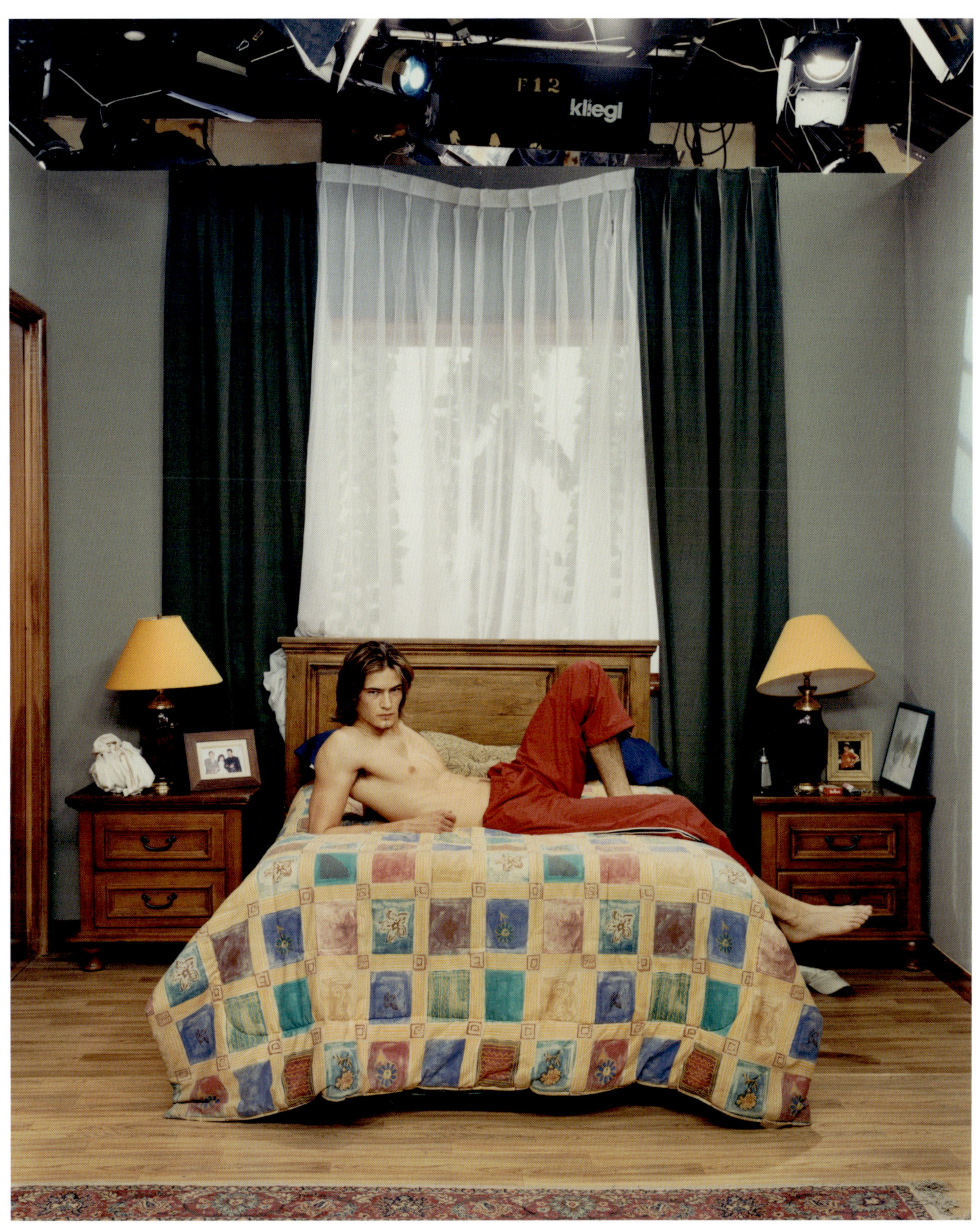

Alejandro Durán Fernández
CEA, Televisa Acting School, 2003

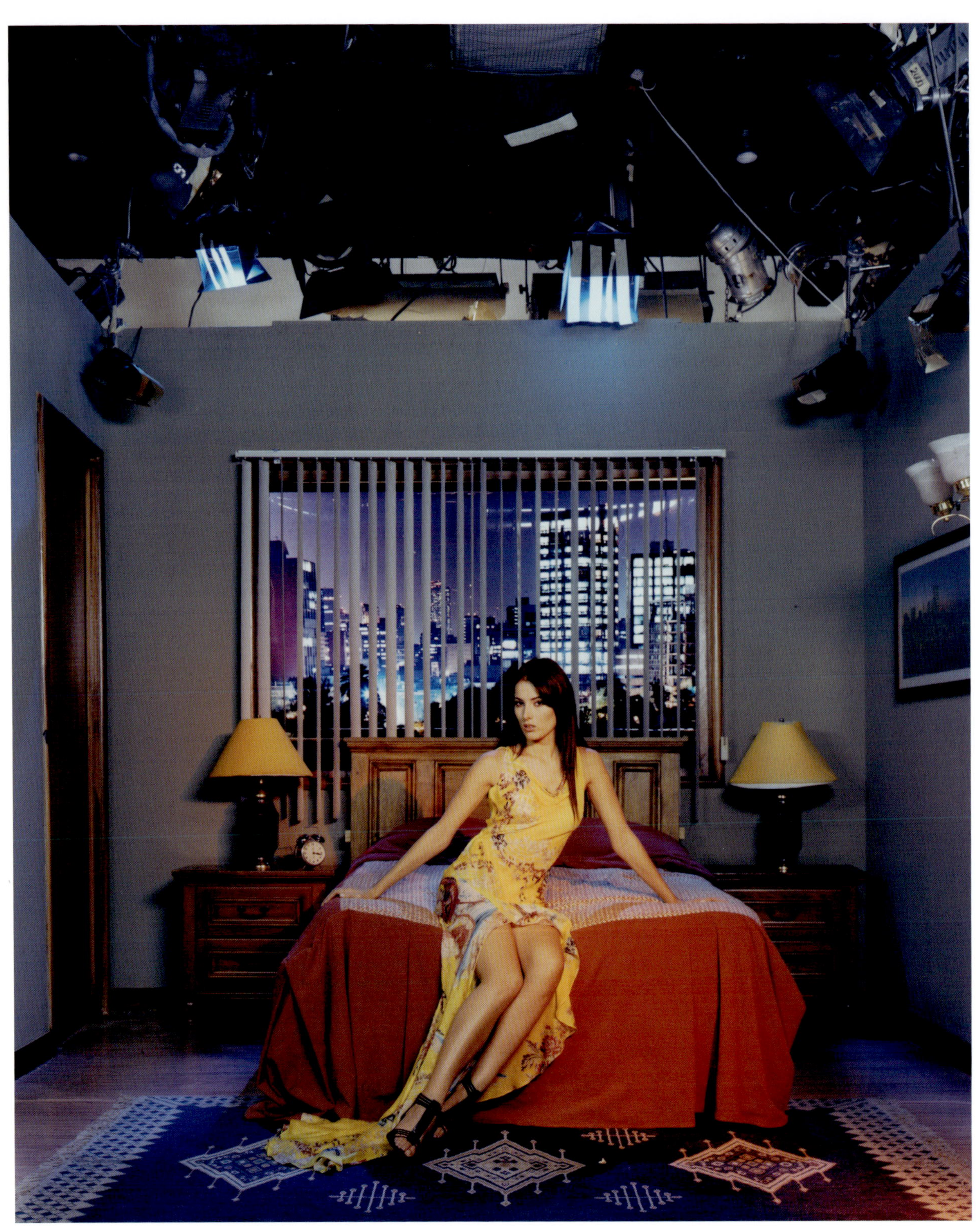

Astrid Chreting
CEA, Televisa Acting School, 2004

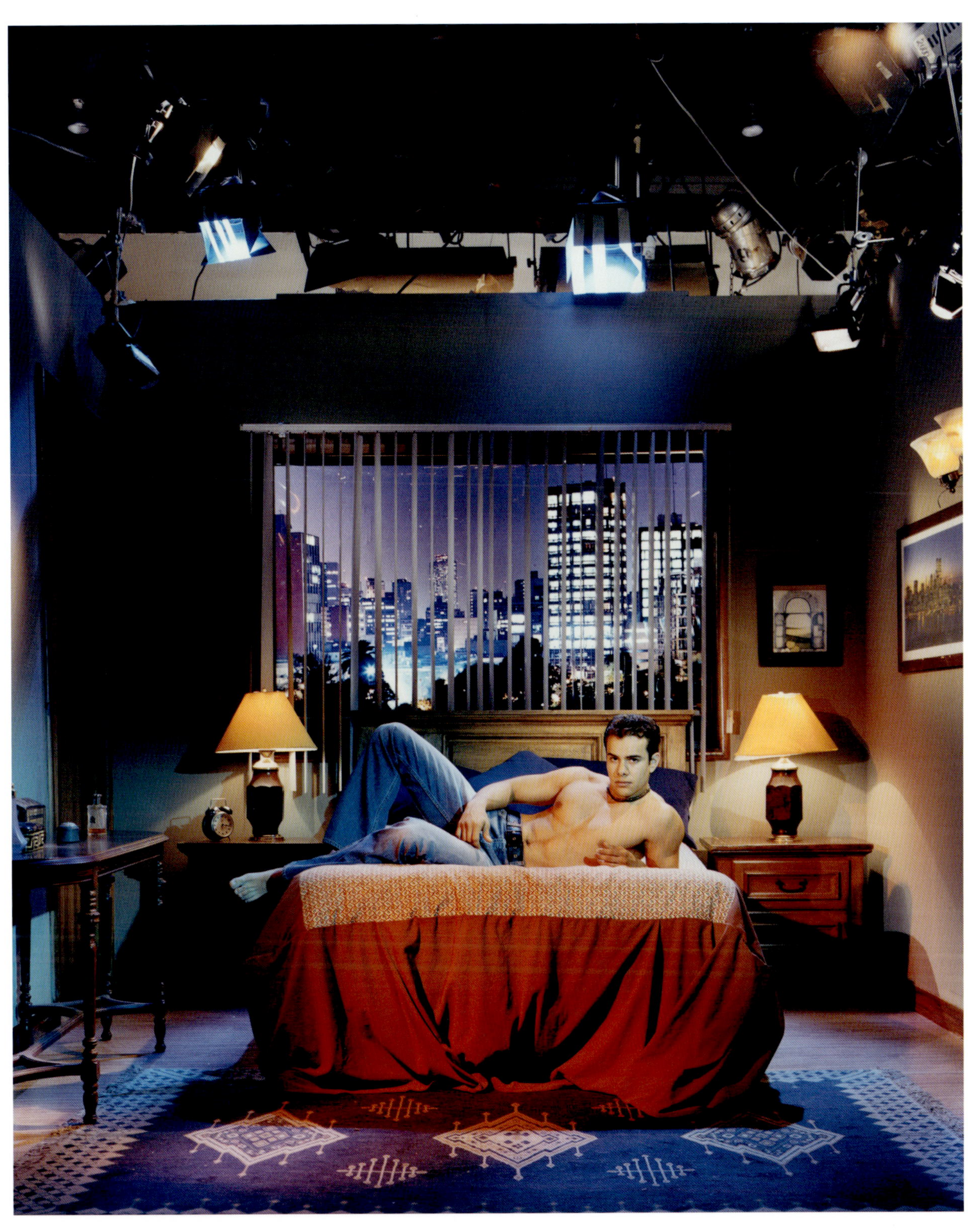

Daniel Cortés
CEA, Televisa Acting School, 2004

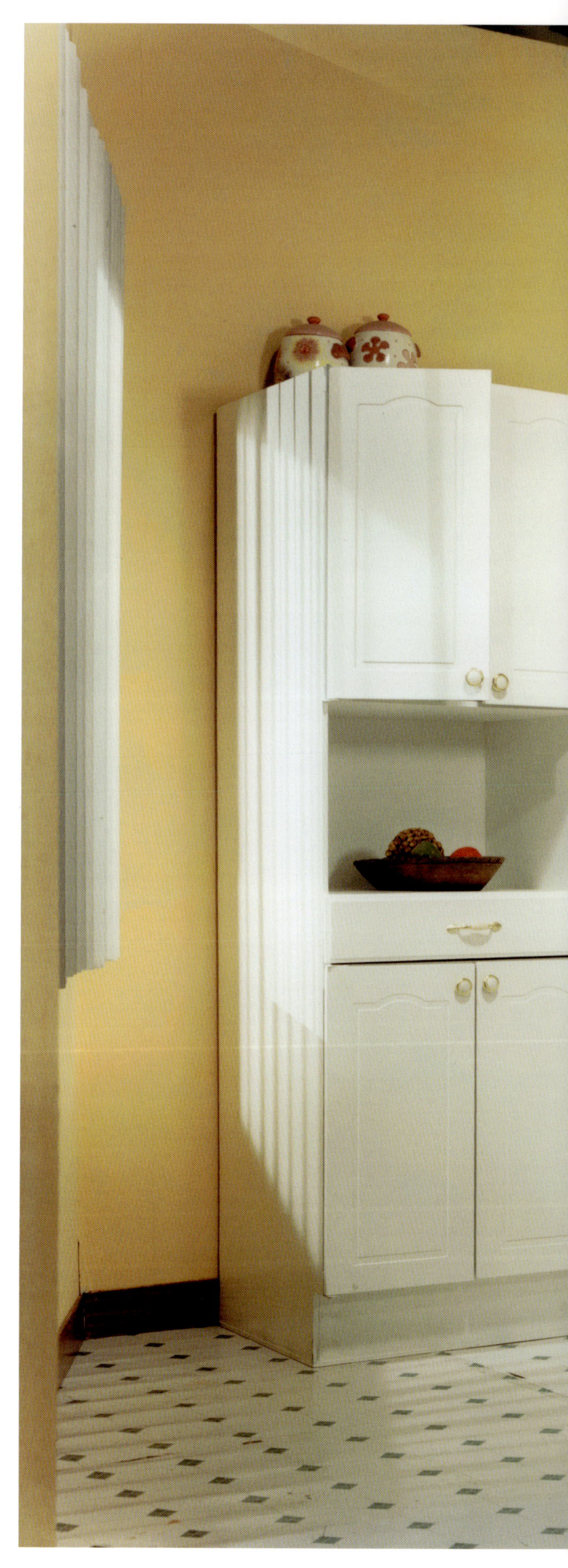

Adrián Martiñón
CEA, Televisa Acting School, 2004

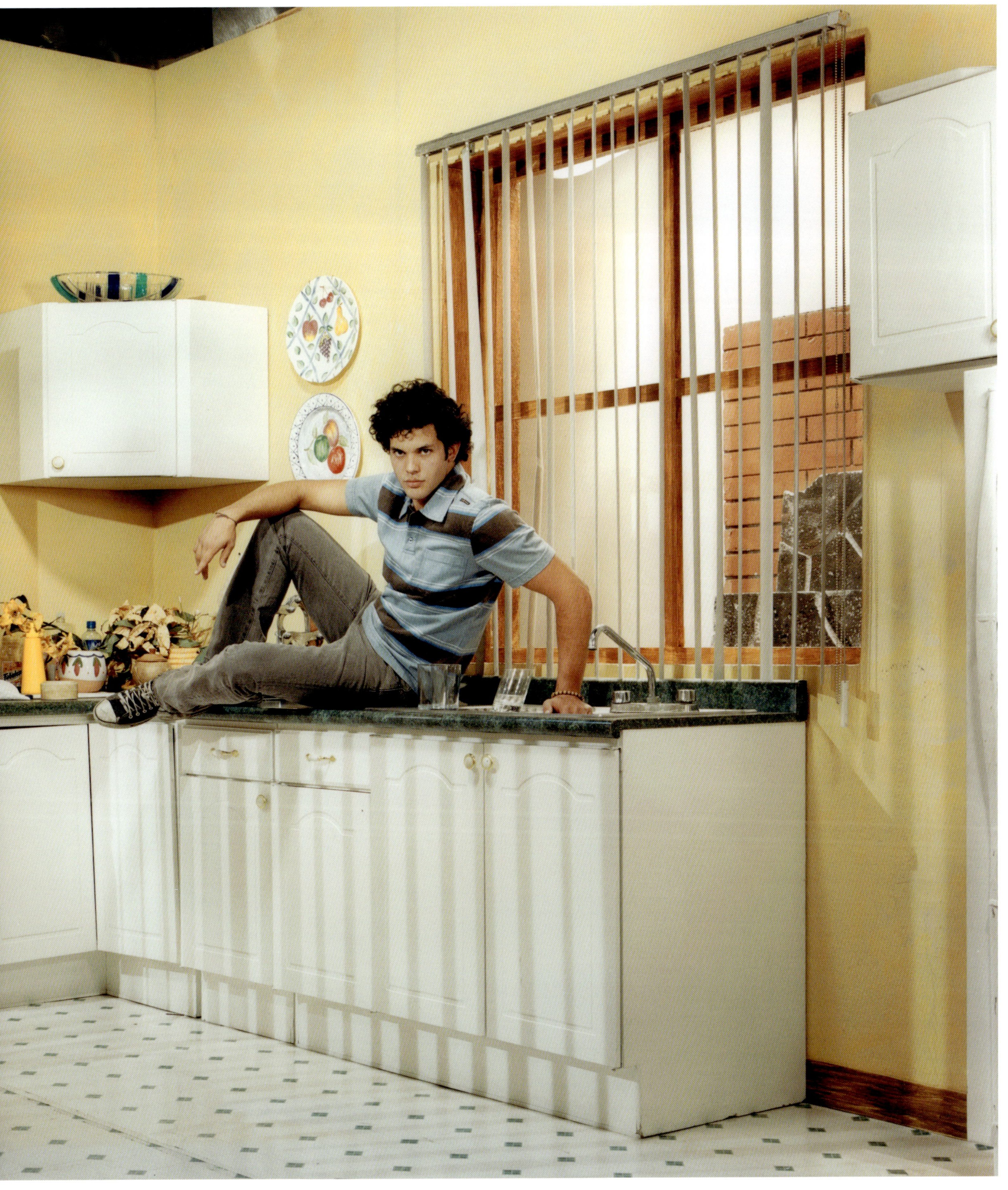

Jorge Garza
CEA, Televisa Acting School, 2003

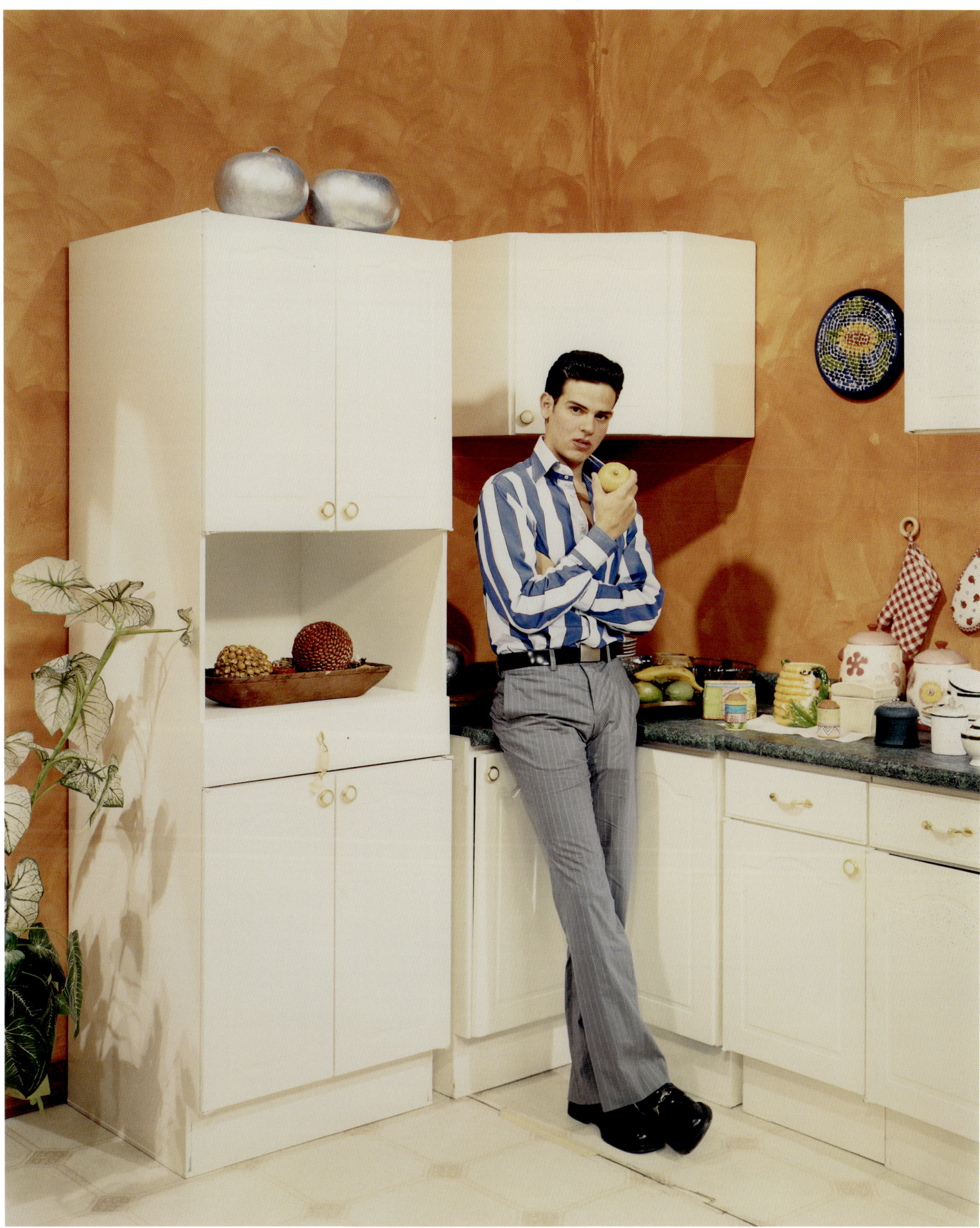

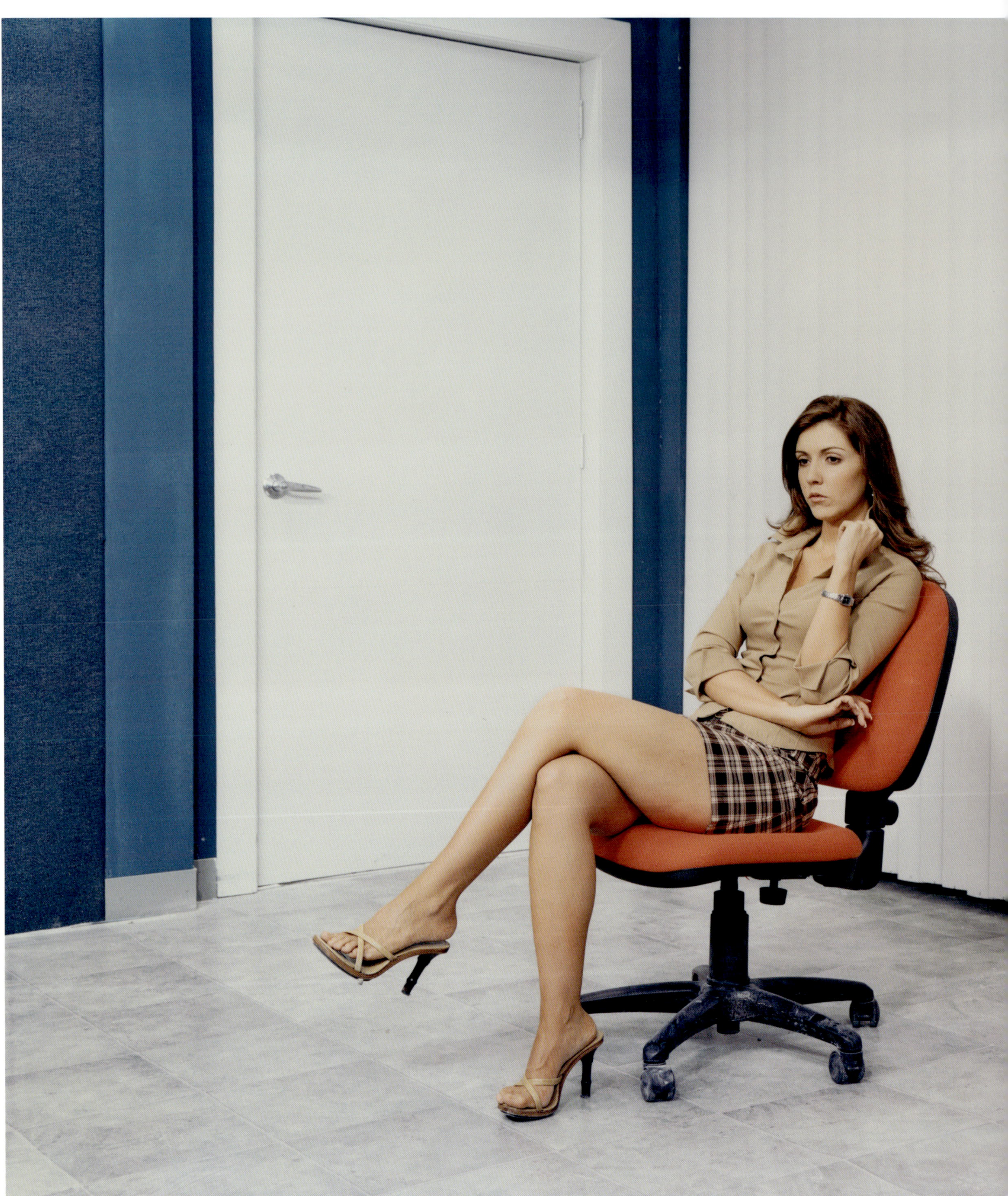

Haydée Navarra as Bianca de la Torre
Corazones al Límite (Hearts to the Limit), 2004

Synopsis of *Corazones al Límite* (Hearts to the Limit)

Diana and Braulio are in love; two adolescents exploring life and love with all the timid intensity of their seventeen years. Handsome, intelligent, and athletic, Braulio is the captain of the rowing team at New Athens High School, an innovative institution that fosters traditional values and hard work among young people.

Diana is Braulio's perfect match, as positive, studious, and enterprising as he is. Both are born leaders, and they face the adventure of each new day, alongside their classmates, with enthusiasm, curiosity, and optimism.

Day by day we are drawn into the fascinating story of this group of teenagers, each of them with his or her own problems and joys: the dangers facing young people—alcoholism, drug addiction, bad choices; their amusing and incredible adventures in school and outside of it; the adrenaline explosion of extreme sports; the frenetic rhythms of their music; the conflicts, tenderness, and drama of their family lives.

Braulio, for example, lost his parents when he was twelve years old and lives with his uncle, aunt, and cousin Esteban—an ambitious man who hates him and will attempt to rob him of his inheritance and supplant him in Diana's affections through lies and deceit, in order to take over her father's million-dollar company.

Diana's father, Doménico, is a cold, uncompromising man who rejects her because she is a woman, and demands that she show herself capable of achieving academic excellence without his money or support. Courageous and determined, Diana accepts the challenge: she goes to live with her aunt Pilar, her mother's sister, and works to support herself and pay for her schooling.

Pilar is a generous, independent woman who loves Diana like a daughter and supports her unconditionally. She wants to keep Diana from suffering the same fate as herself: she lost Álvaro, the love of her life, because of her father's social prejudices.

Álvaro is now the owner and principal of New Athens High School. As he encounters Pilar again, life has given him a new chance to be happy. But their love is threatened by his partner Emma, who wants to marry him and is incensed to see them together. She schemes relentlessly to separate them.

Diana's and Braulio's love is also endangered by the jealousy of Conny, an arrogant, envious girl who dreams of being Braulio's girlfriend and allies herself with Emma to achieve her goal. Amidst a storm of lies and blackmail, Braulio and Diana can count on the support and affection of their friends: healthy, vibrant, and hopeful young people who are joined by strong ties of lasting friendship.

We will share with them the joy of being young, the pride of triumph and the bitterness of failure, their refusal to accept defeat, their passion for danger, and the confused but intense emotions of first love.

René Casados as Dante Lacalfari
Corazones al Límite (Hearts to the Limit), 2004

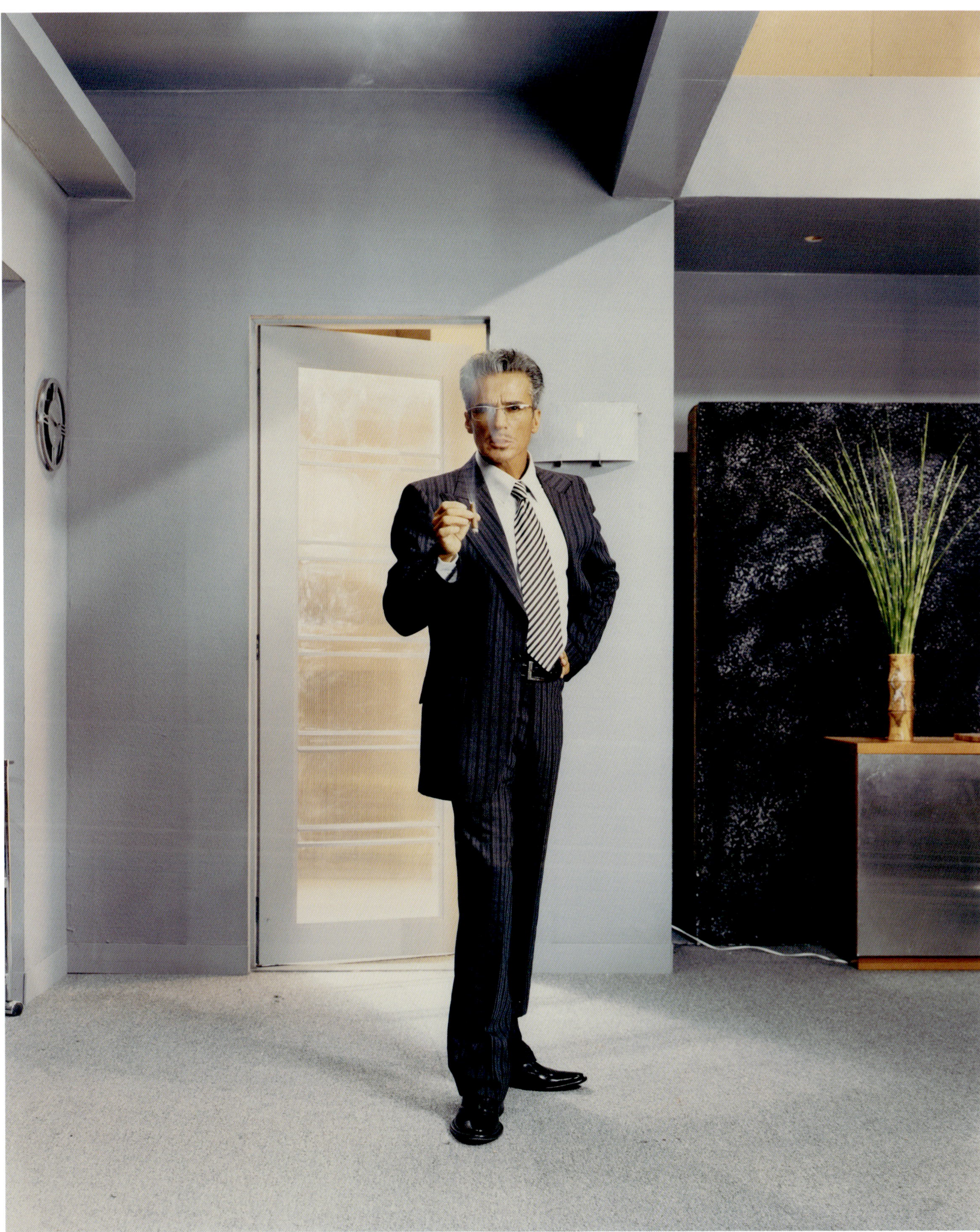

39 *Rubí*, 2004

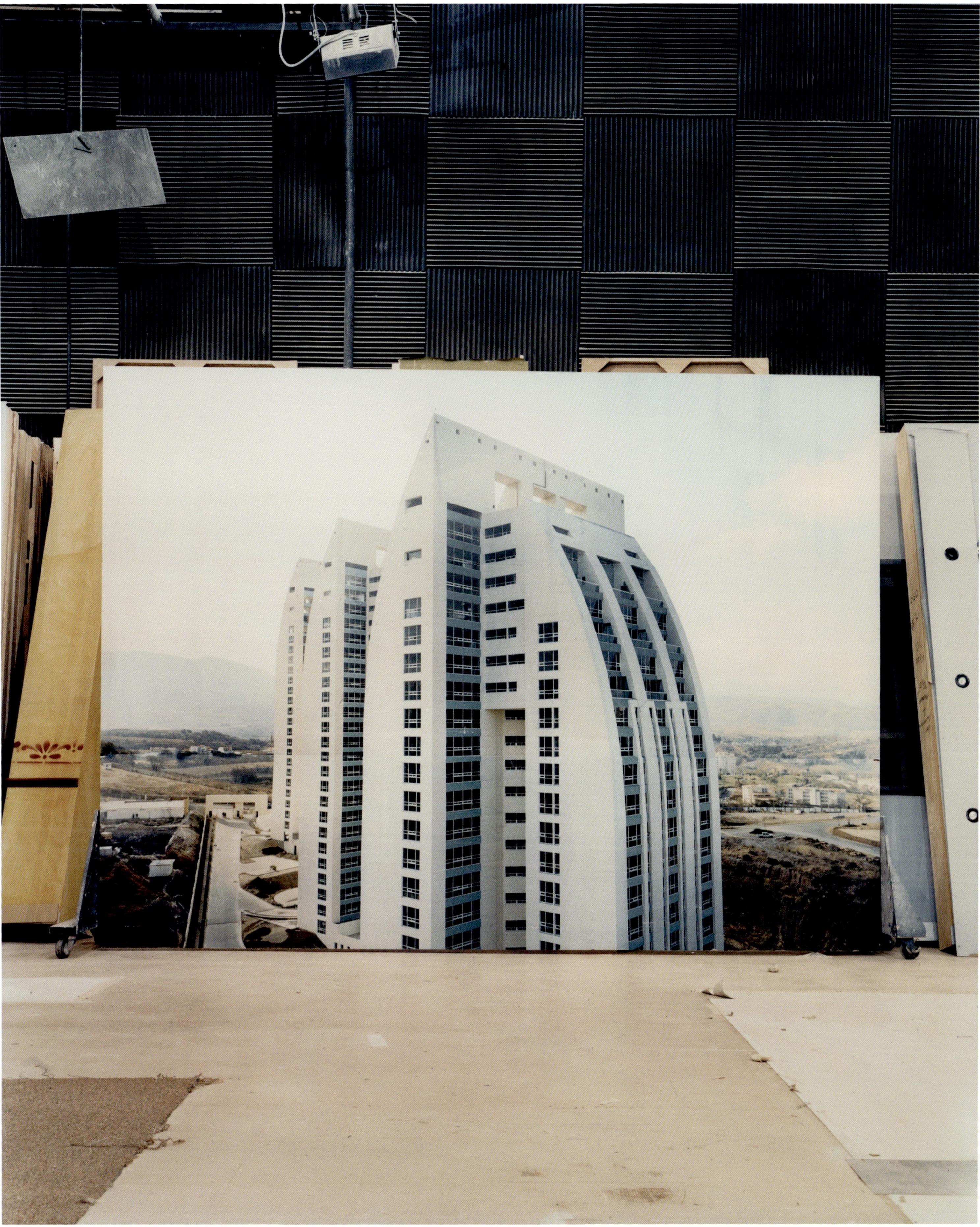

40 *Amorcito Corazón* (Darling Sweetheart), 2011

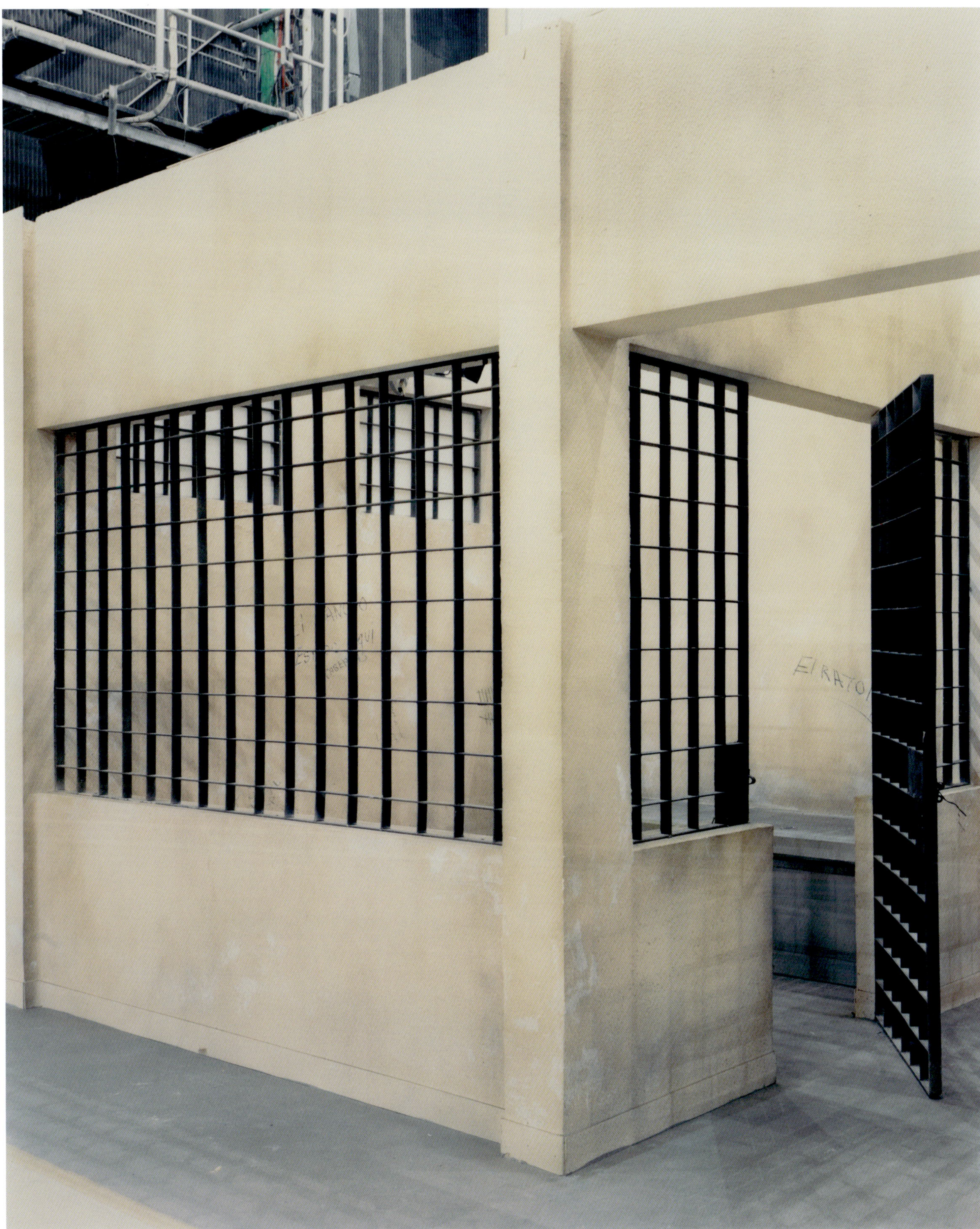

ÁNGELA LANDA DE DUPRÍS

Sweet, beautiful, balanced, understanding, and charitable, Ángela is the very best mother in the world. Having abandoned her career as a ballerina for Franco, she lives only to love him and their children. She gives dance classes. She is a strong-willed woman, able to stand up for her convictions. When Franco dies, Ángela falls victim to Lucrecia, but she struggles to go on, and will eventually find a new love.

Bianca Marroquín as Ángela Landa de Duprís
Esperanza del Corazón (Hope of the Heart), 2011

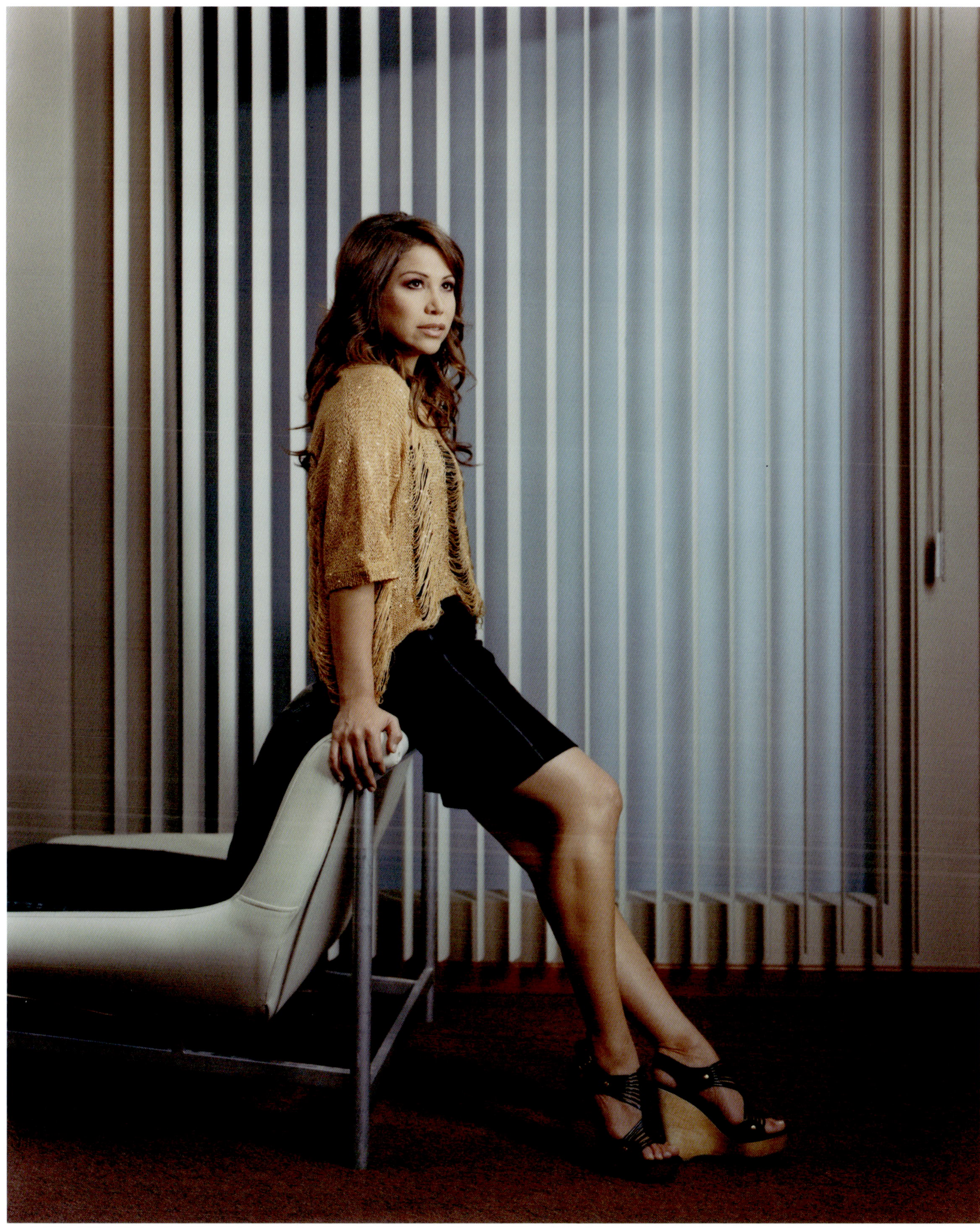

ORLANDO DUARTE

The patriarch of the Duarte family, and a famous television and movie actor in his younger days. A wise man, full of optimism. Widowed for many years, he is devoted to his son and grandchildren. He gets along very badly with Camila, of whose malice he is well aware. Mariano's best friend, he steadies and enlightens the family with his deep experience of life.

Fernando Allende as Orlando Duarte
Esperanza del Corazón (Hope of the Heart), 2011

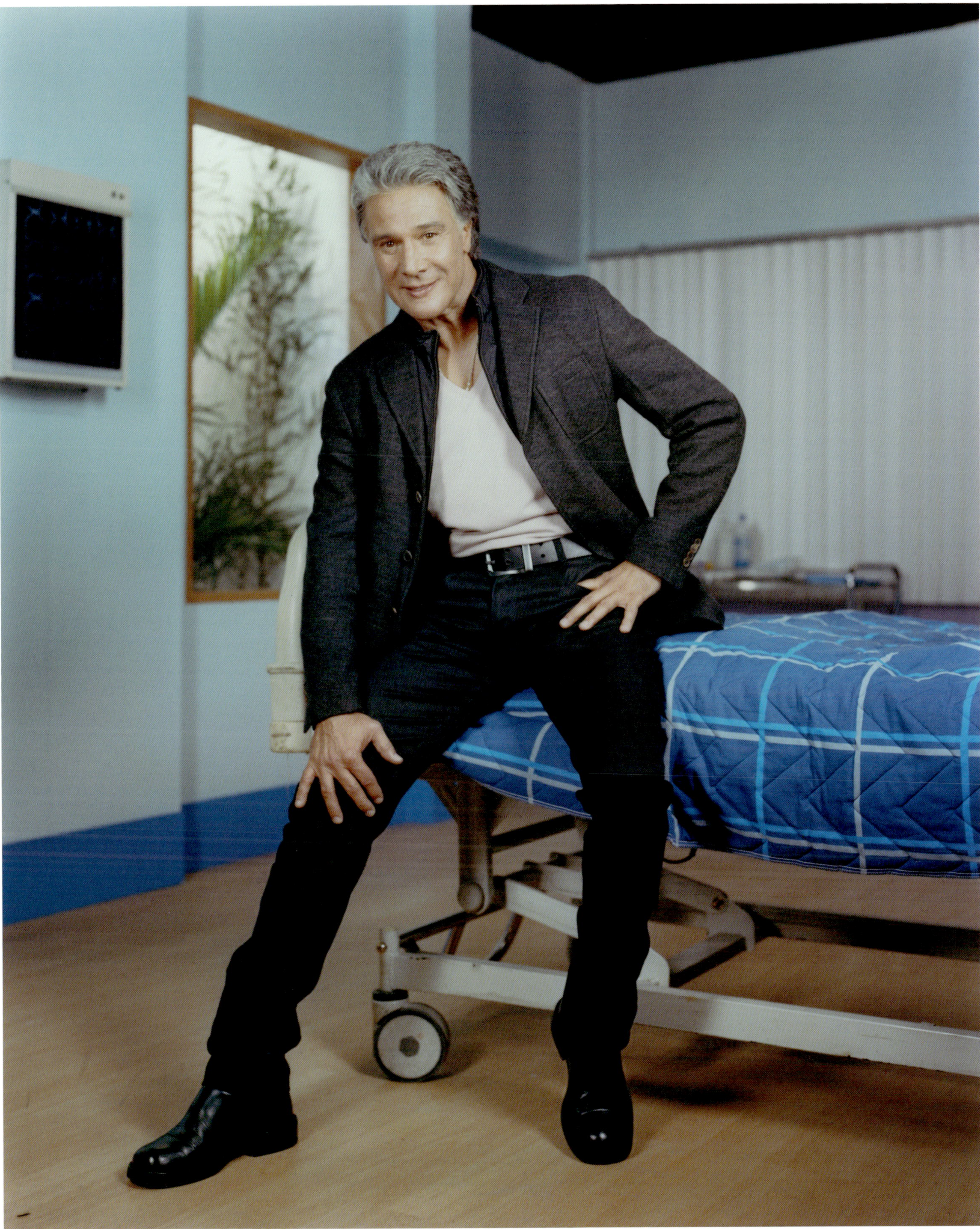

REFUGIO URBINA

A homemaker, the mother of Cristina and Óscar, and Cristóbal's wife. She loves Cristóbal and admires him for his honesty, without suspecting the secret he conceals. Conservative by nature, attractive, sincere, and faithful, she is the cornerstone of the family. She loves music.

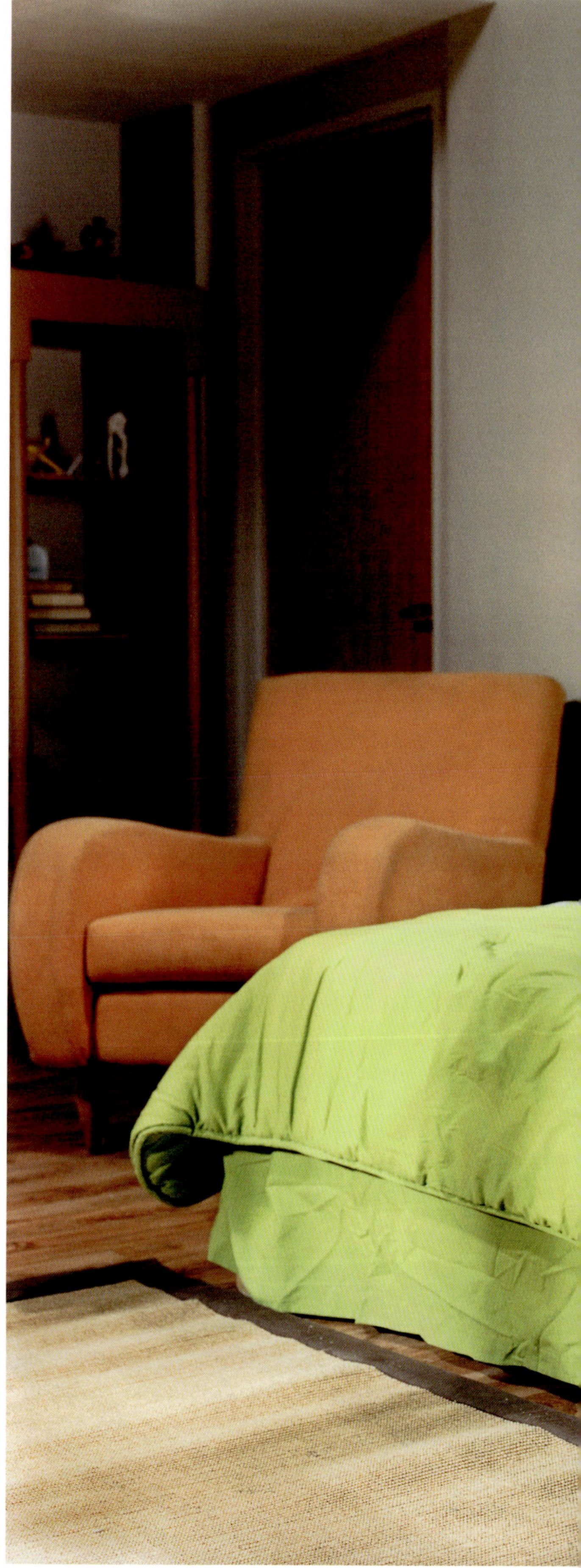

Laura León "La Tesorito" as Refugio Urbina
Dos Hogares (Double Life), 2011

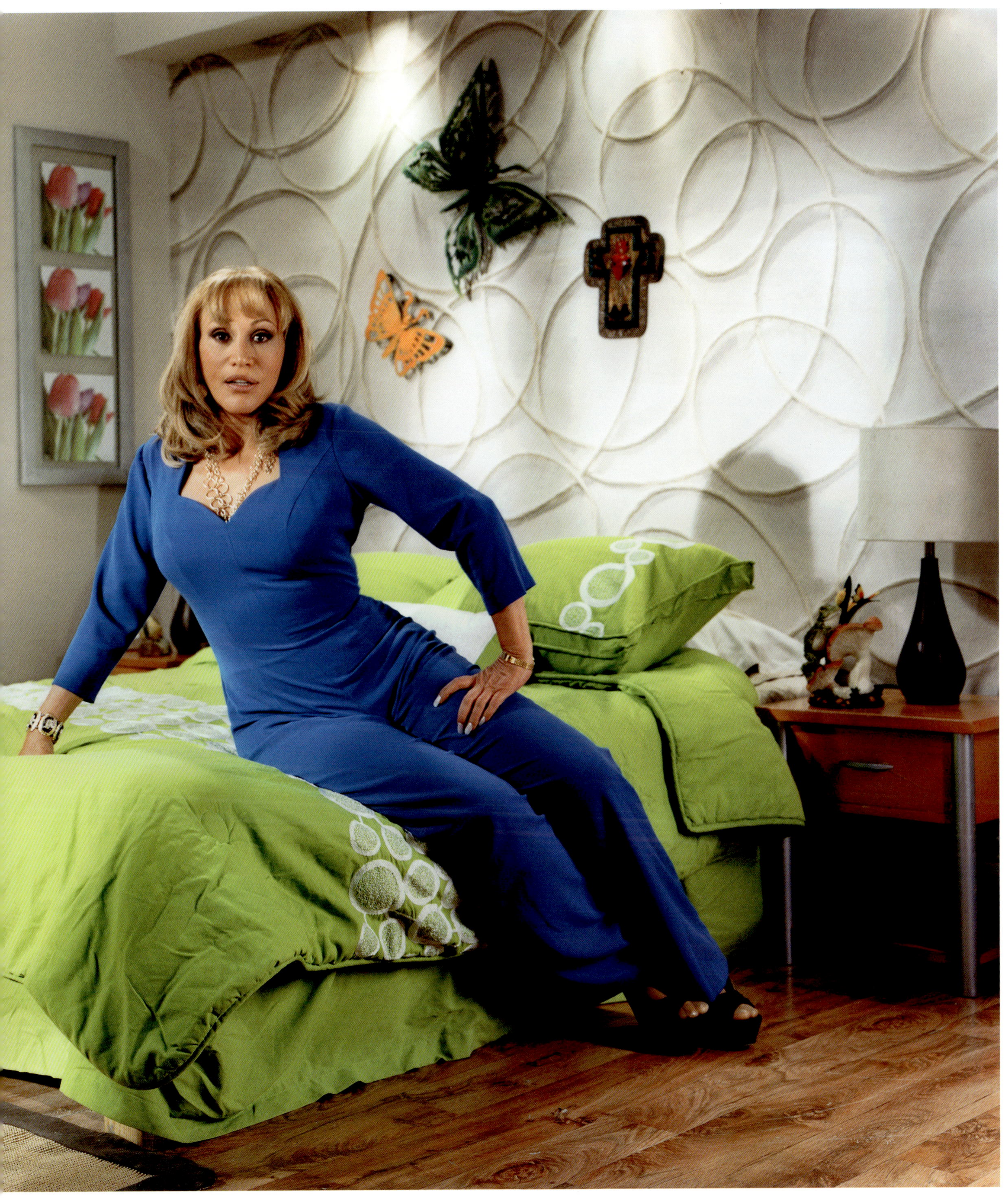

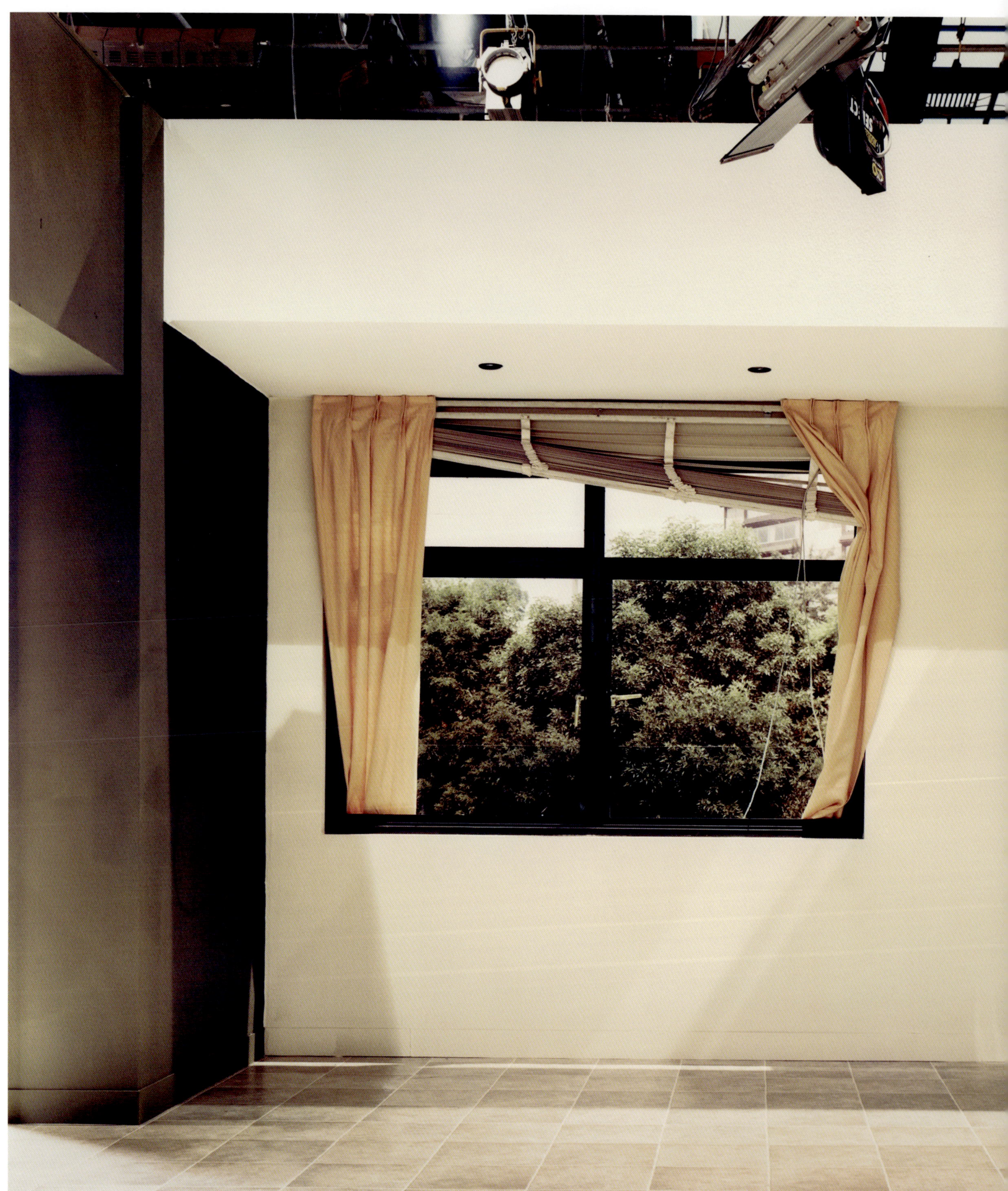

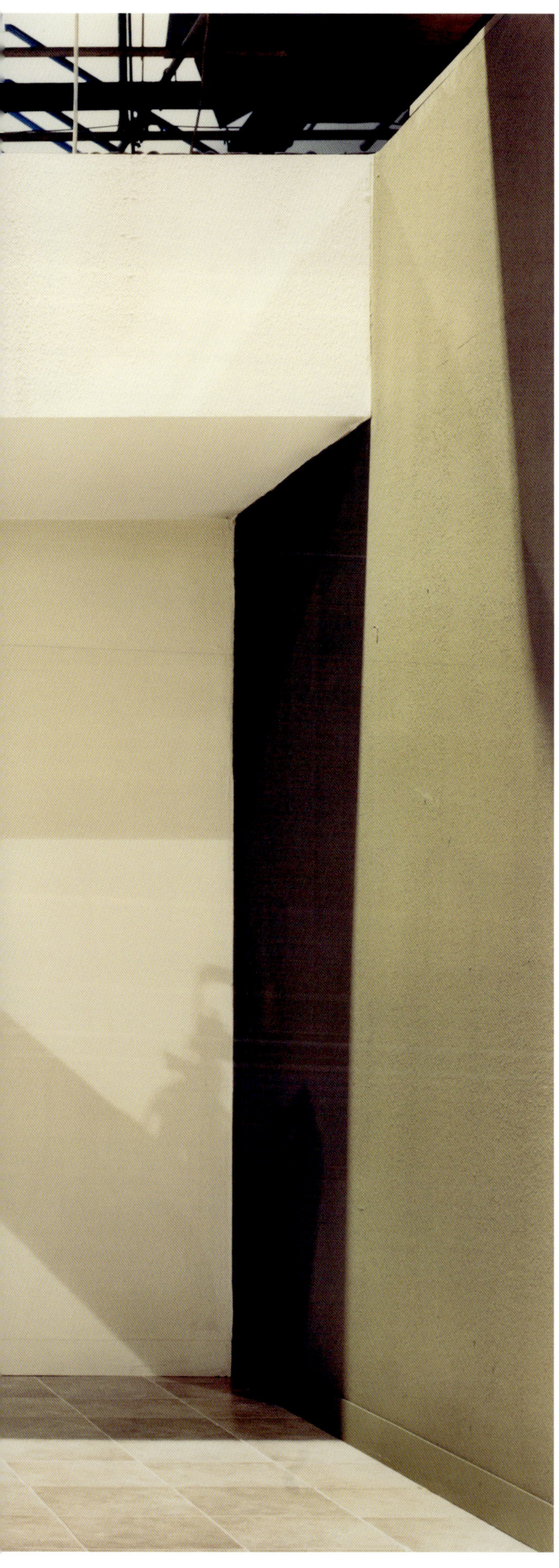

44 *Amarte es mi Pecado* (Loving You Is My Sin), 2003

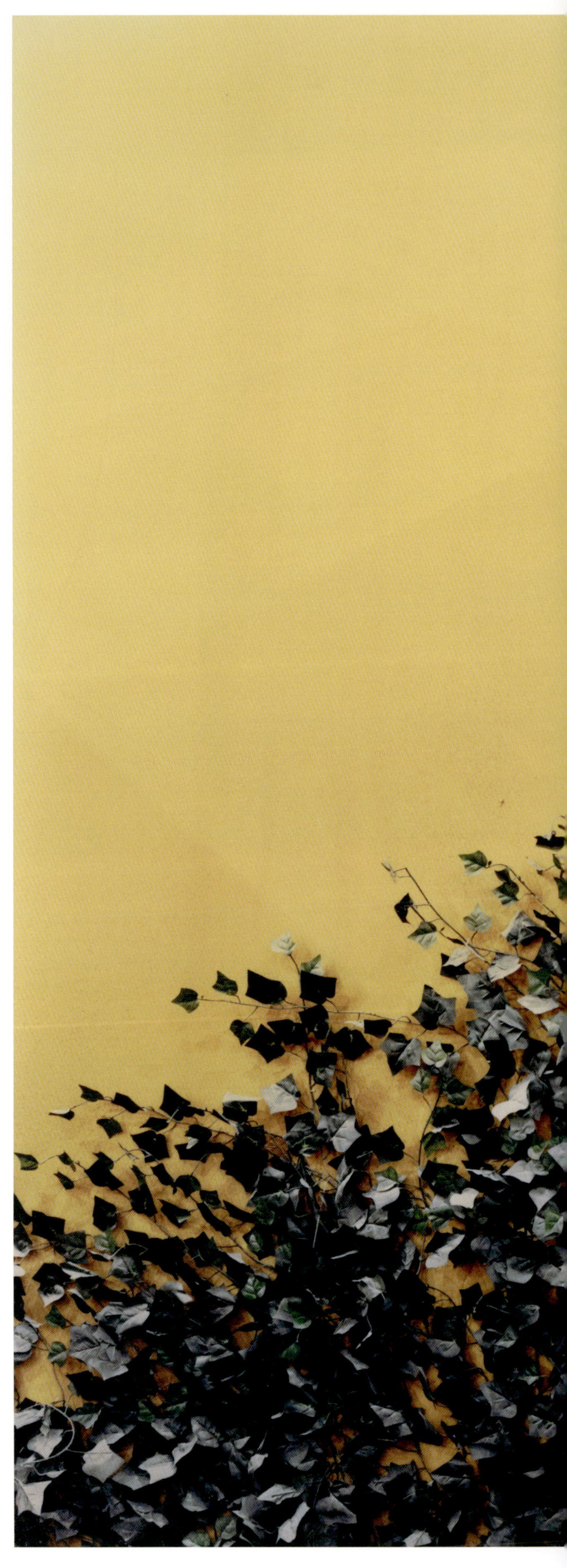

45 *Alma de Hierro* (Iron Soul), 2009

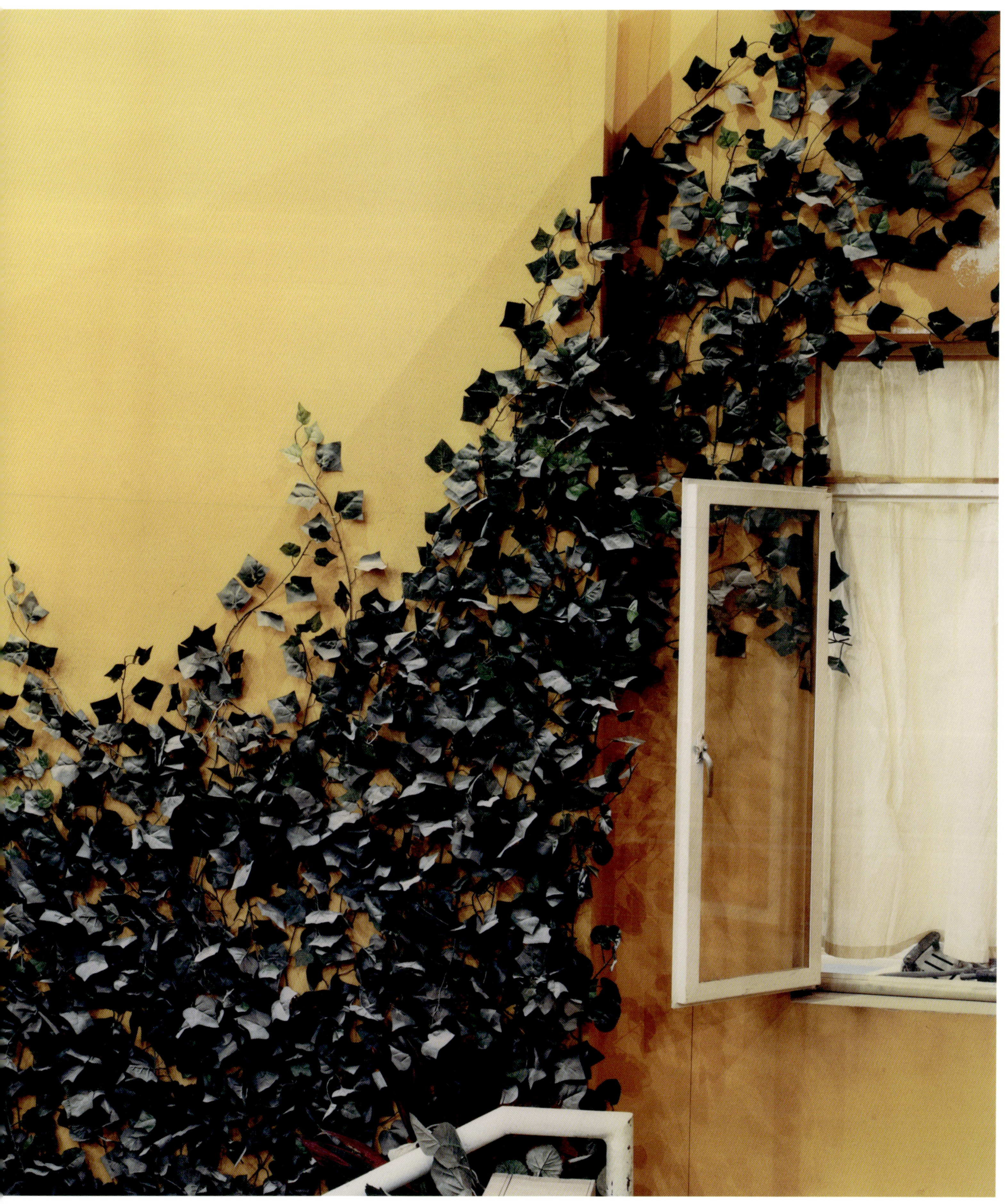

 Un Gancho al Corazón (A Blow to the Heart), 2009

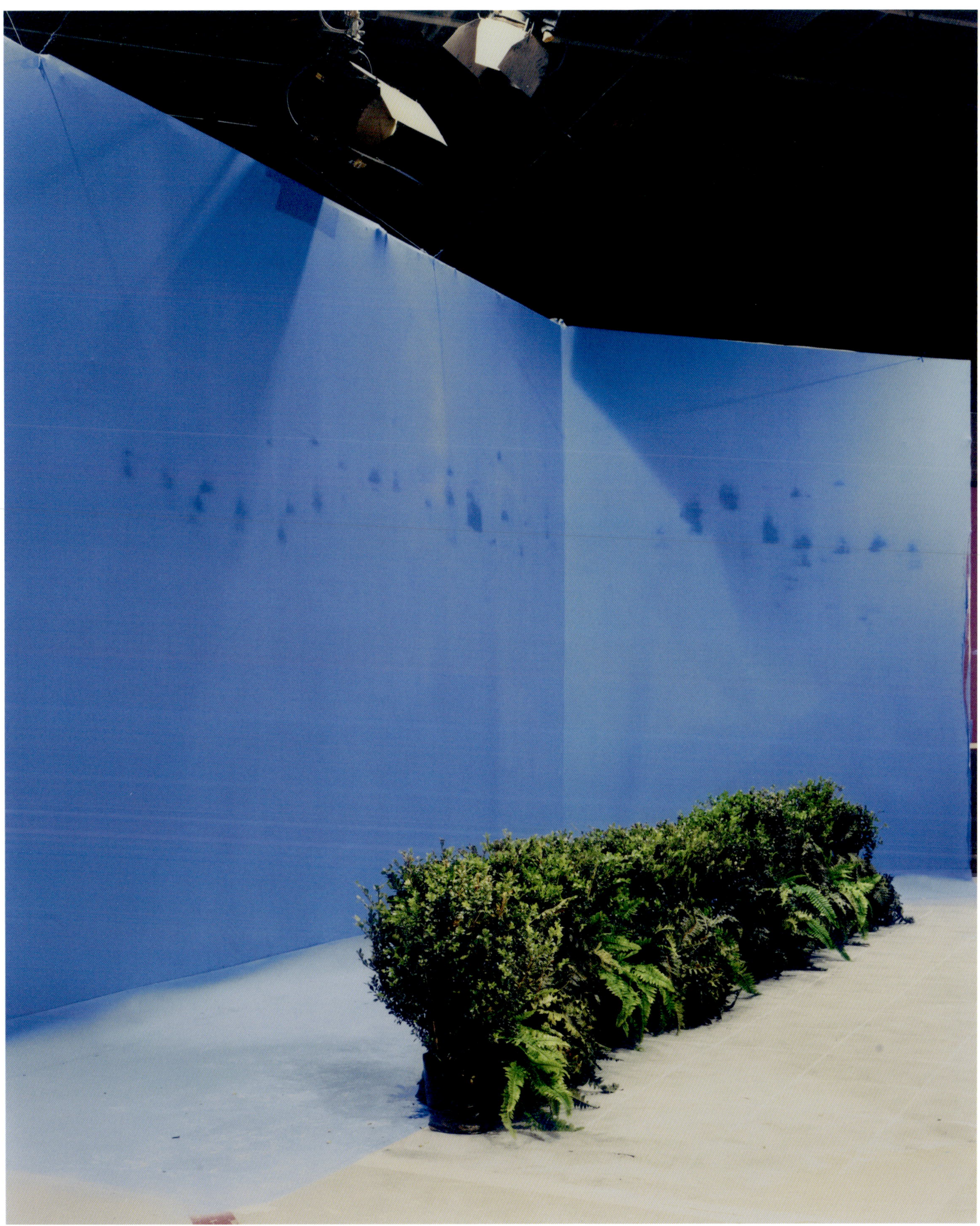

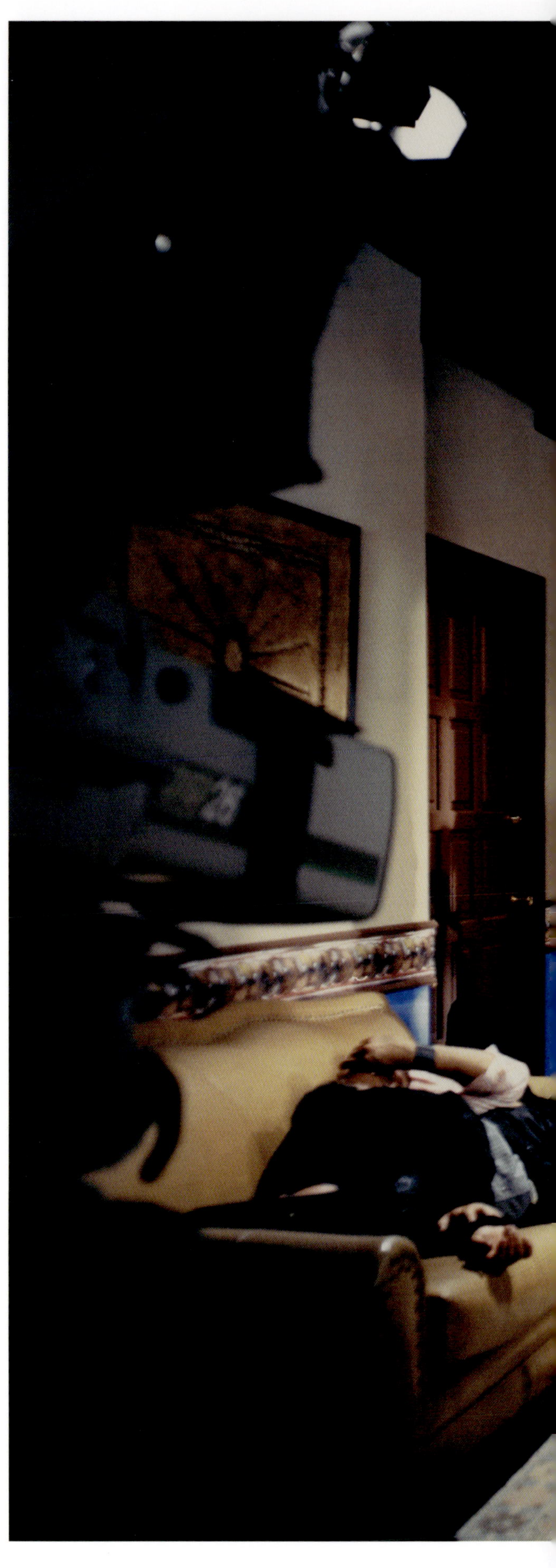

Pablo Montero and Gilberto de Anda as Emilio Valtierra and Hugo
Duelo De Pasiones II (Duel of Passions), 2006

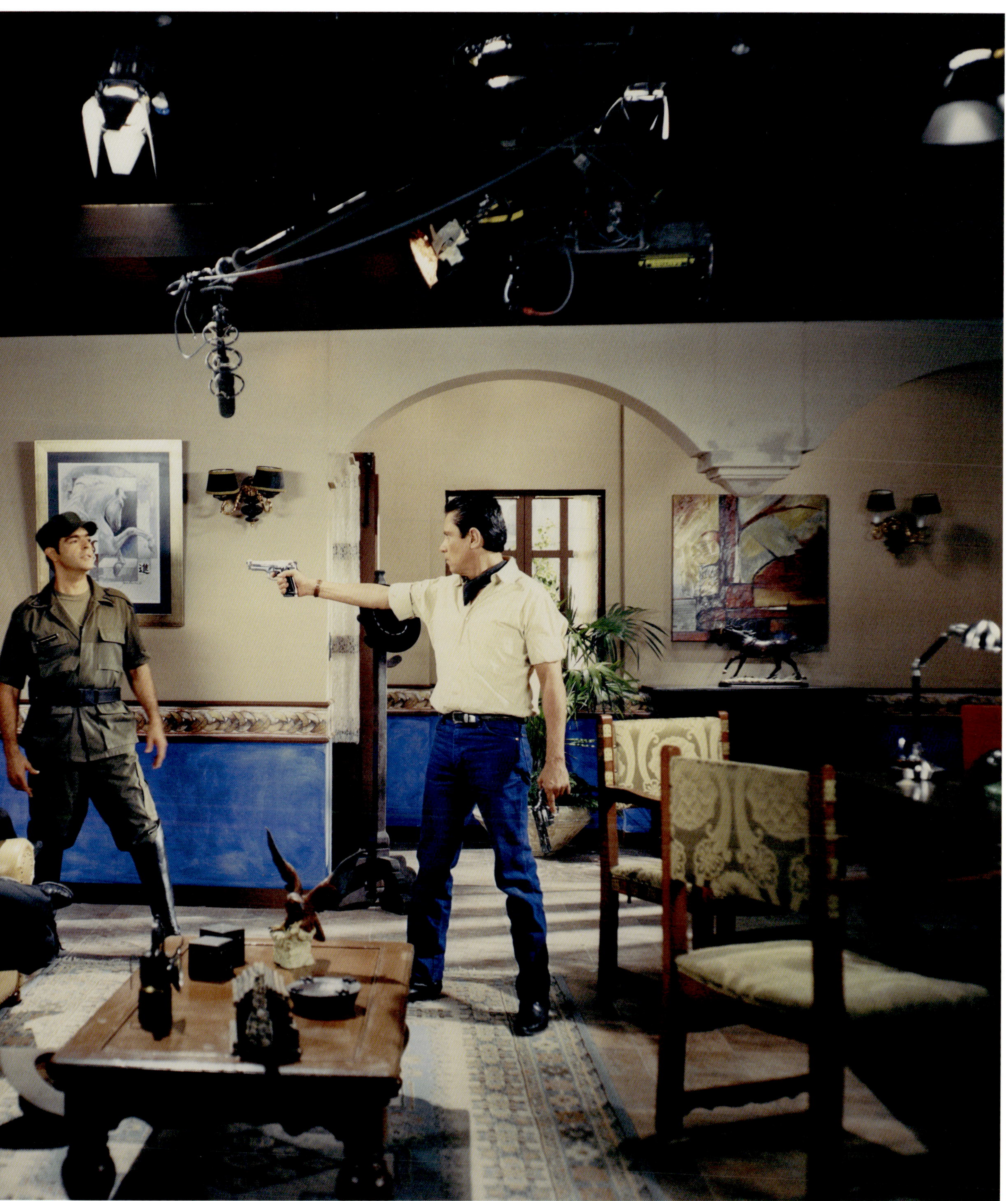

ARTURO SANDOVAL DE ANDA

A temperamental young man who cannot endure lies or betrayal. Even so, by the hazards of fate, it is he who will betray Nora's love.

LEONORA "NORA" GUZMÁN MADRIGAL DE ORTA DE PALACIOS-GARCÍA

She is young and beautiful, a dreamer who believes in true love. But the treachery of those she has loved turn her into a cruel, calculating woman who uses her beauty to keep men in thrall.

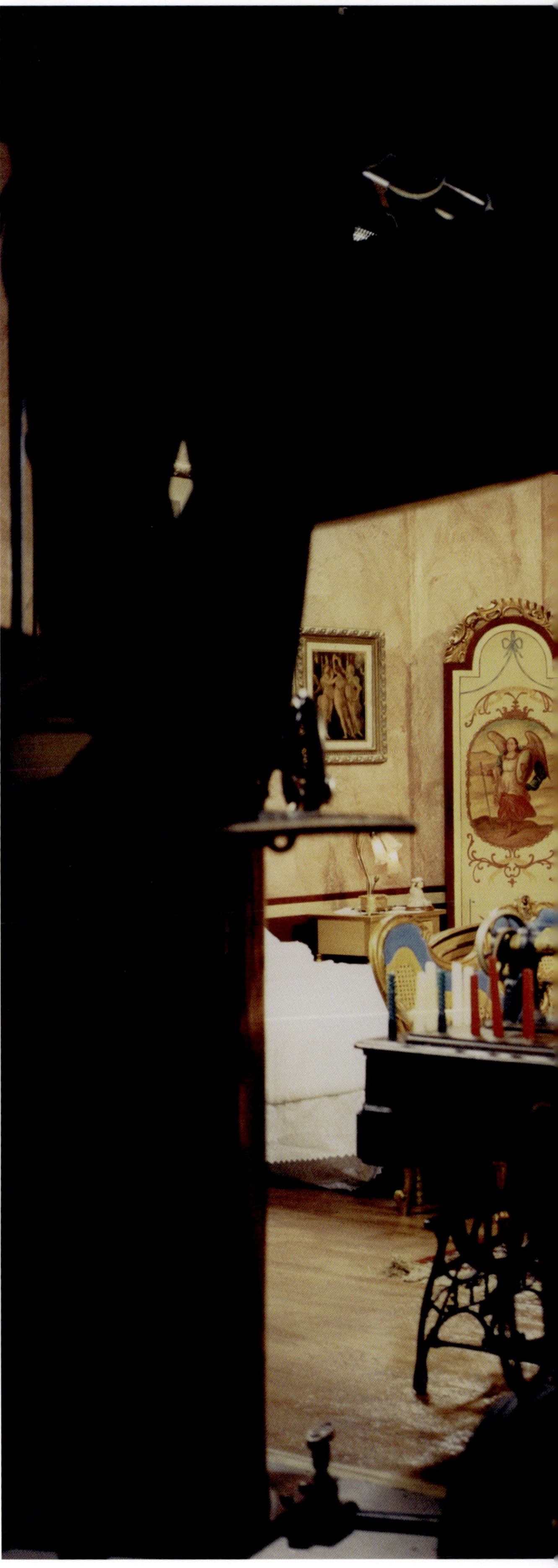

Sergio Sendel and Yadhira Carrillo as Arturo and Nora
Amarte es mi Pecado (Loving You Is My Sin), 2003

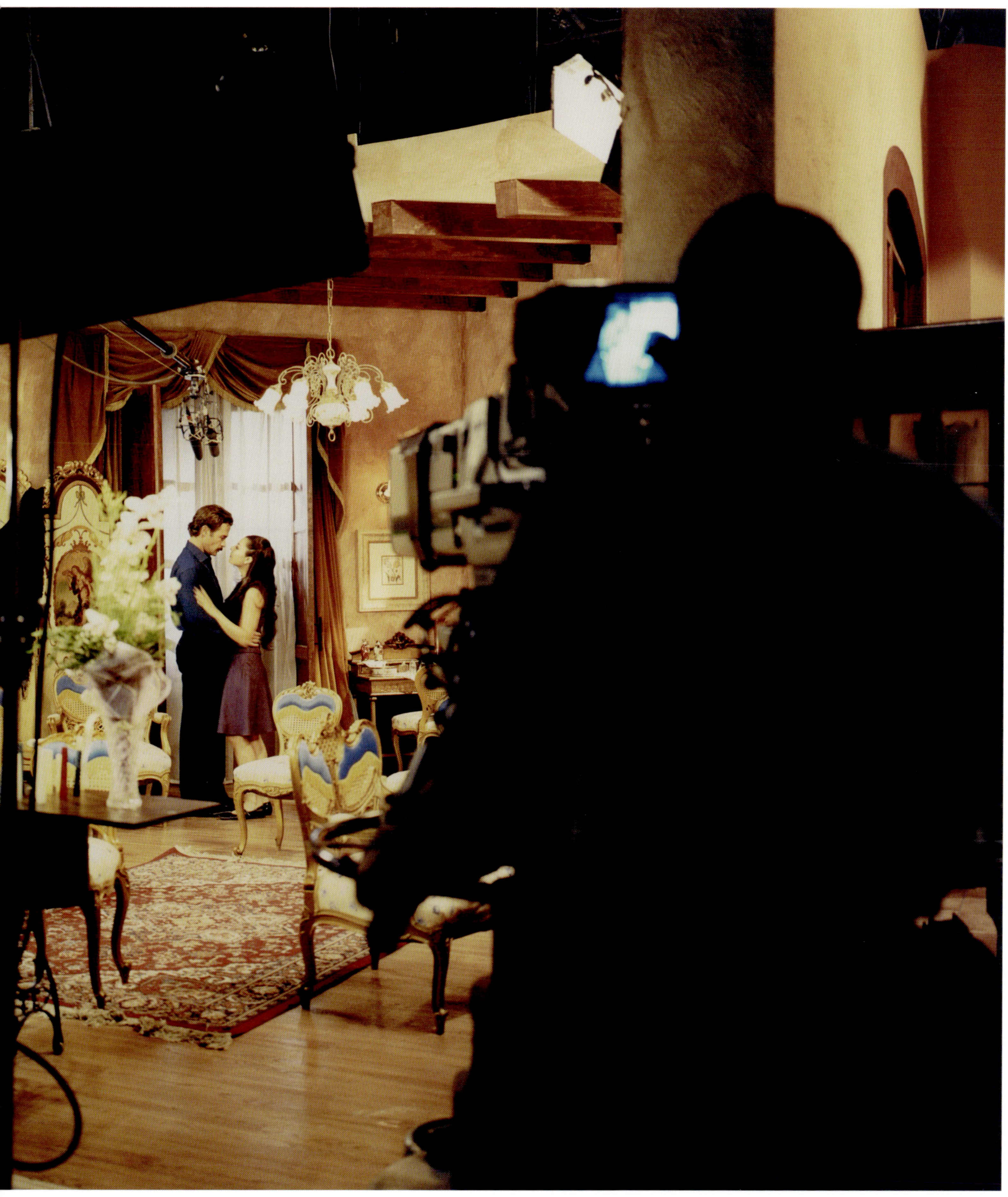

Tania Vázquez as Venus García "Lovely Norton"
 Mañana es para Siempre (Tomorrow Is Forever), 2009

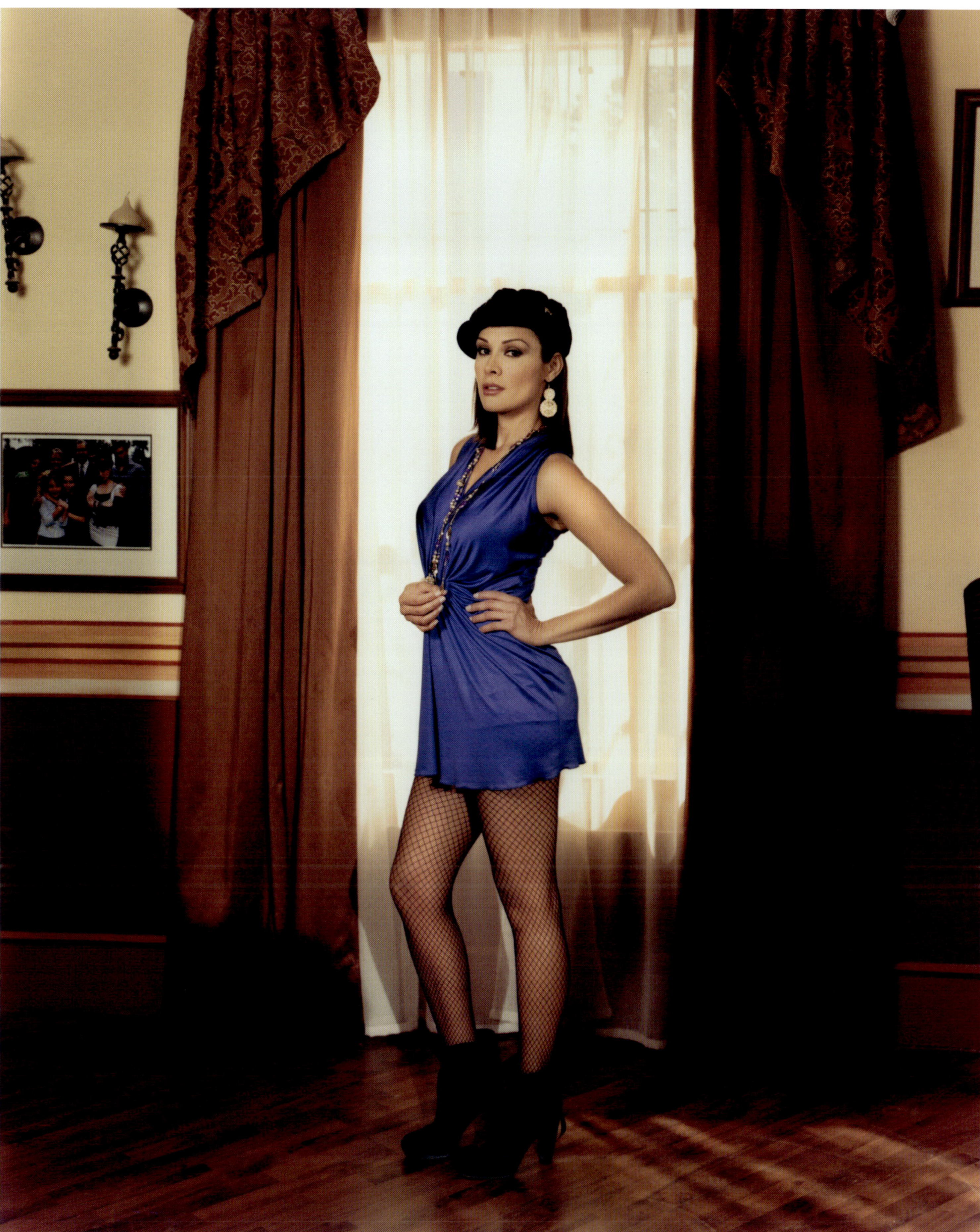

EFRAÍN RÍOS

Poor, tough, and highly sensual, he is the overseer of the Hacienda del Fuerte. He maintains a passionate relationship with Cinthia, but he knows it will go no further. He is Rogelio's right-hand man. A womanizer, he is toying with Consuela's love for him.

Fabián Robles as Efraín Ríos
La Que No Podía Amar (The One Who Could Not Love), 2011

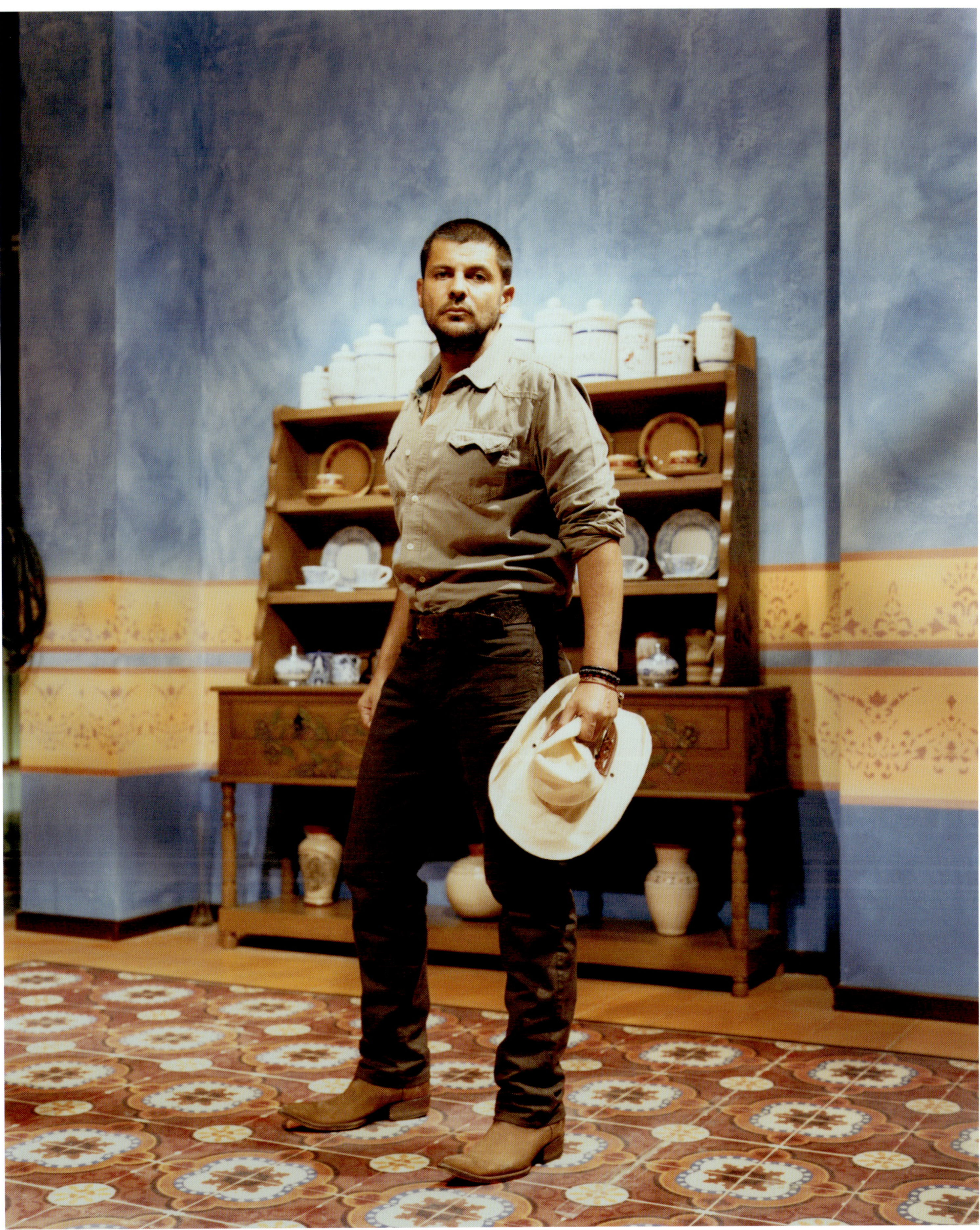

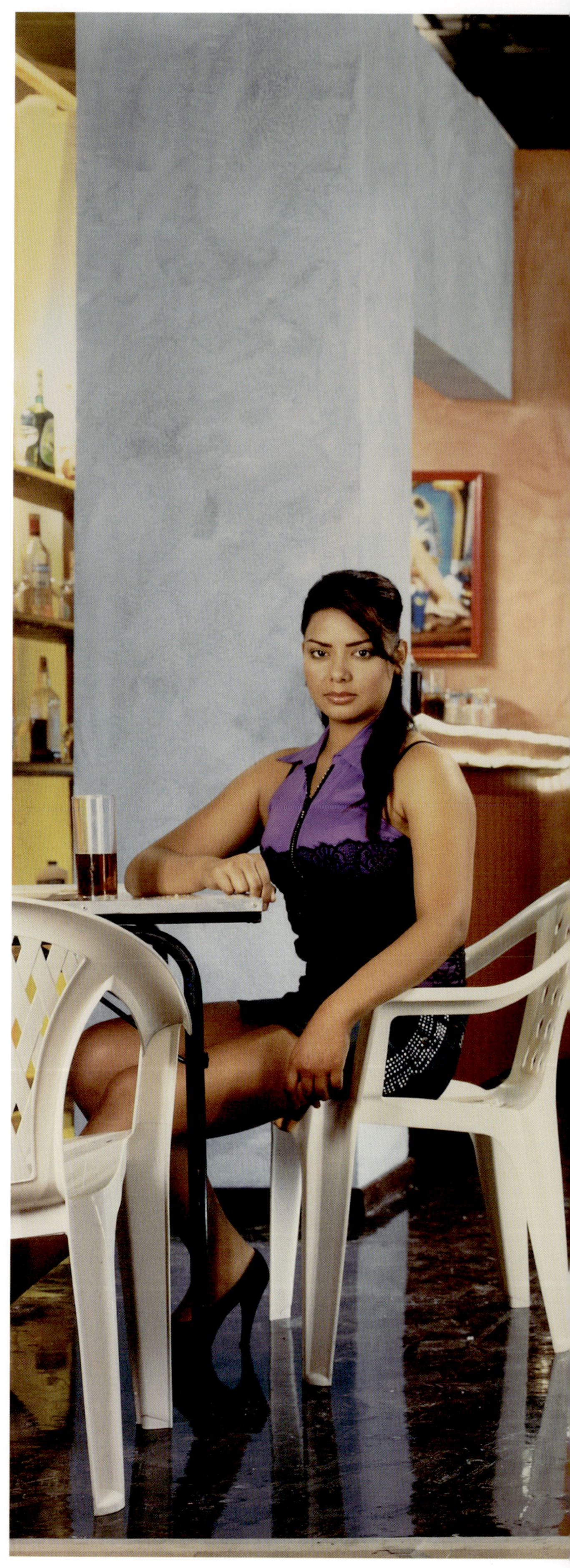

Maribel Velázquez and Sergio Acosta
as Bar Patron and Cornelio "Sergio" Mendoza
Dos Hogares (Double Life), 2011

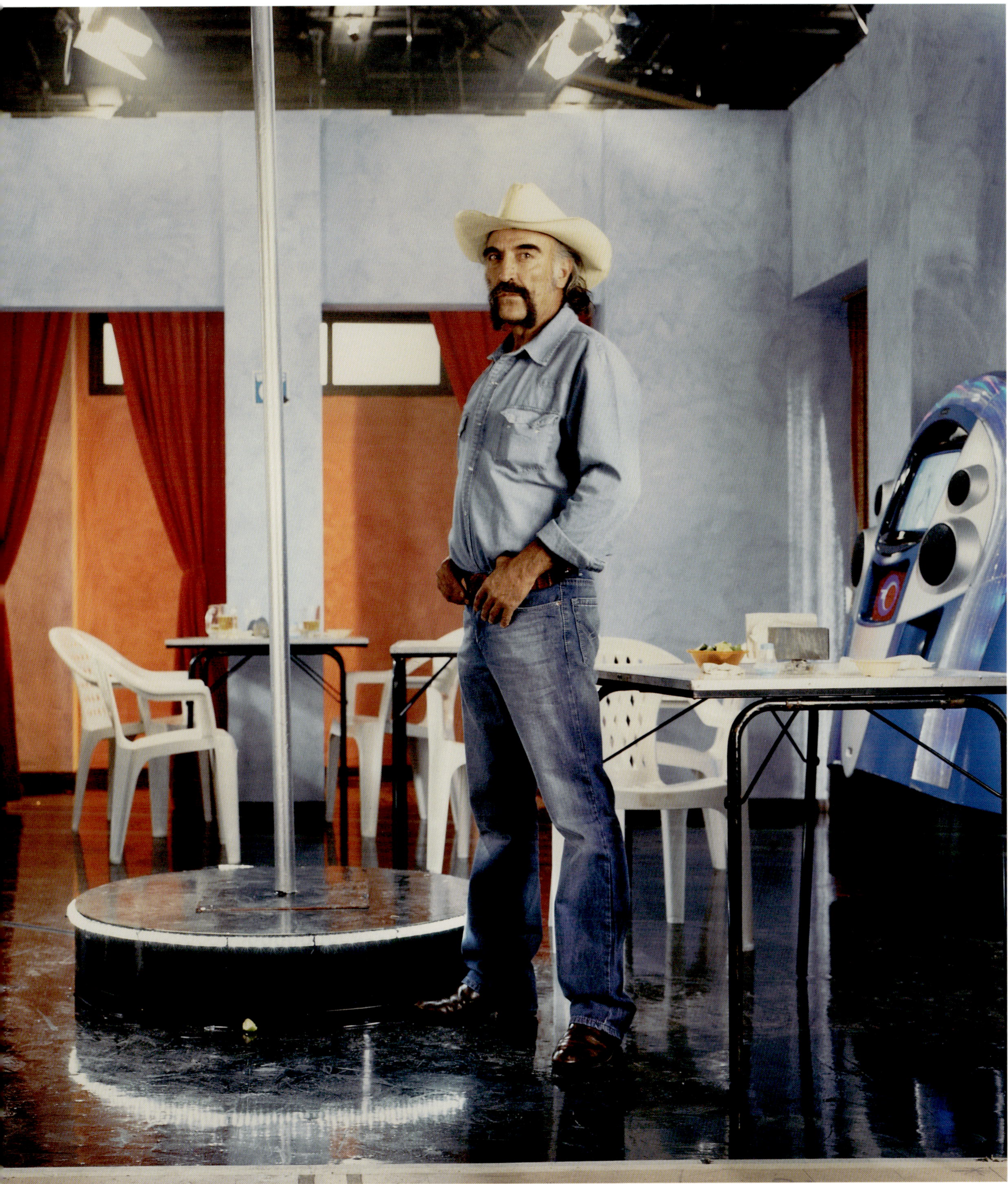

Margarita Magaña as Estrella Falcón
Un Gancho al Corazón (A Blow to the Heart), 2009

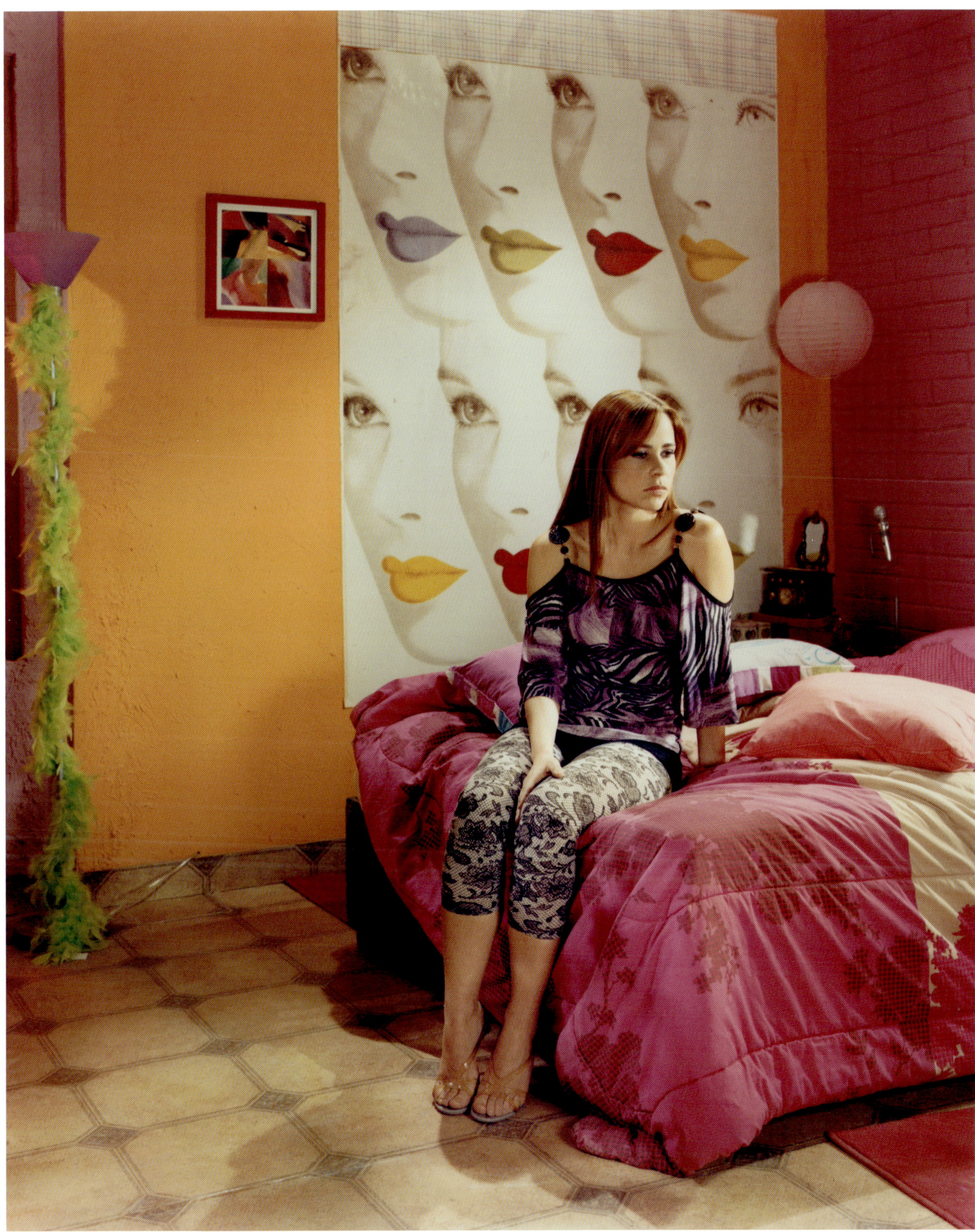

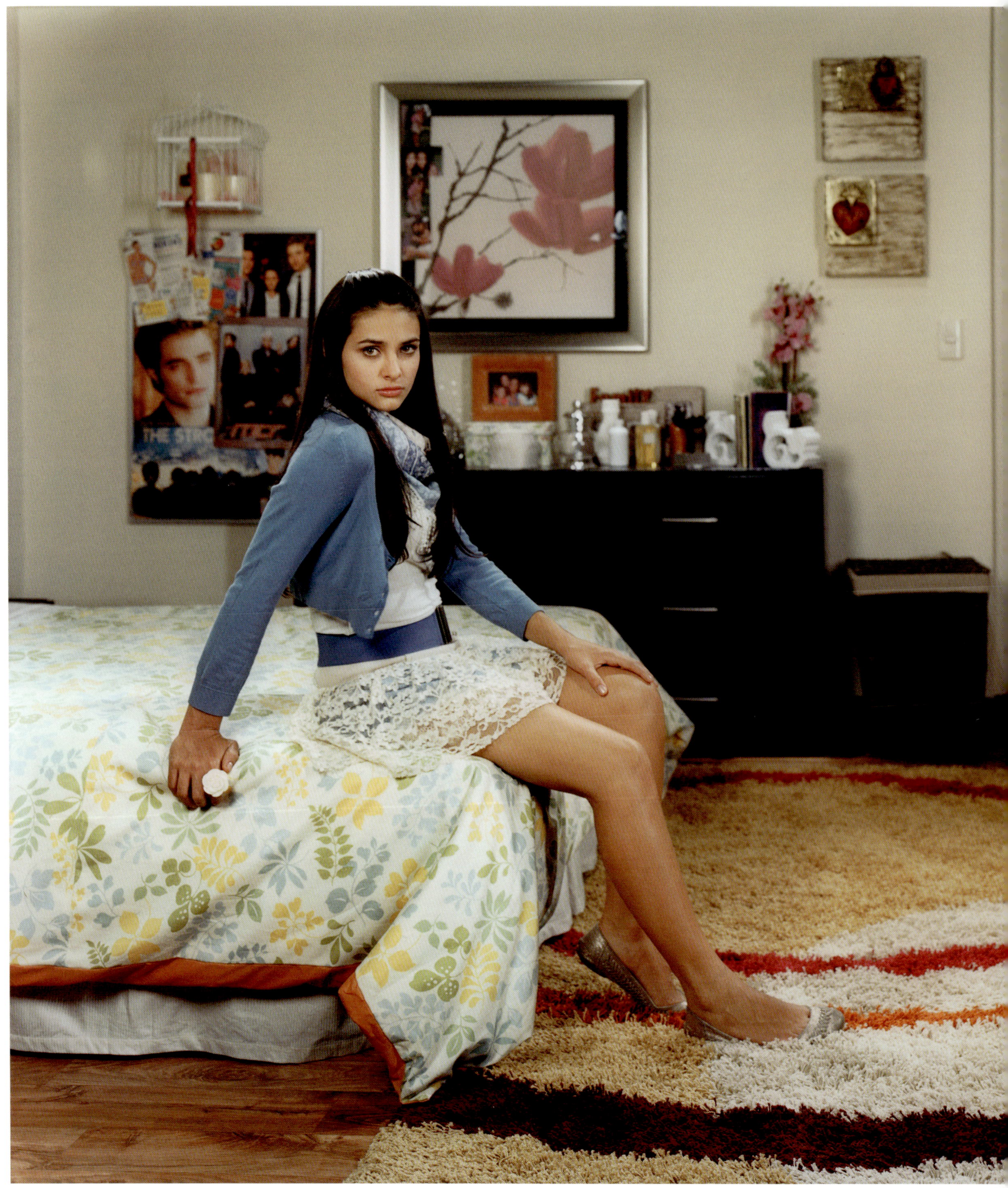

MARISOL

At sixteen, a difficult age, Marisol is a rebellious teenager. She is sincere and passionate, very much like her father. She has good principles, but makes bad decisions. Always positive, Marisol tries to do the right thing, but it never works out for her. She is deeply in love with Juancho, but fate has decreed her love unrequited; and she must pay the consequences of her actions. She lives with her Aunt Lucía for a time.

Renata Notni as Marisol
Amorcito Corazón (Darling Sweetheart), 2011

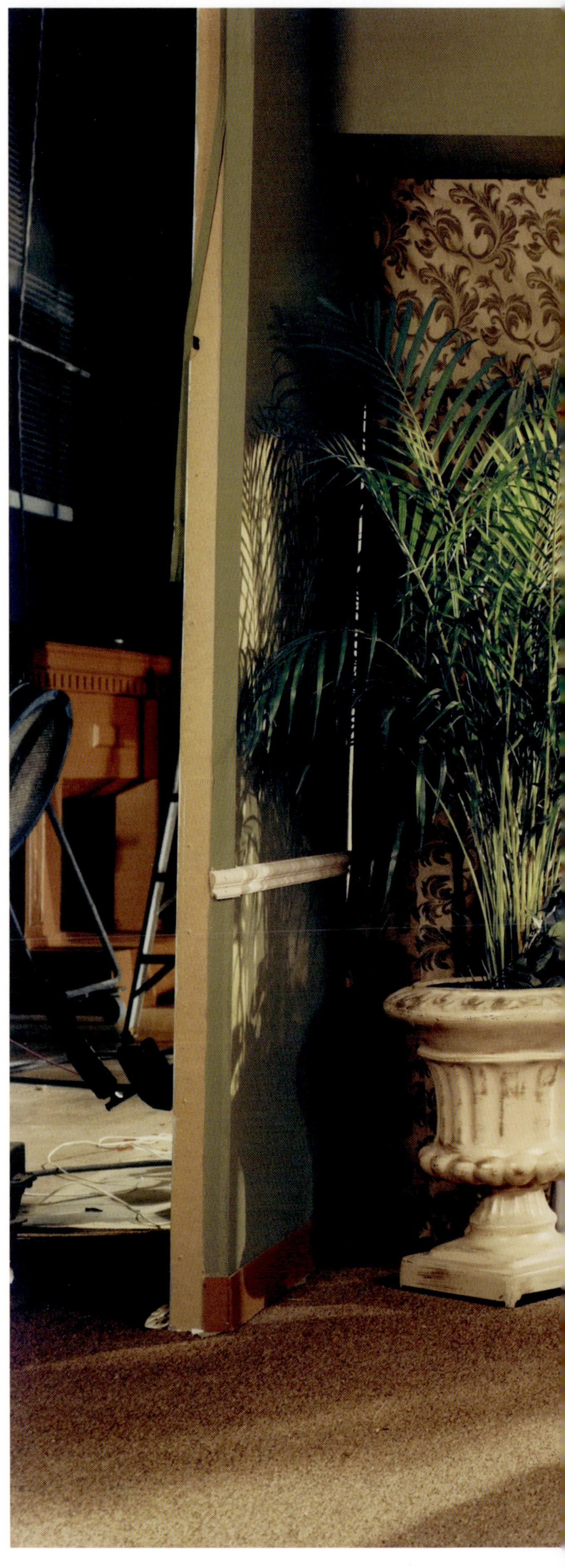

Leonore Hilda Ochoa as Dolores Herrera Guzmán
Rubí, 2004

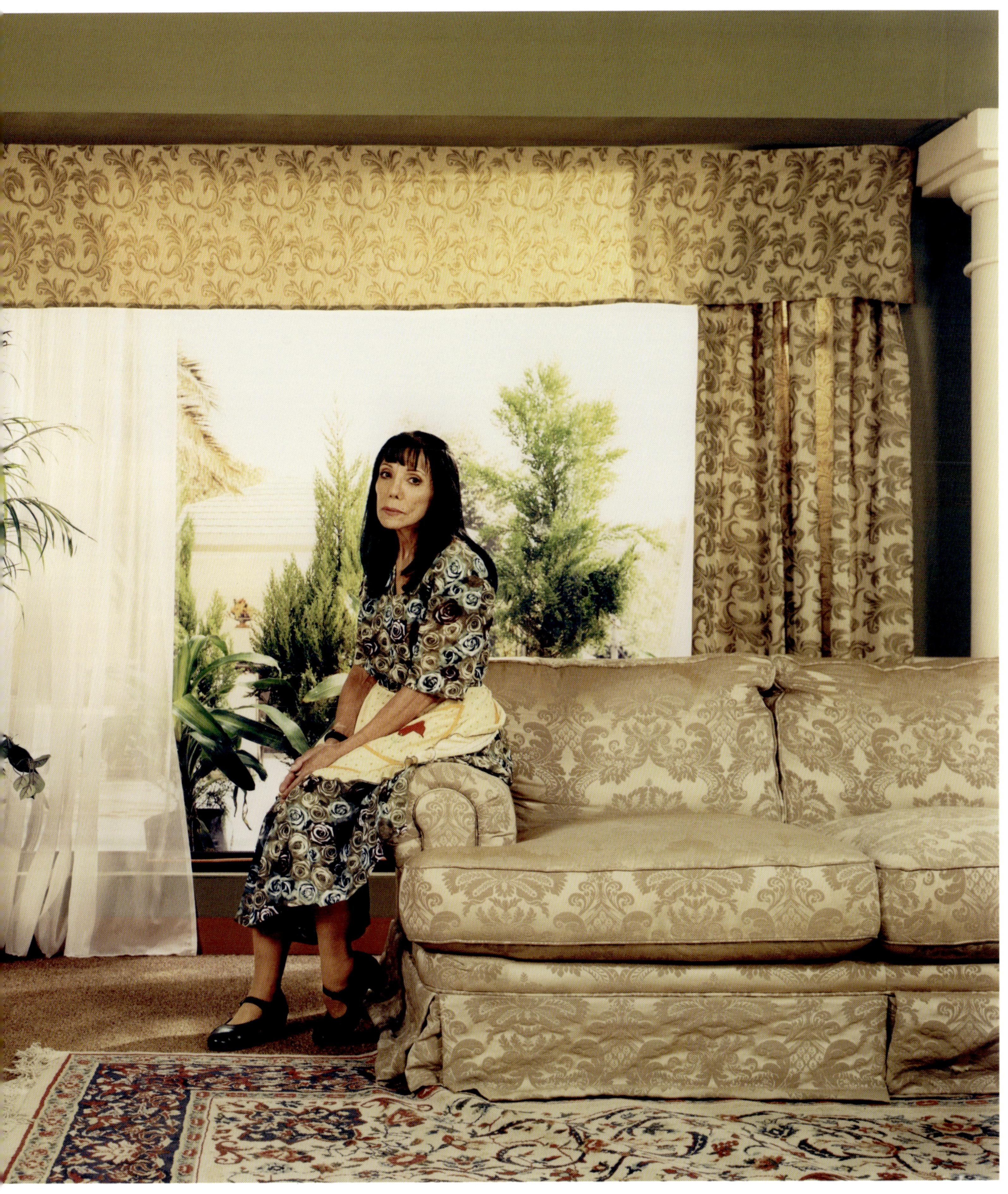

55 *Dos Hogares* (Double Life), 2011

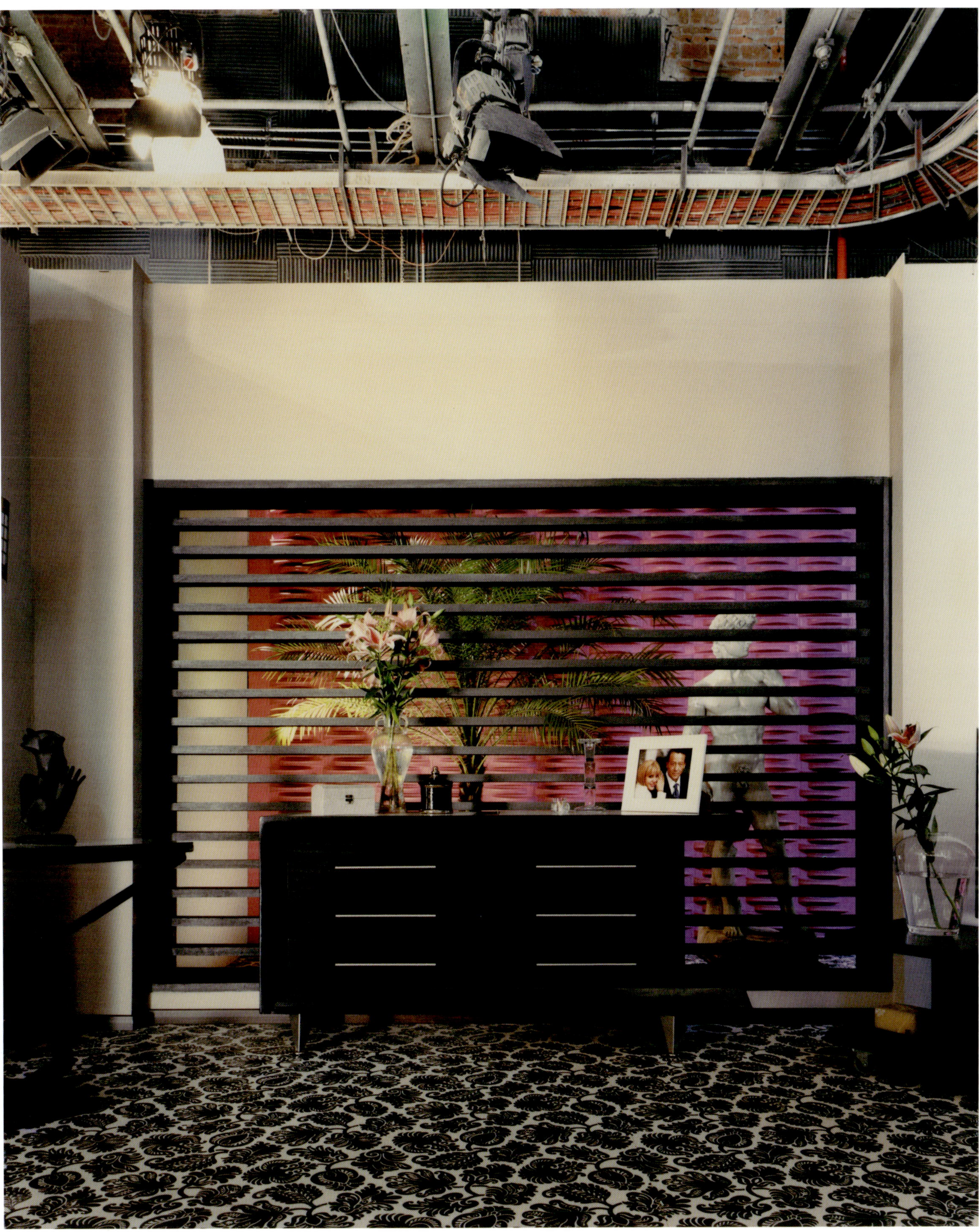

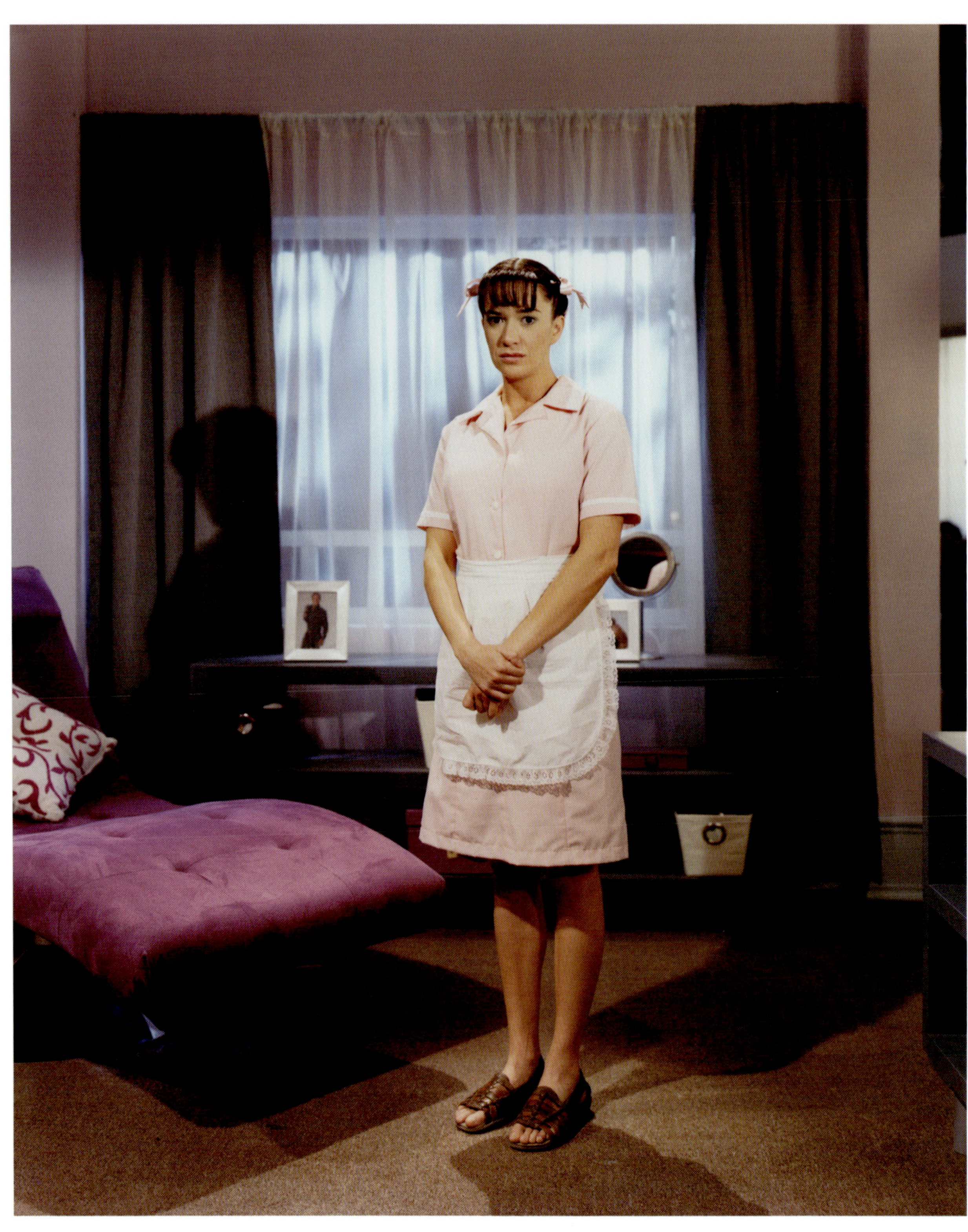

Helena Guerrero as Adoración
Una Familia Con Suerte (One Family with Luck), 2011

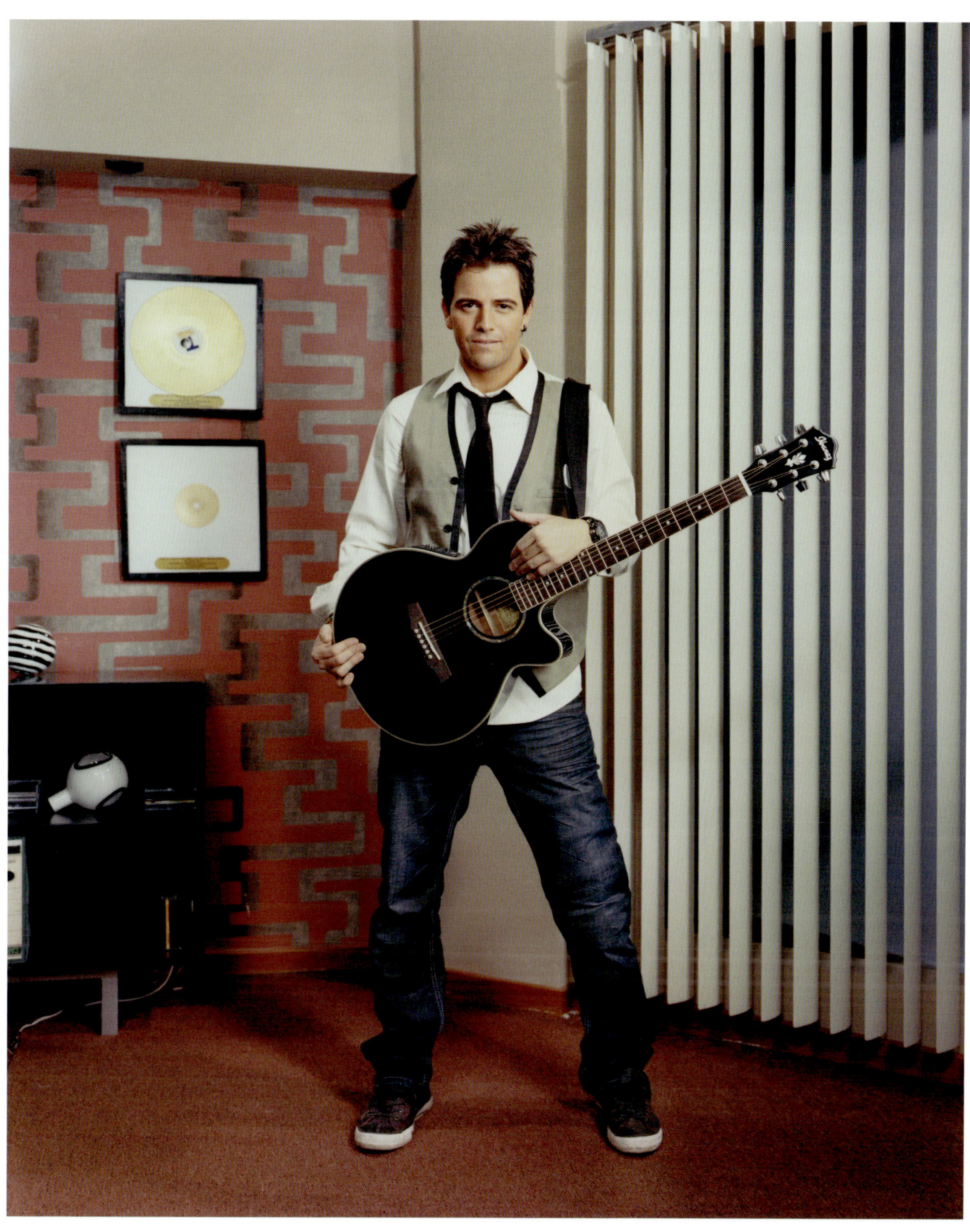

Mané de la Parra as Alexis Duarte
Esperanza del Corazón (Hope of the Heart), 2011

58 *Una Familia Con Suerte* (One Family with Luck), 2011

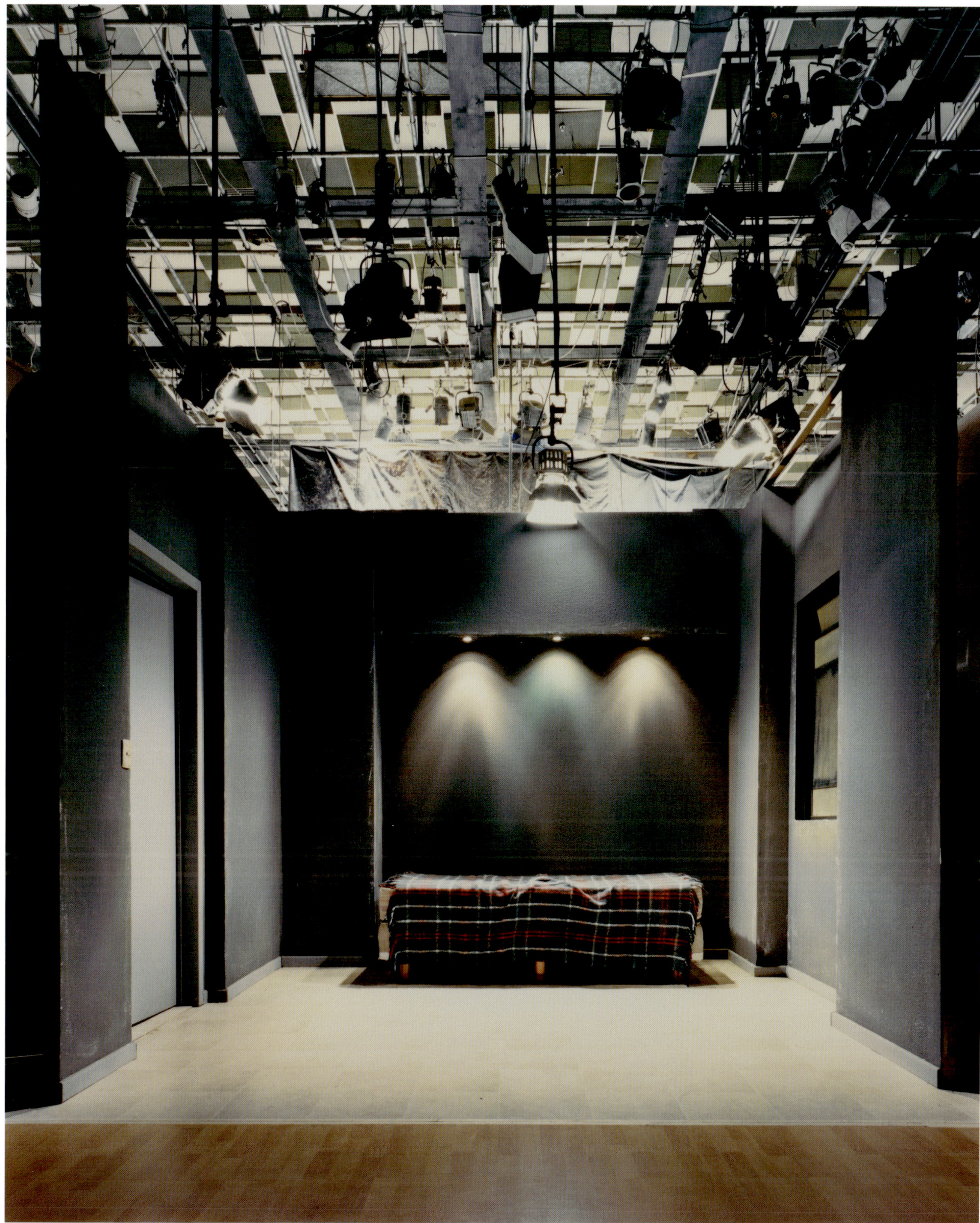

59 *Esperanza del Corazón* (Hope of the Heart), 2011

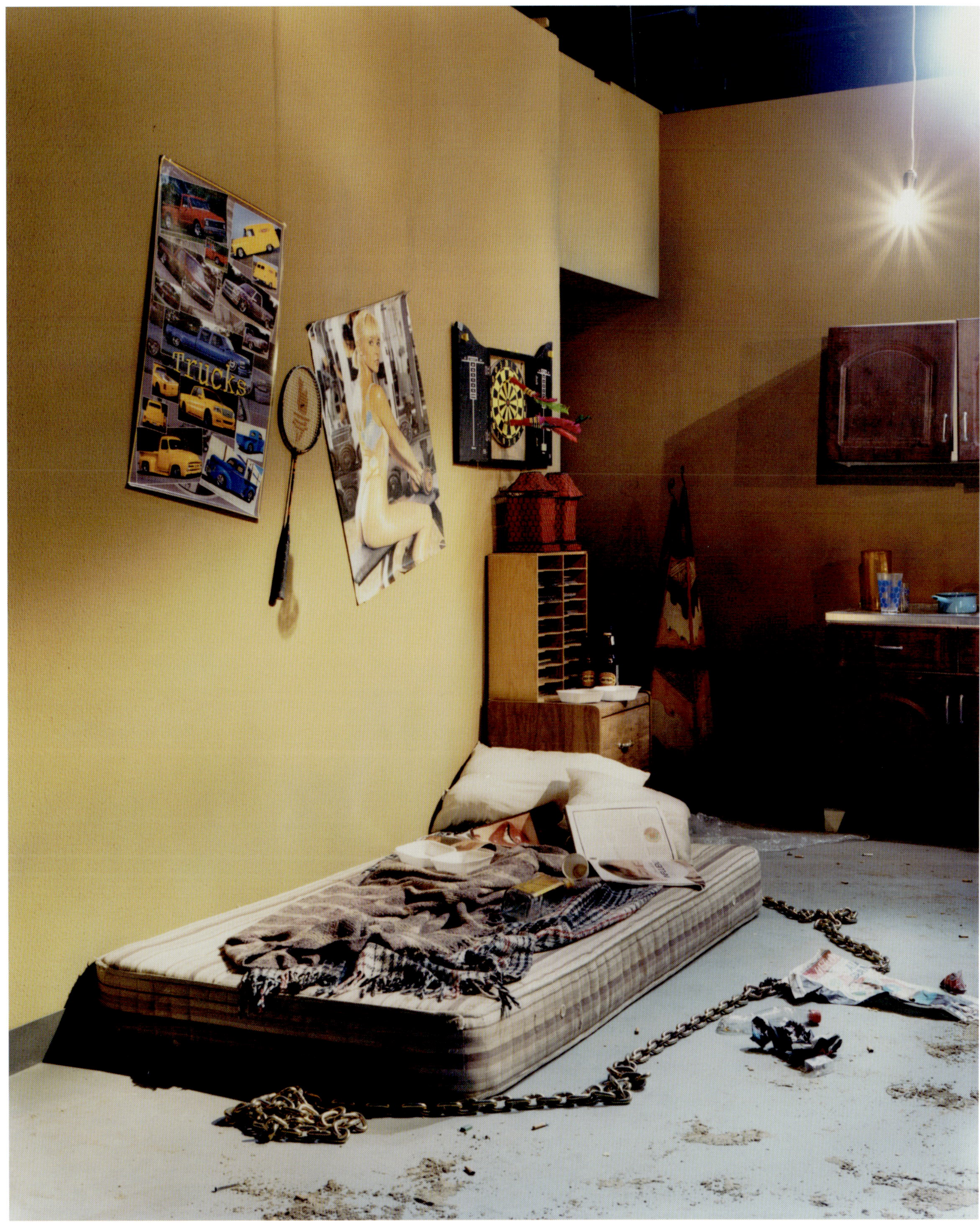
Trucks

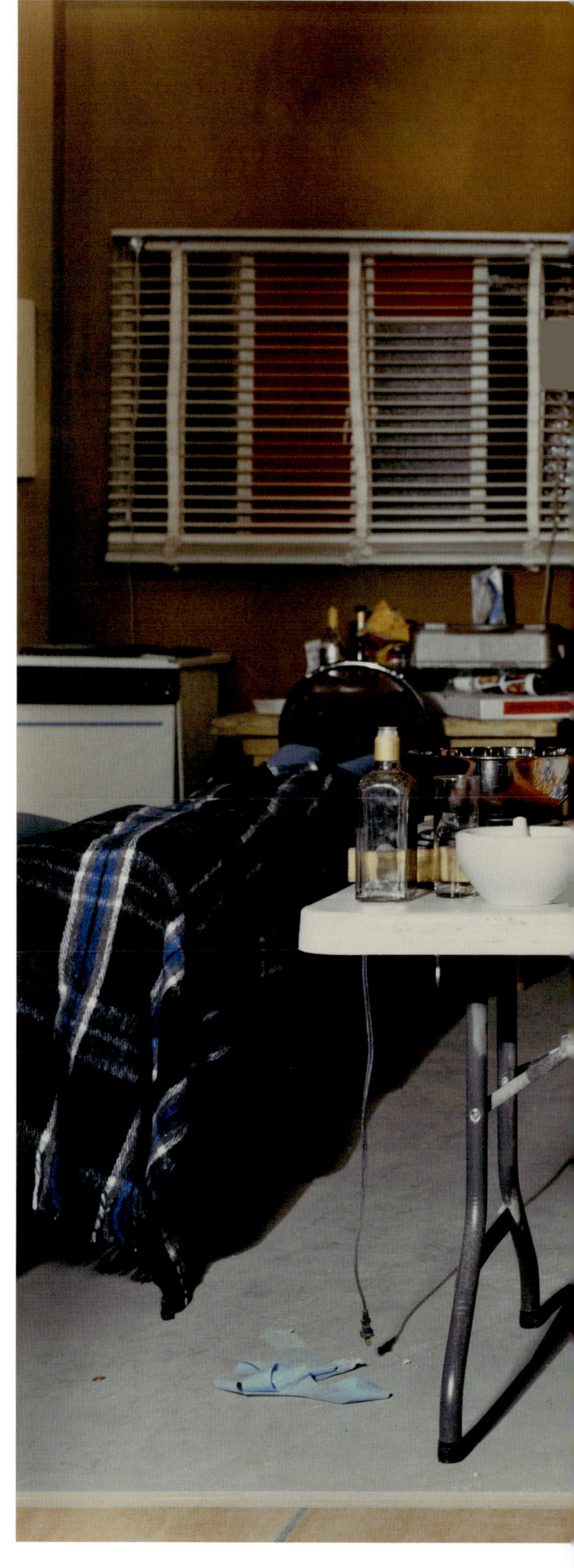

Alfredo Gatica as El Cobra
Esperanza del Corazón (Hope of the Heart), 2011

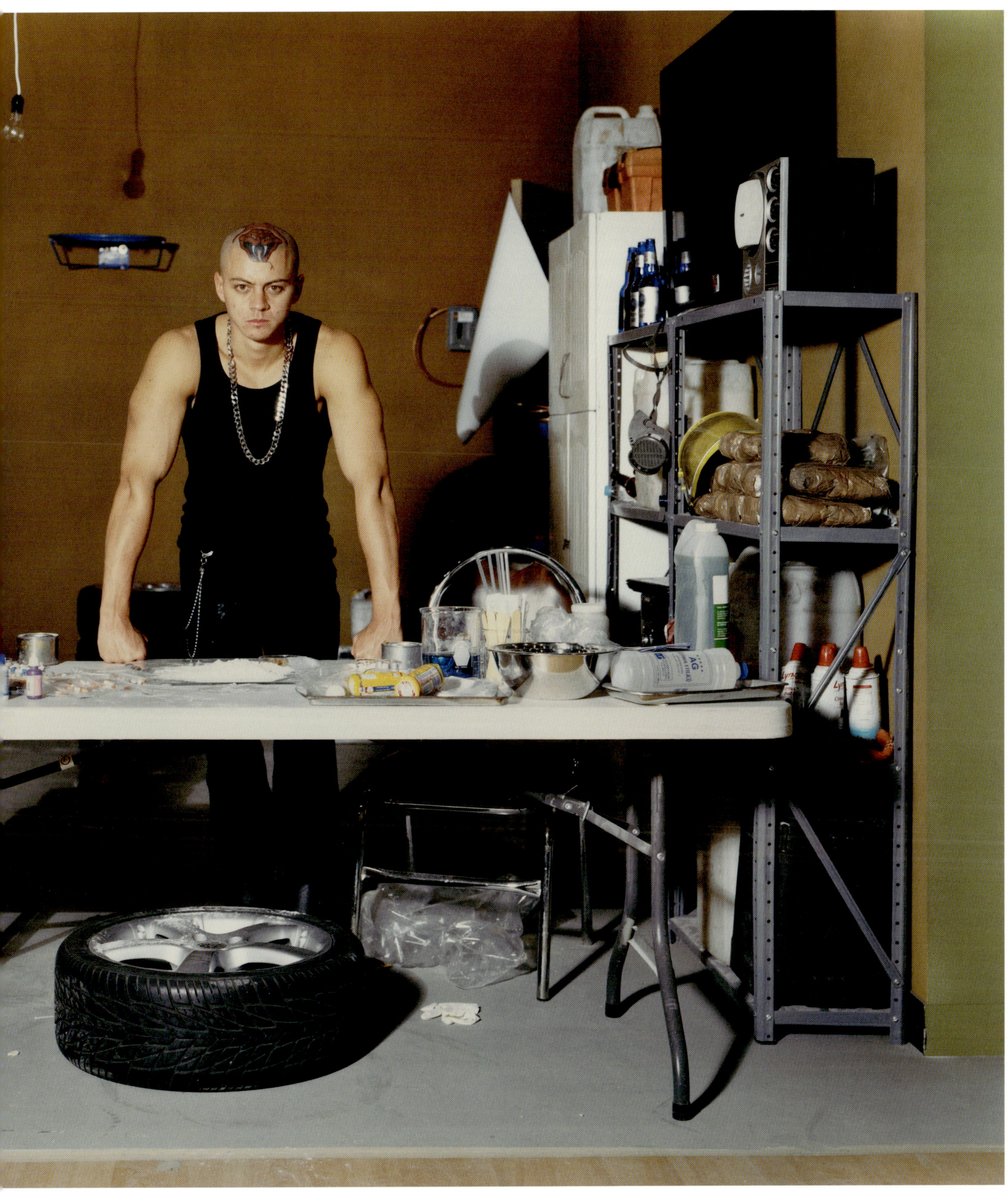
AG

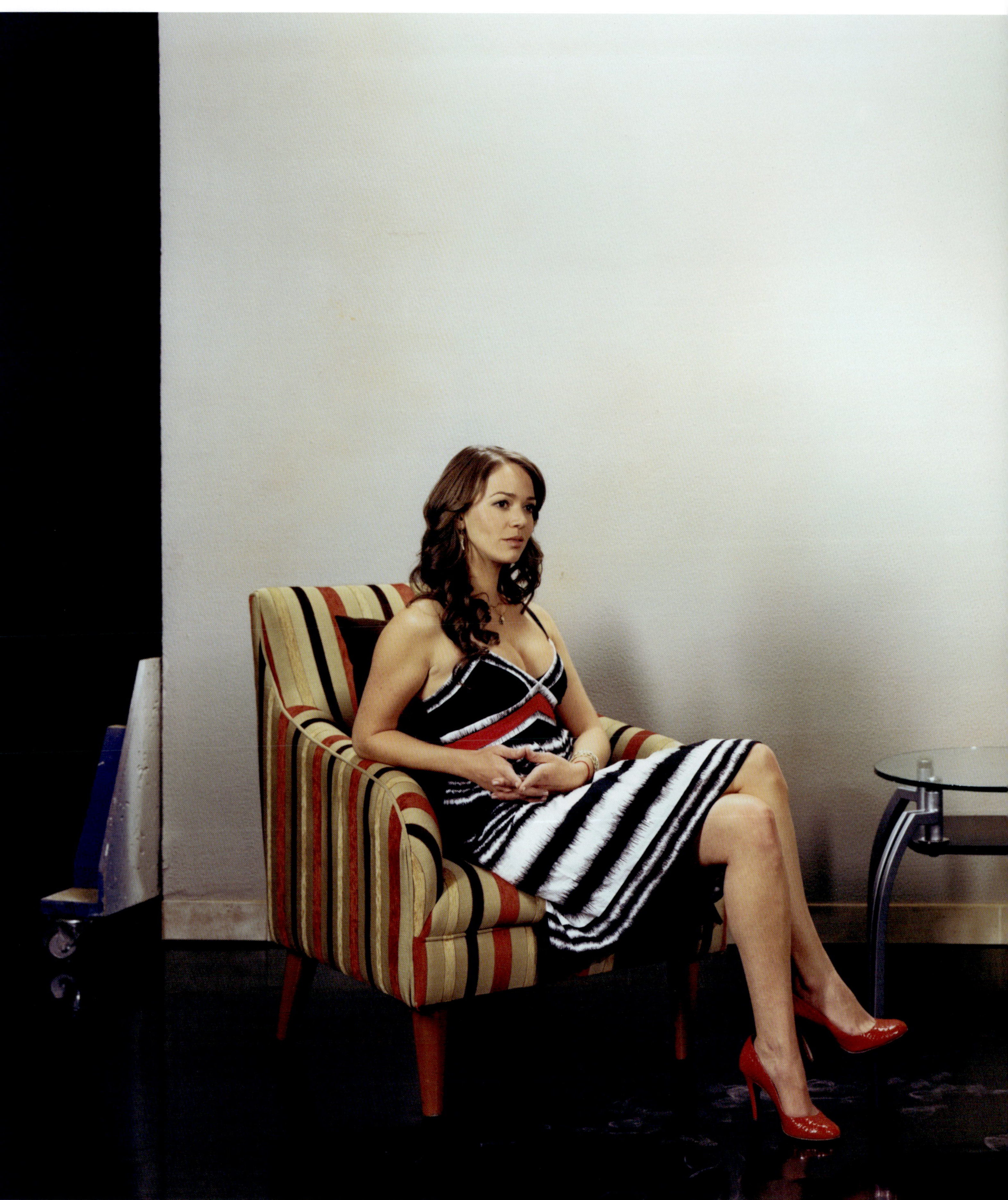

CONSTANZA LERDO DE TEJADA

Mauricio's girlfriend. A society woman, proud, haughty, and arrogant. She will do anything to keep up appearances. She wants to marry Mauricio,but mainly because of what it would mean for her socially and economically, and not for Mauricio himself. She allies herself with Jerónimo and Óscar in order to prevent Mauricio and Valentina from getting married. She feels a strange passion for Beto, the wrestler boyfriend of "la Monita."

Laisha Wilkins as Constanza Lerdo de Tejada
Un Gancho al Corazón (A Blow to the Heart), 2009

FERNANDA ELIZALDE RIVERA

Beautiful, sweet, and generous, without social prejudices, she holds strong convictions and is concerned about others. Her innocent heart is dealt a blow when she is separated from Eduardo and when her mother dies shortly thereafter. Her positive outlook helps her to overcome her loss. As she works and grows in the family business, she decides to open a handicraft center in her community.

Silvia Navarro as Fernanda Elizalde Rivera
Mañana es para Siempre (Tomorrow Is Forever), 2009

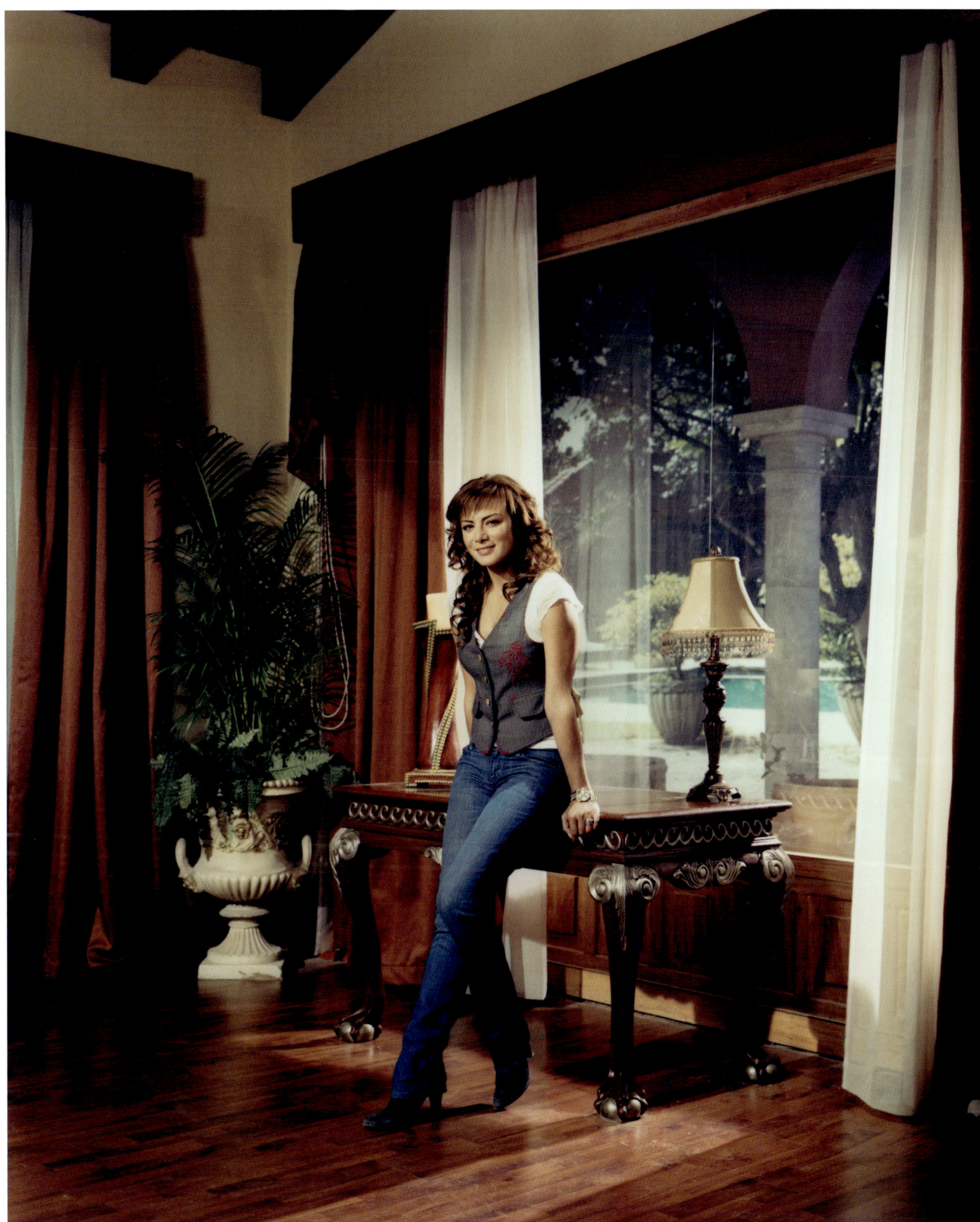

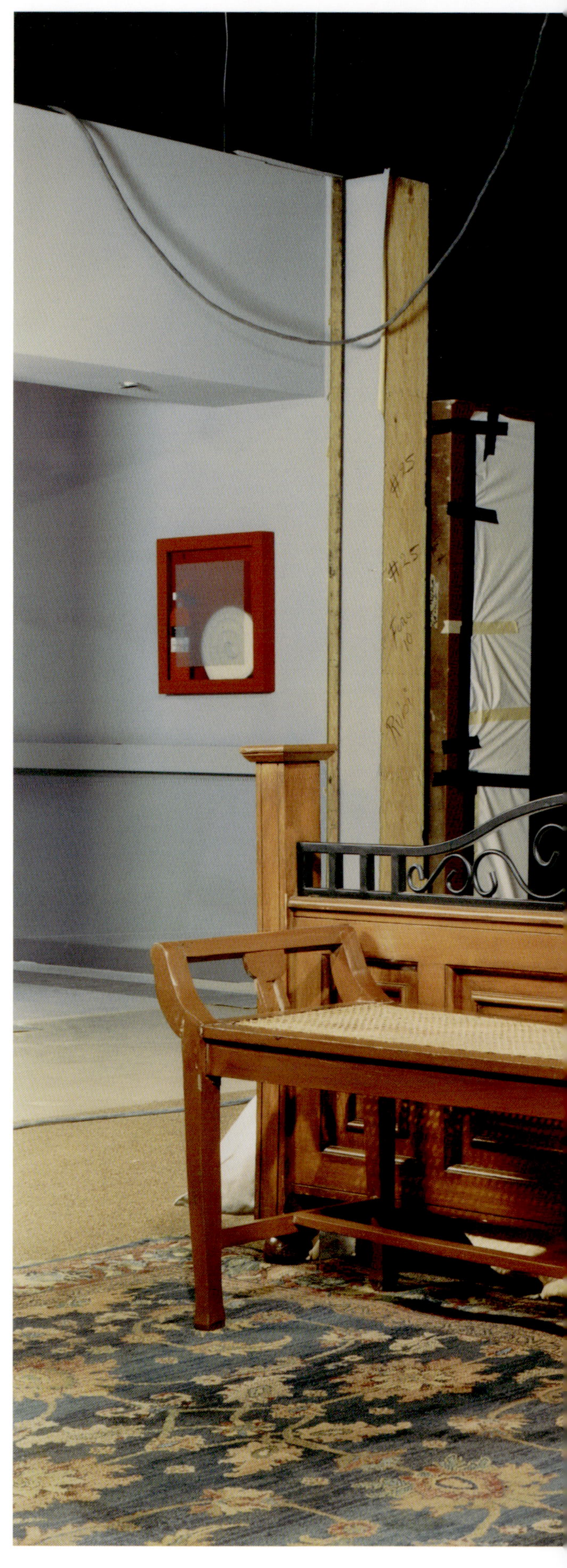

63 *Rubí*, 2004

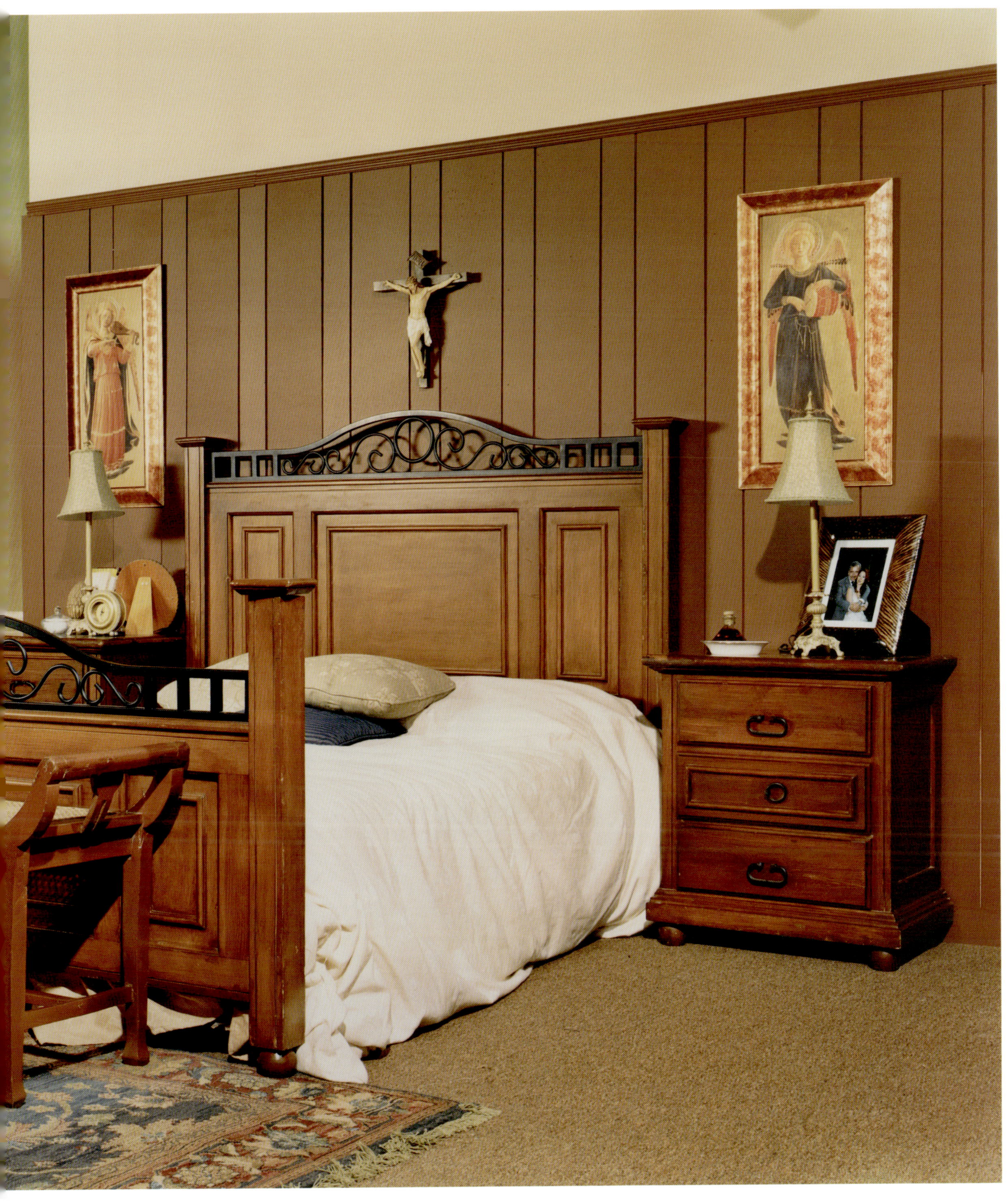

Ana Brenda Contreras as Ana Paula Carmona
La Que No Podía Amar (The One Who Could Not Love), 2011

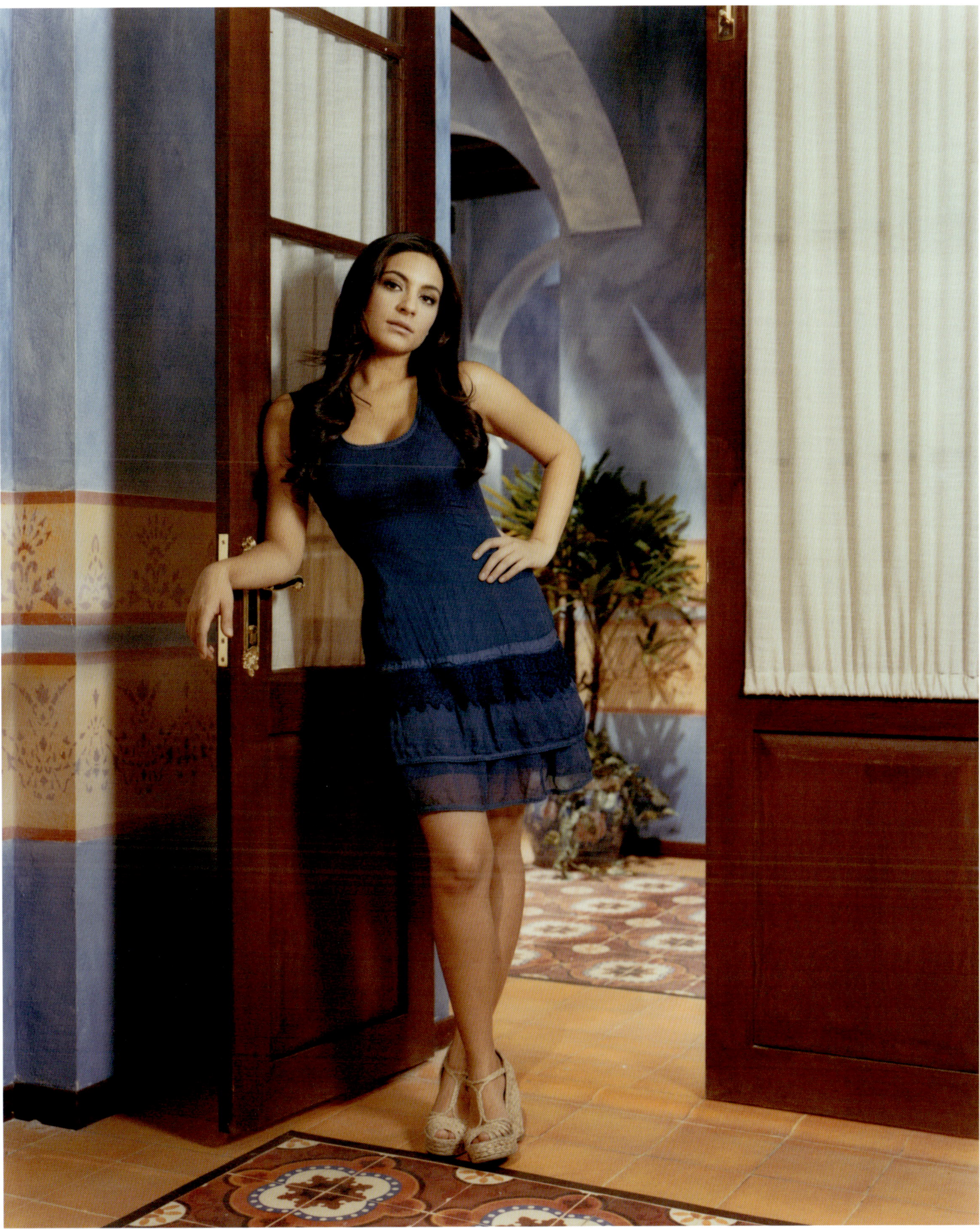

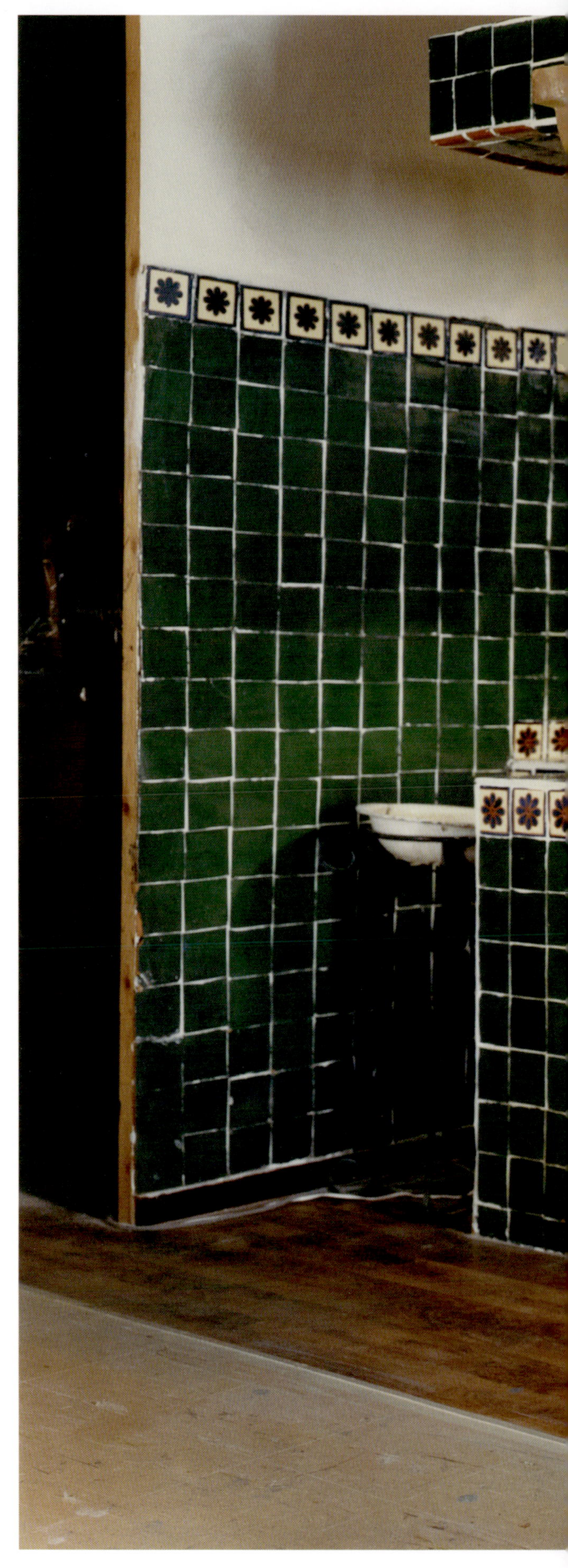

Elsa Marín as Euduviges
Dos Hogares (Double Life), 2011

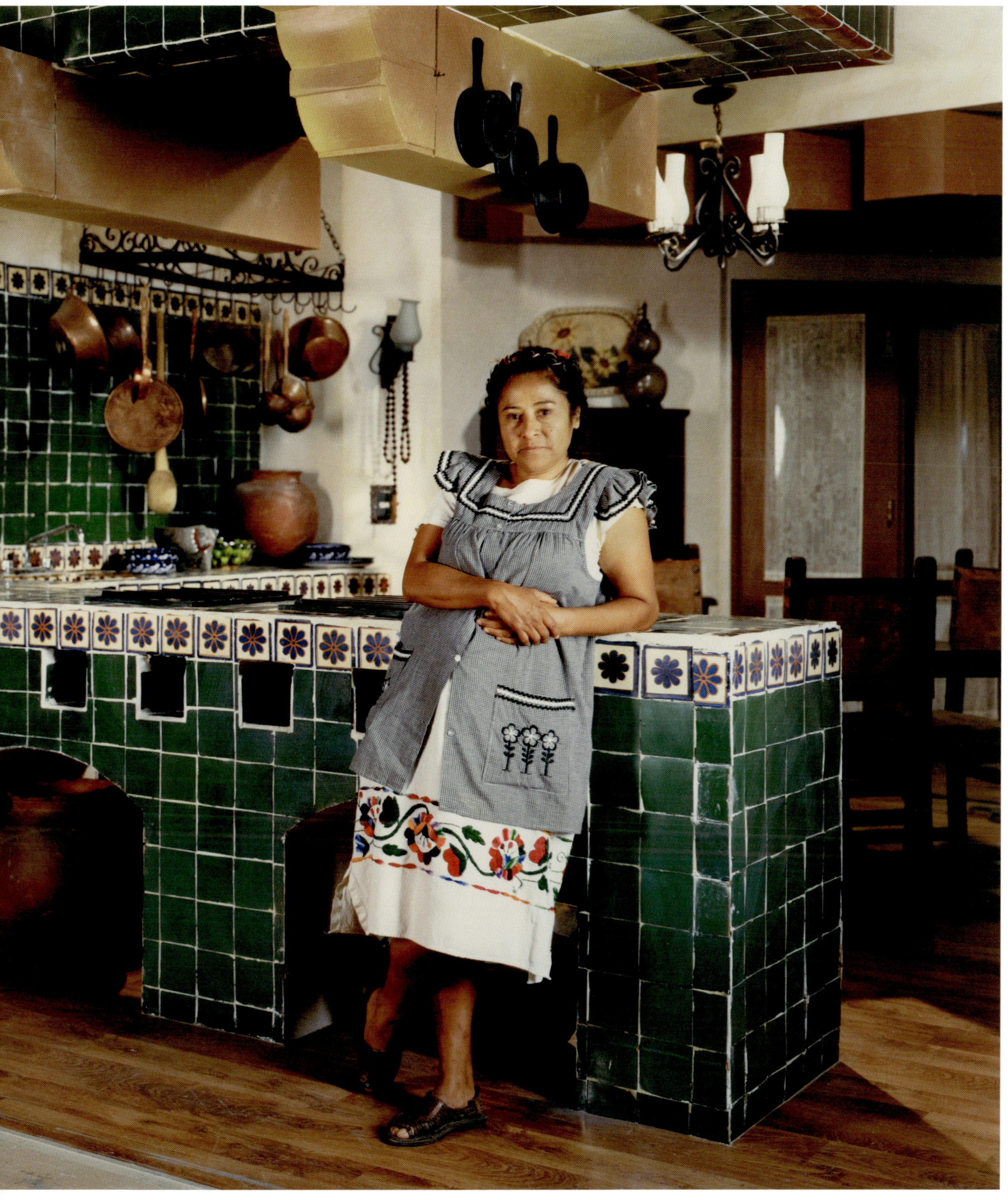

 Dos Hogares (Double Life), 2011

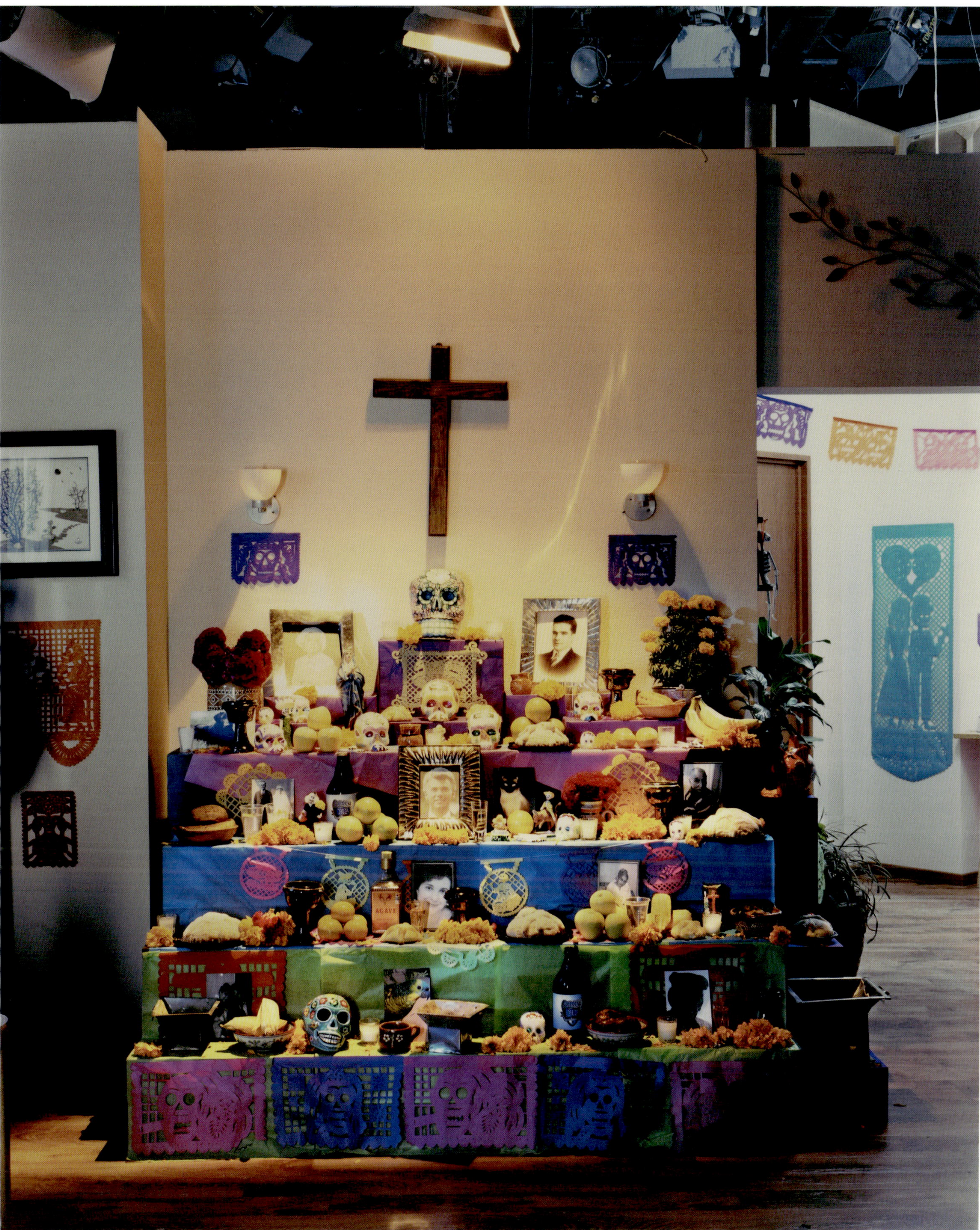
AGAVE

Ricardo Abarca as Aldo
Un Gancho al Corazón (A Blow to the Heart), 2009

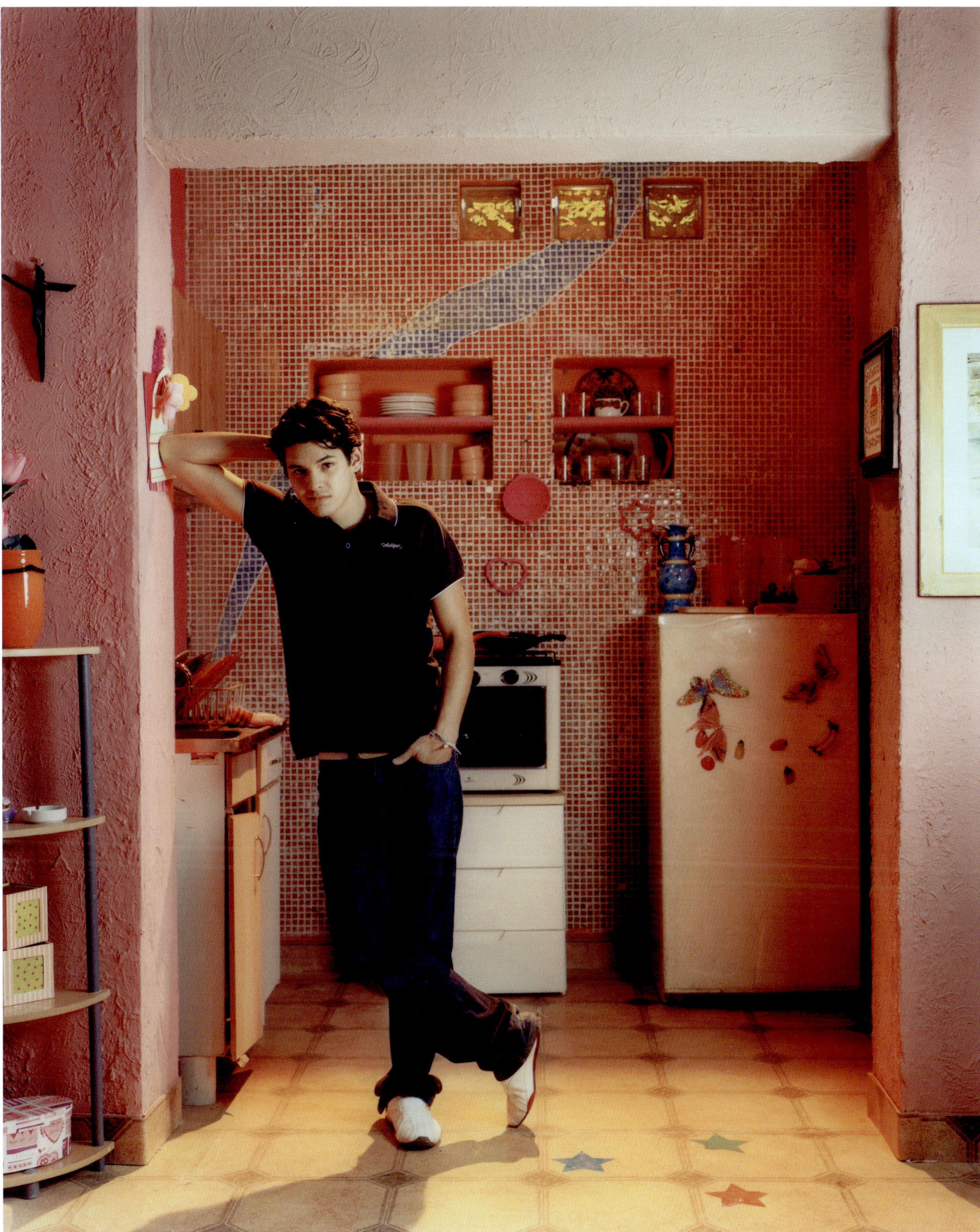

CARLOTA ESPINOZA DE LOS MONTEROS

Although people think she is generous and good, she is really cruel and manipulative; a woman with a strong and domineering personality who was brought up with iron discipline and complete repression. From a young age, she has had to take care of her siblings, and she uses blackmail and insults to maintain her authority. She is not happy and will not allow anyone else to be so, least of all her sister Macarena. And, she would be willing to kill to prevent her niece from escaping her domination.

Leticia Calderón as Carlota Espinoza de los Monteros
En Nombre del Amor (In the Name of Love), 2009

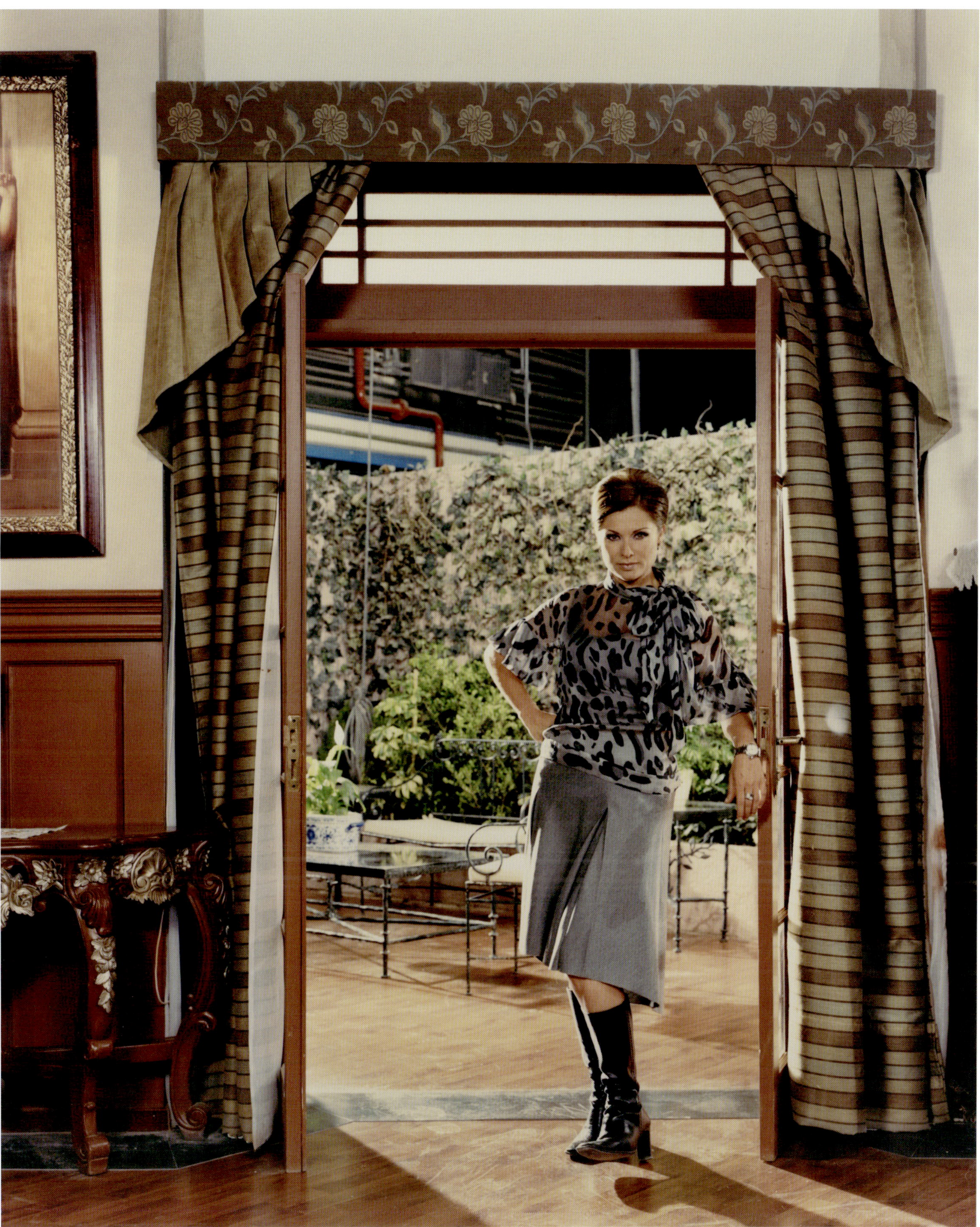

69 *Duelo De Pasiones II* (Duel of Passions), 2009

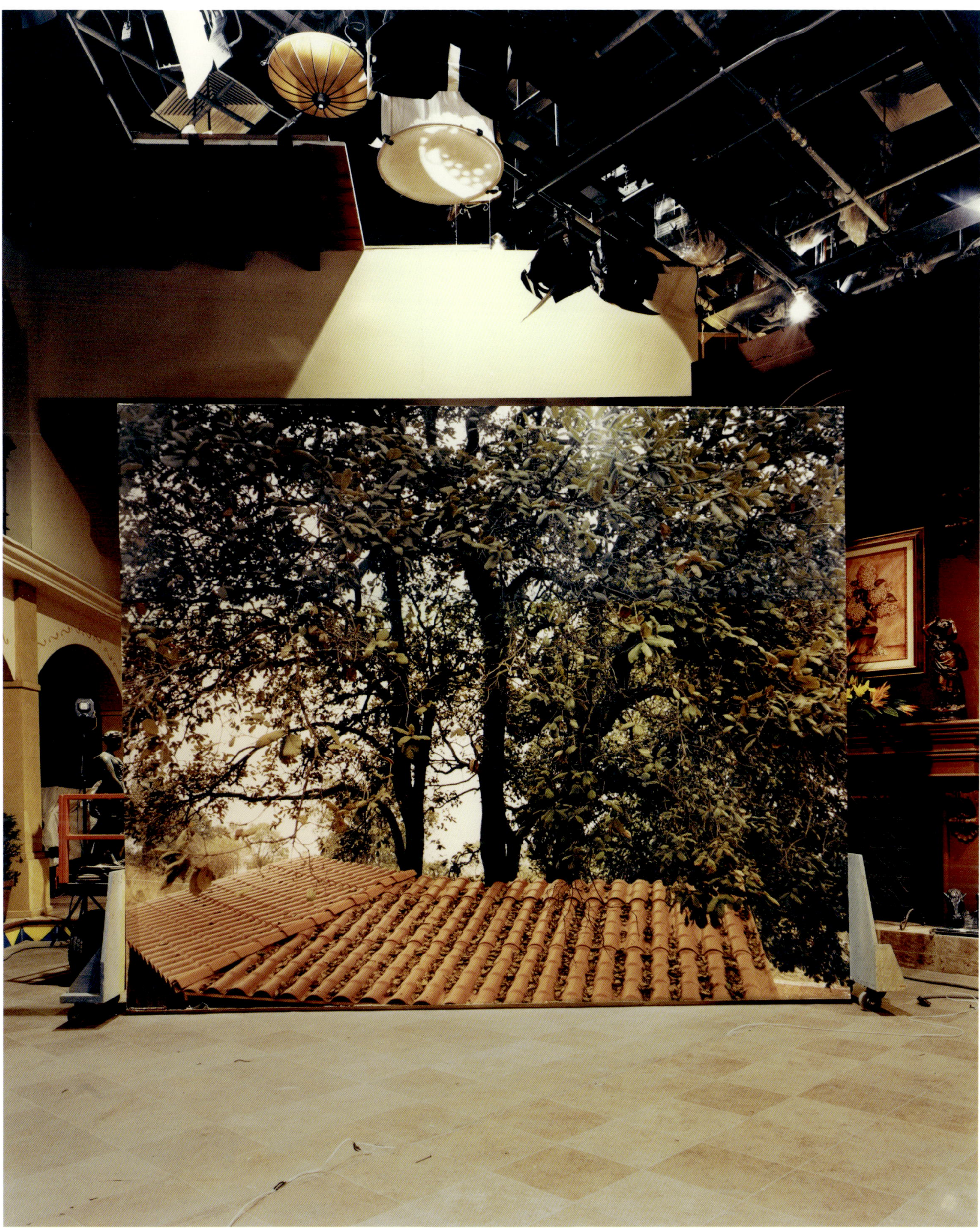

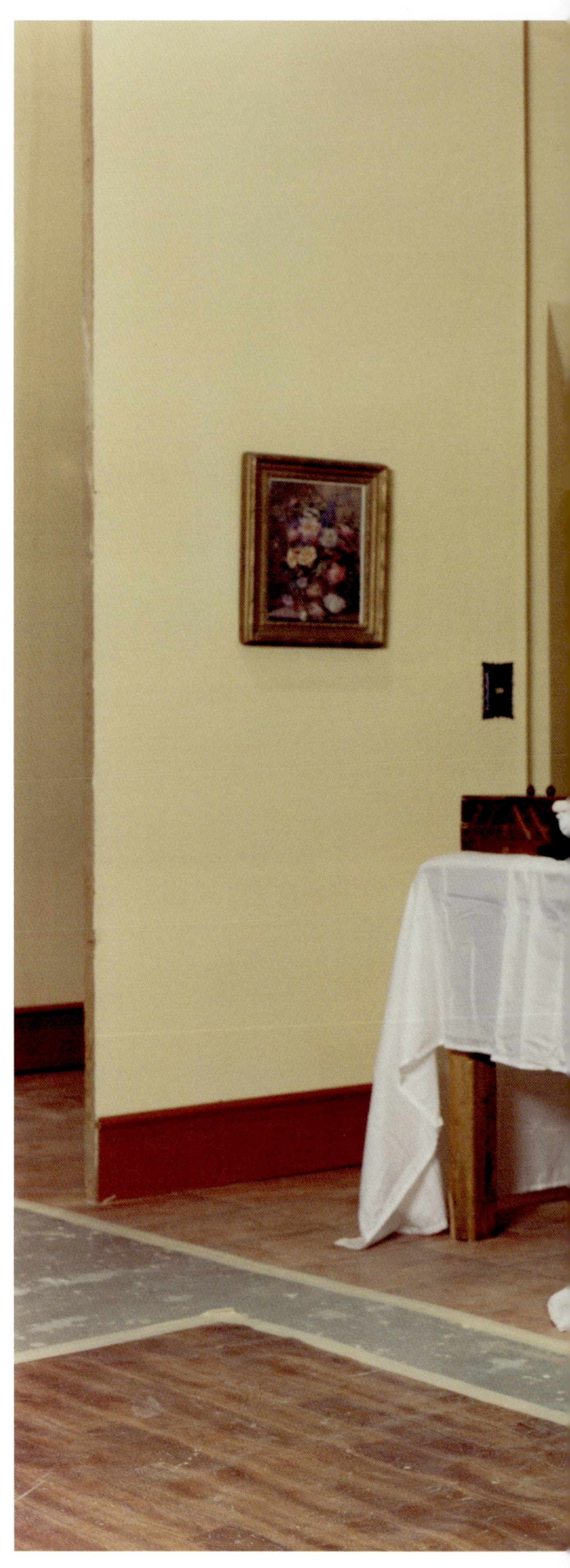

Adanely Núñez as Ana Gregoria
Mañana es para Siempre (Tomorrow Is Forever), 2009

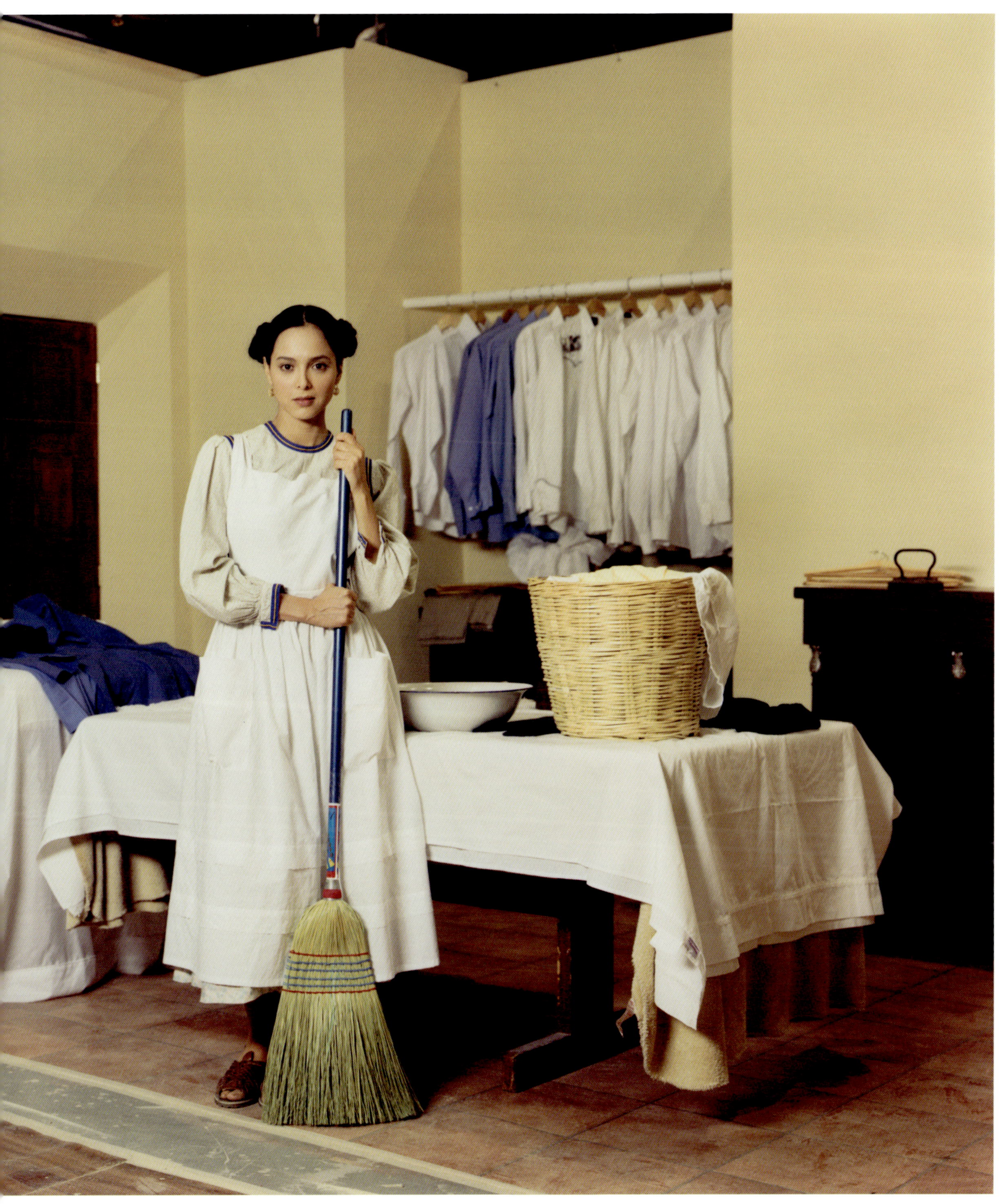

Aleida Núñez as Gardenia Campillo
Mañana es para Siempre (Tomorrow Is Forever), 2009

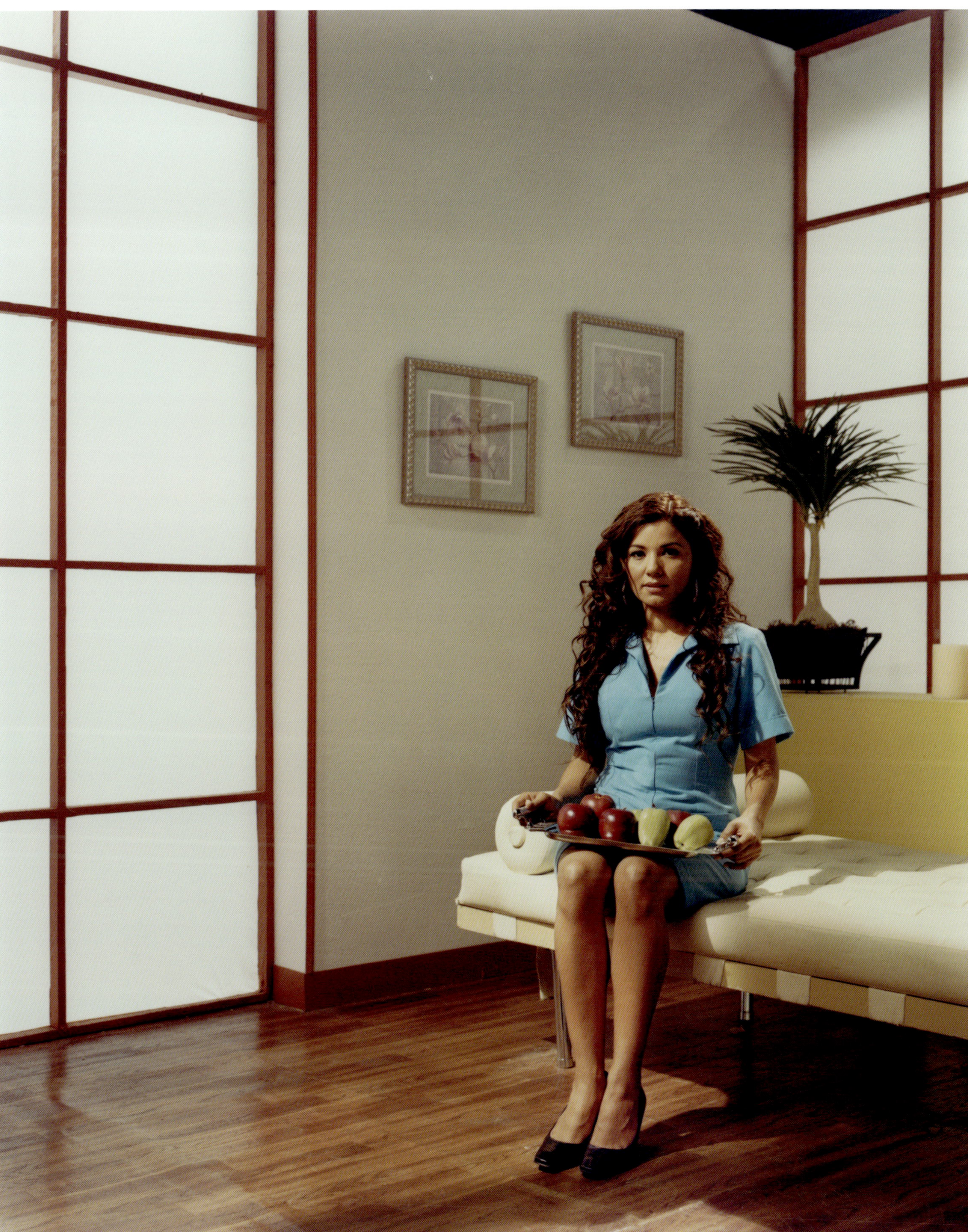

Alejandro Ávila as Dr. Ernesto Cortés
La Que No Podía Amar (The One Who Could Not Love), 2011

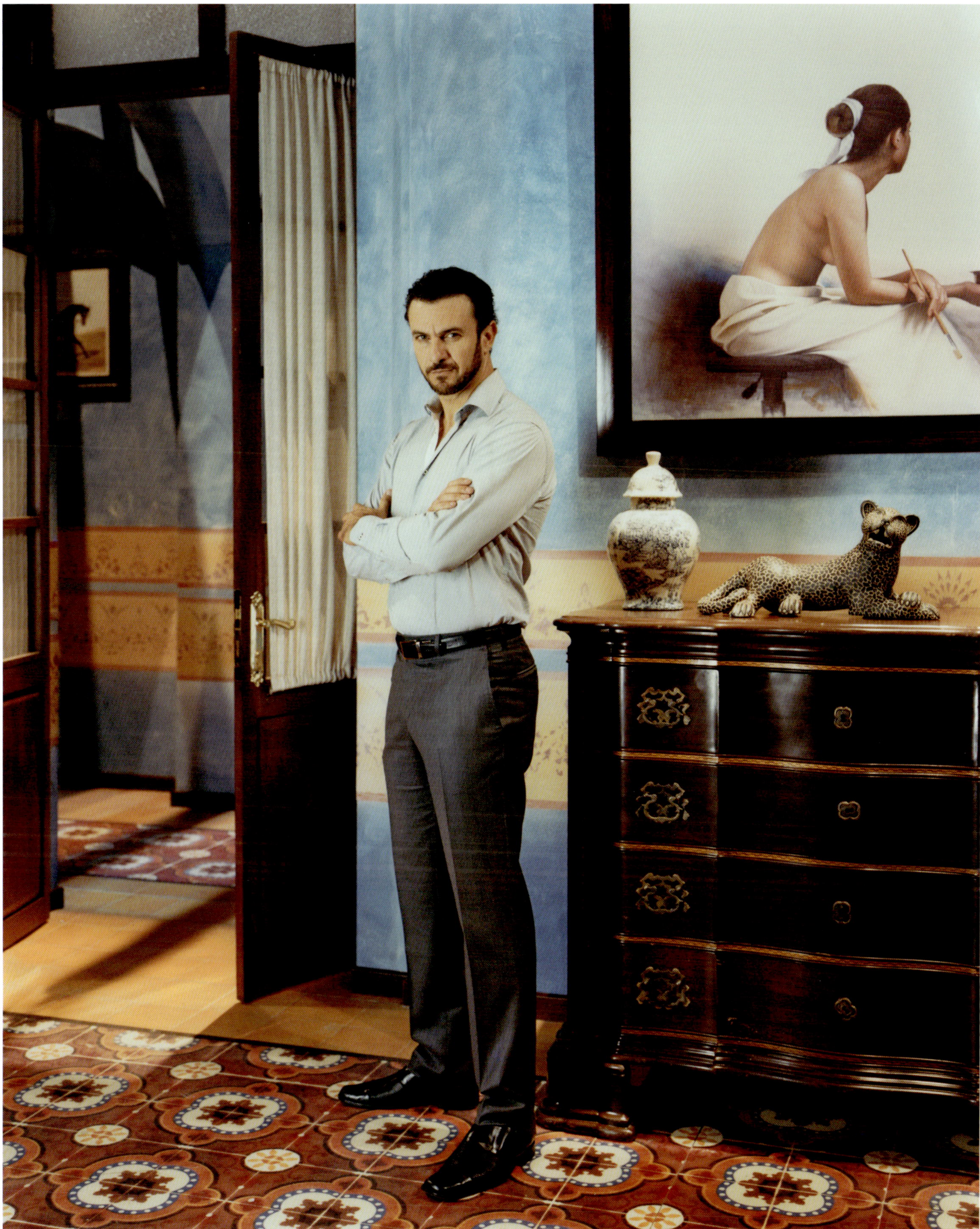

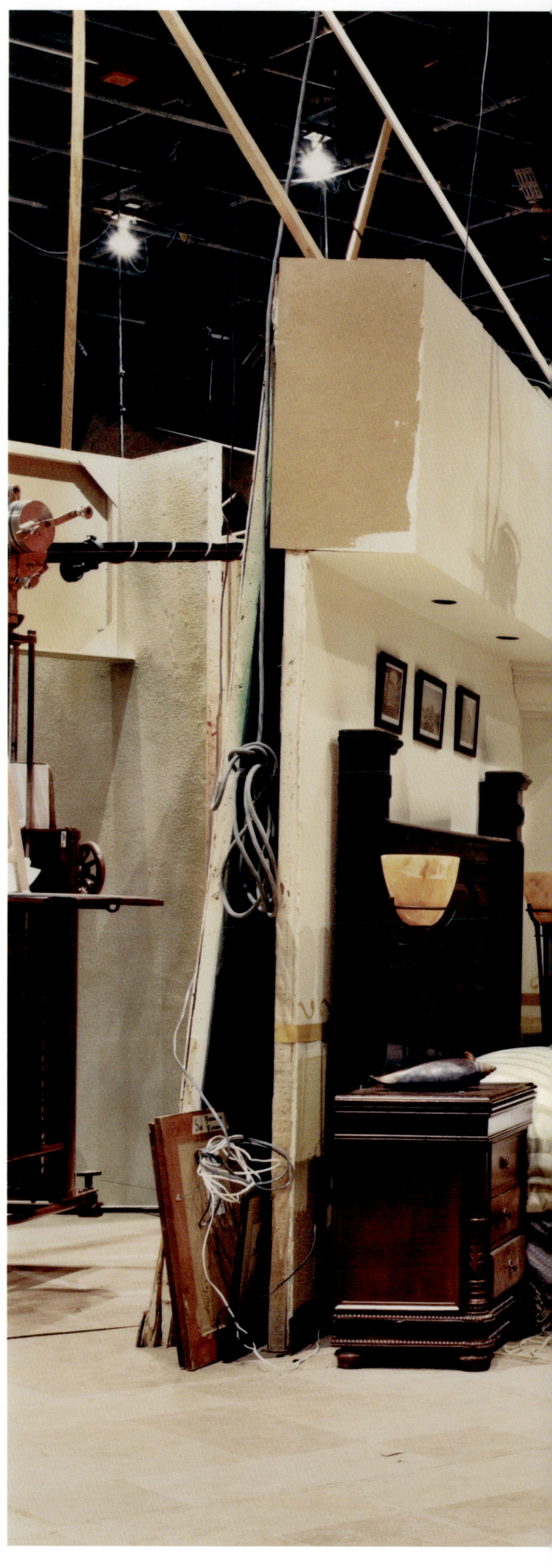

73 *Duelo de Pasiones II* (Duel of Passions), 2006

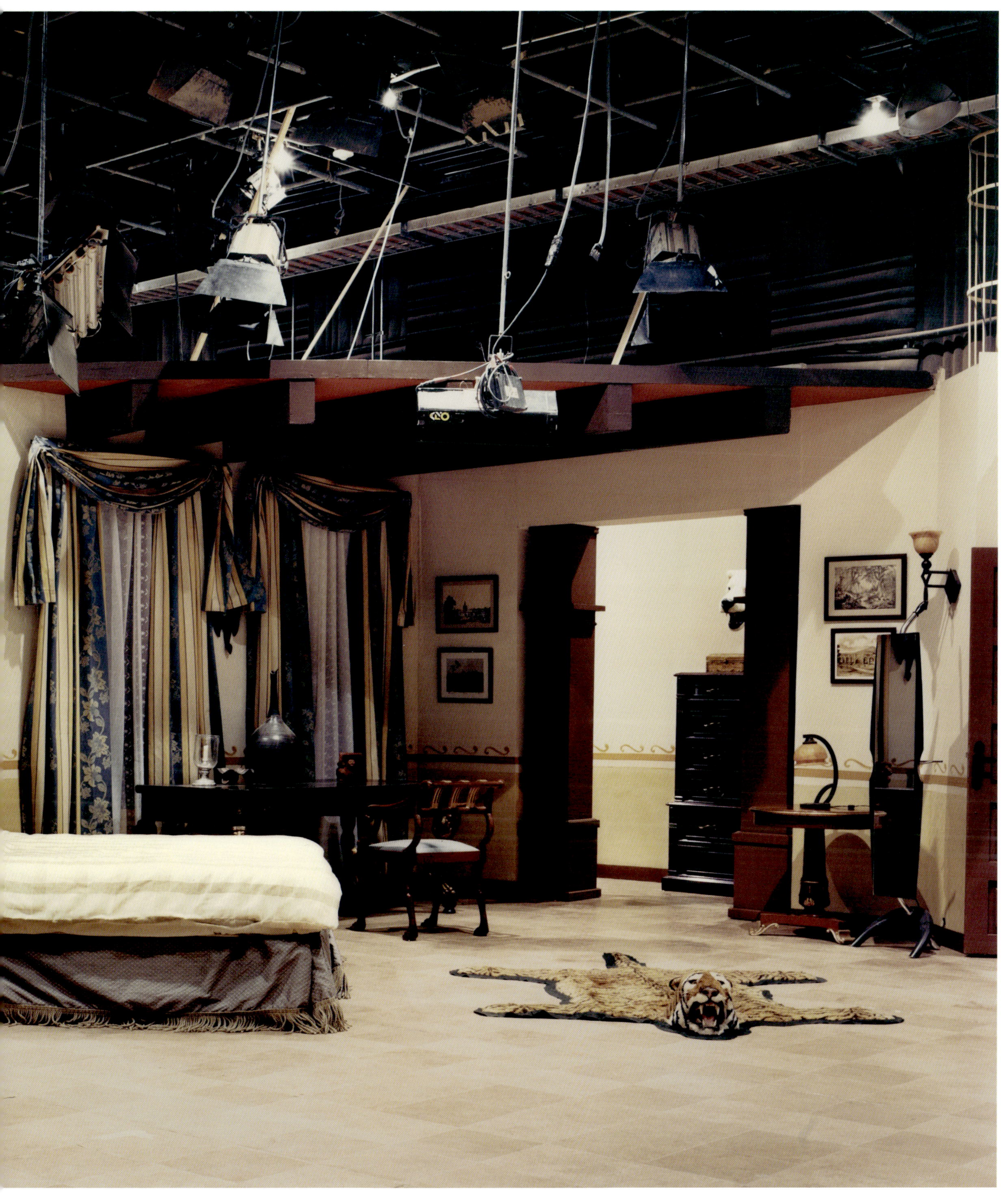

Alexis Ayala as Leonardo

Amarte es mi Pecado (Loving You Is My Sin), 2003

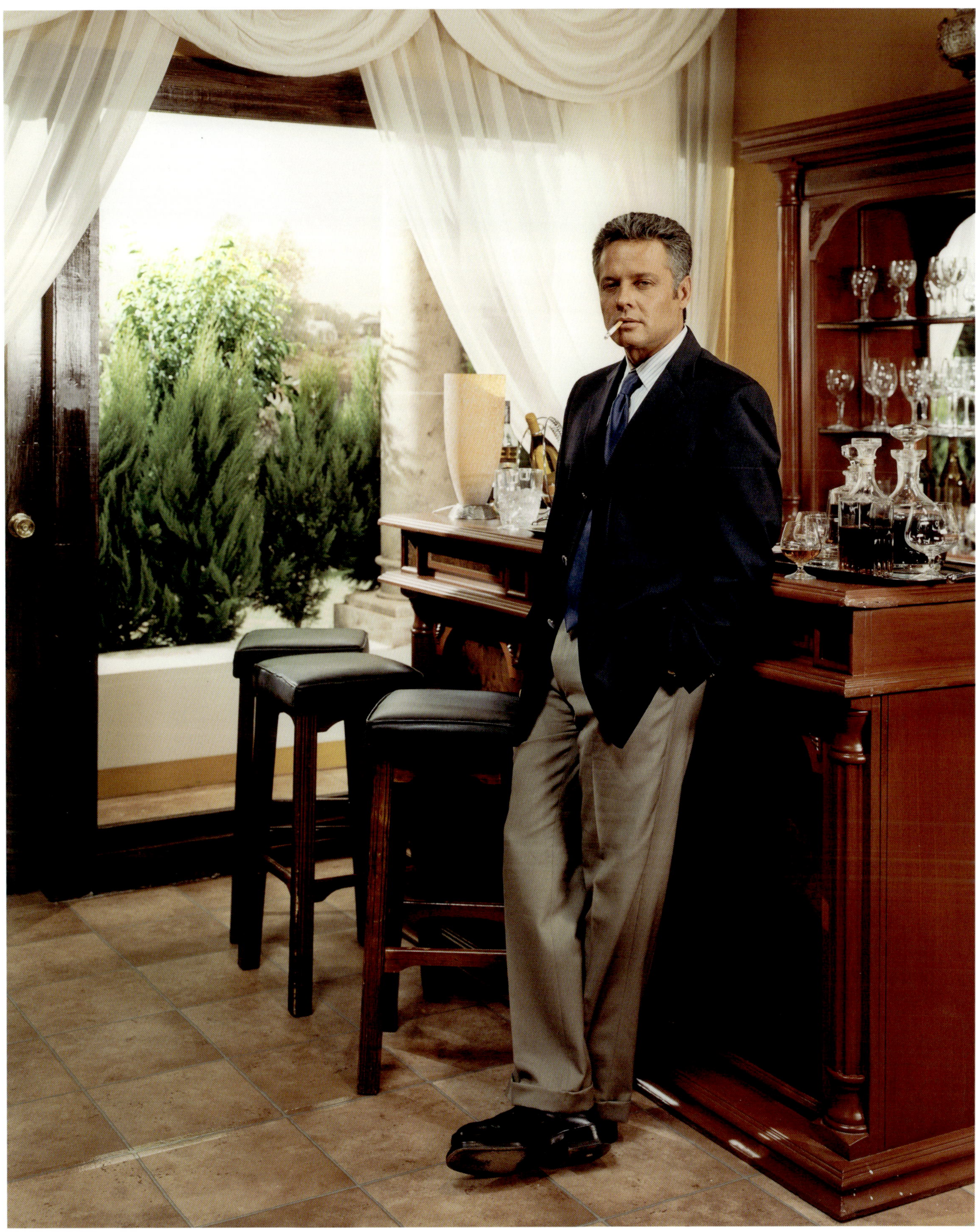

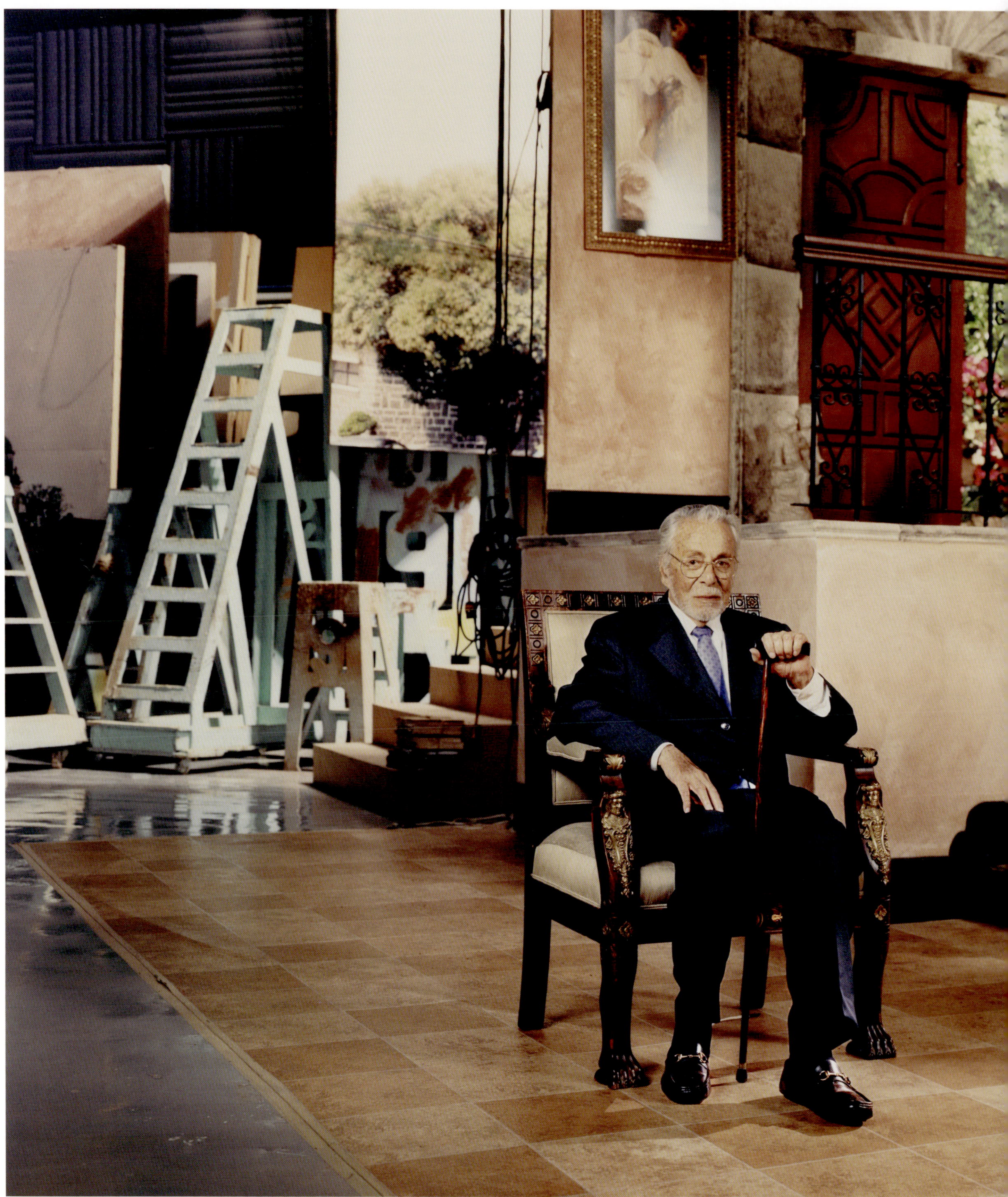

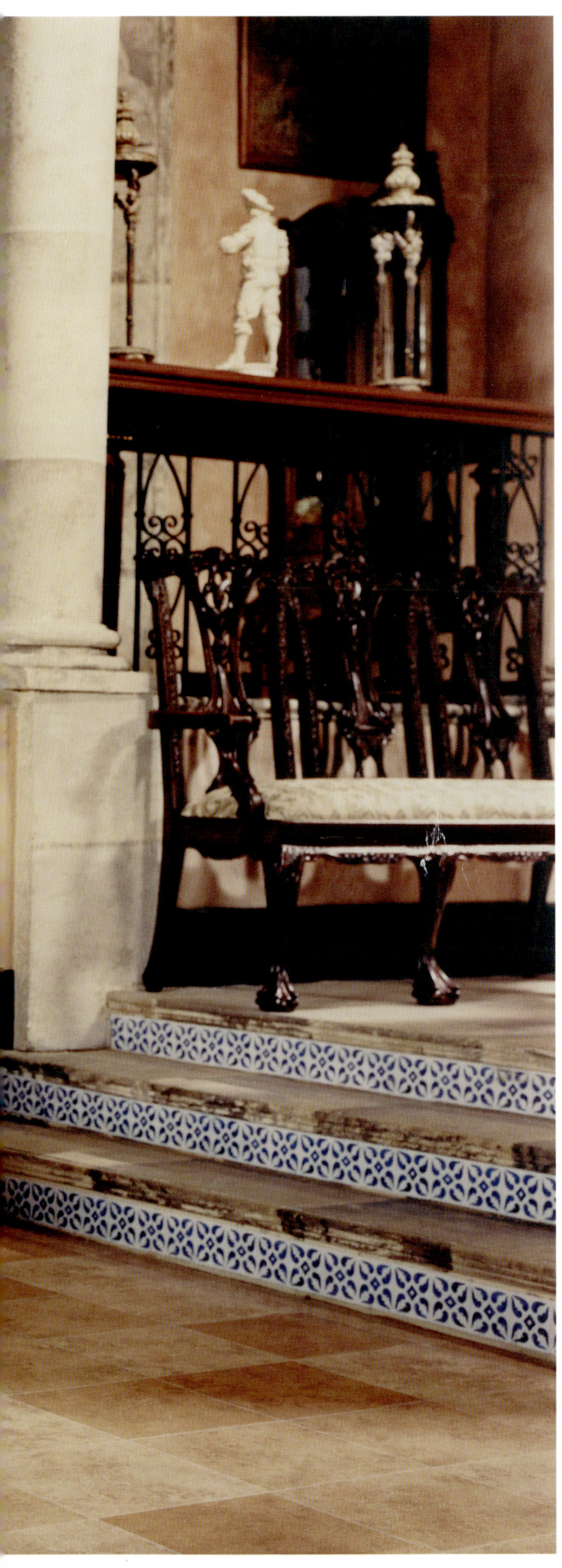

Ernesto Alonso on the set of *Amarte es mi Pecado* (Loving You Is My Sin), 2003

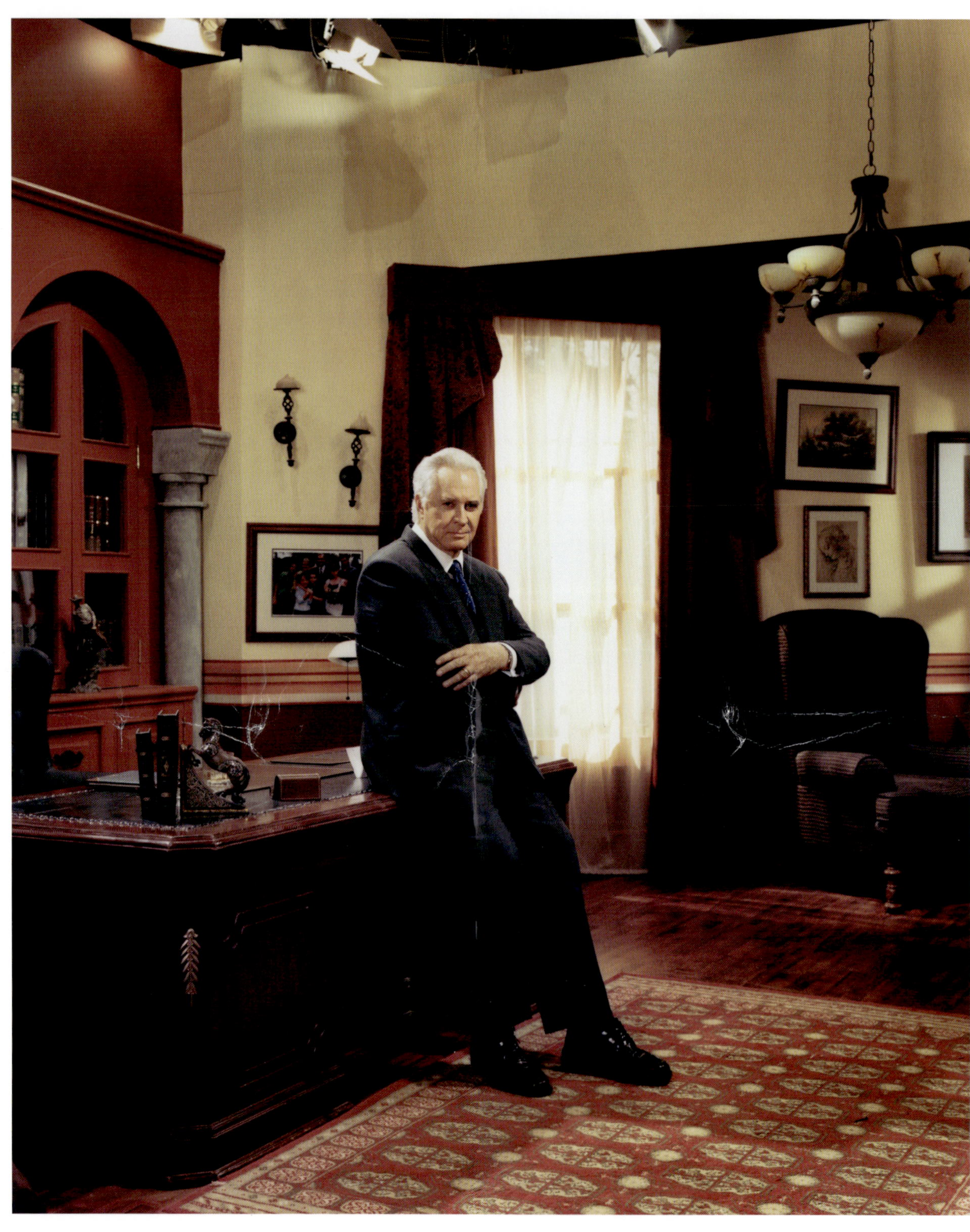

Rogelio Guerra as Gonzalo Elizalde
Mañana es para Siempre (Tomorrow Is Forever), 2009

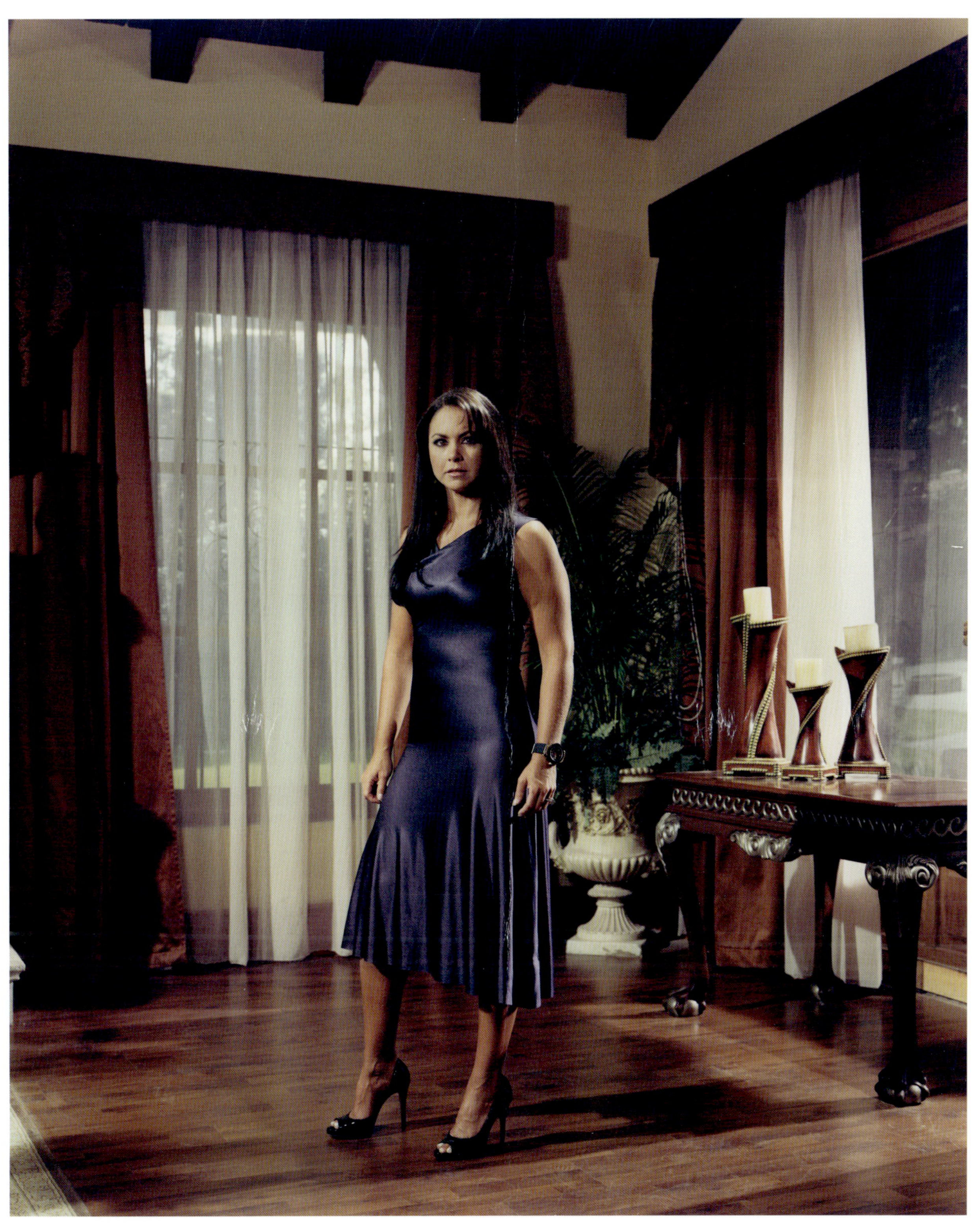

Lucero as Bárbara Greco de Elizalde/Rebeca Sánchez
Mañana es para Siempre (Tomorrow Is Forever), 2009

ROLANDO KLUNDER

Physically attractive, but vain and spiteful. Mauricio's rival in car racing. He dresses in the latest style and is always competing with others, especially Mauricio, whom he considers his fiercest rival. He has always been envious of him. A strong and impulsive personality, but hypocritical, dishonest, and rancorous. He doesn't care what he has to do to get his way.

Alejandro Sirvent as Rolando Klunder
Un Gancho al Corazón (A Blow to the Heart), 2009

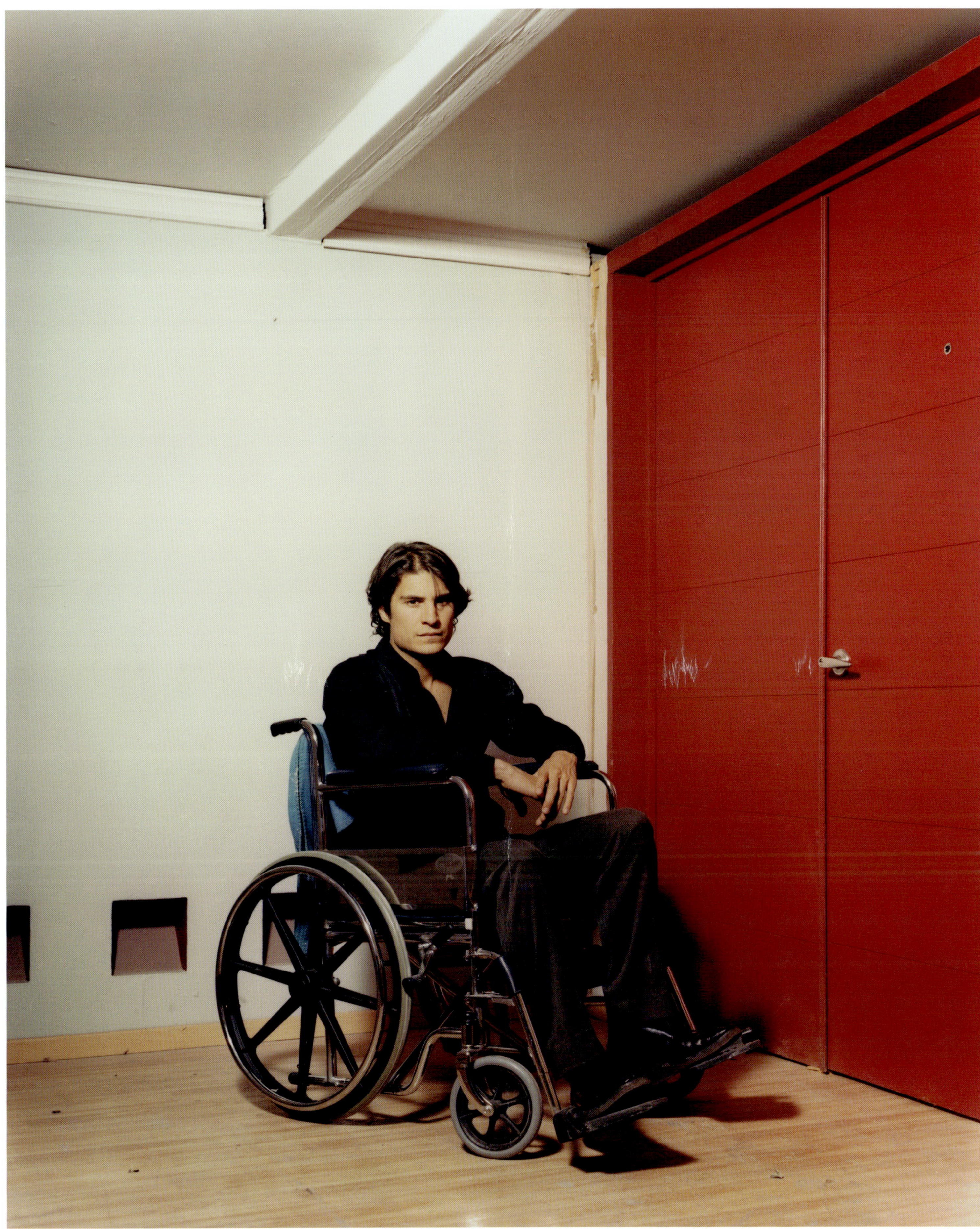

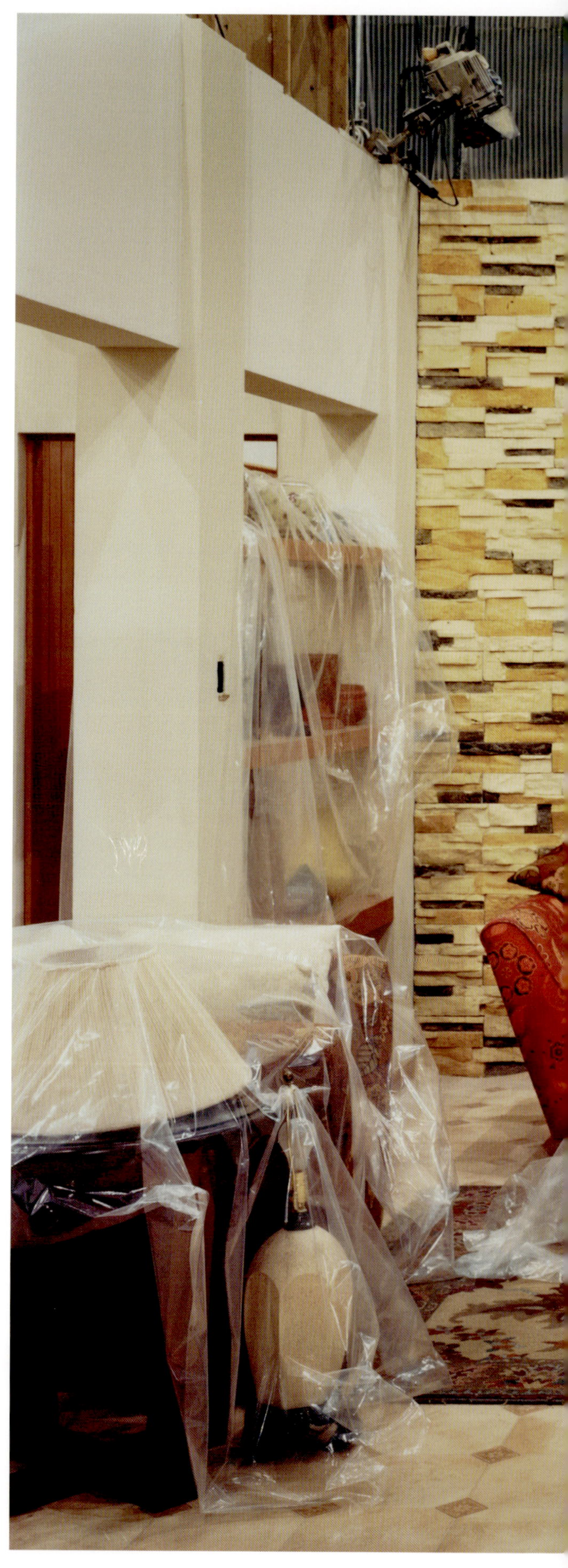

79 *Alma de Hierro* (Iron Soul), 2009

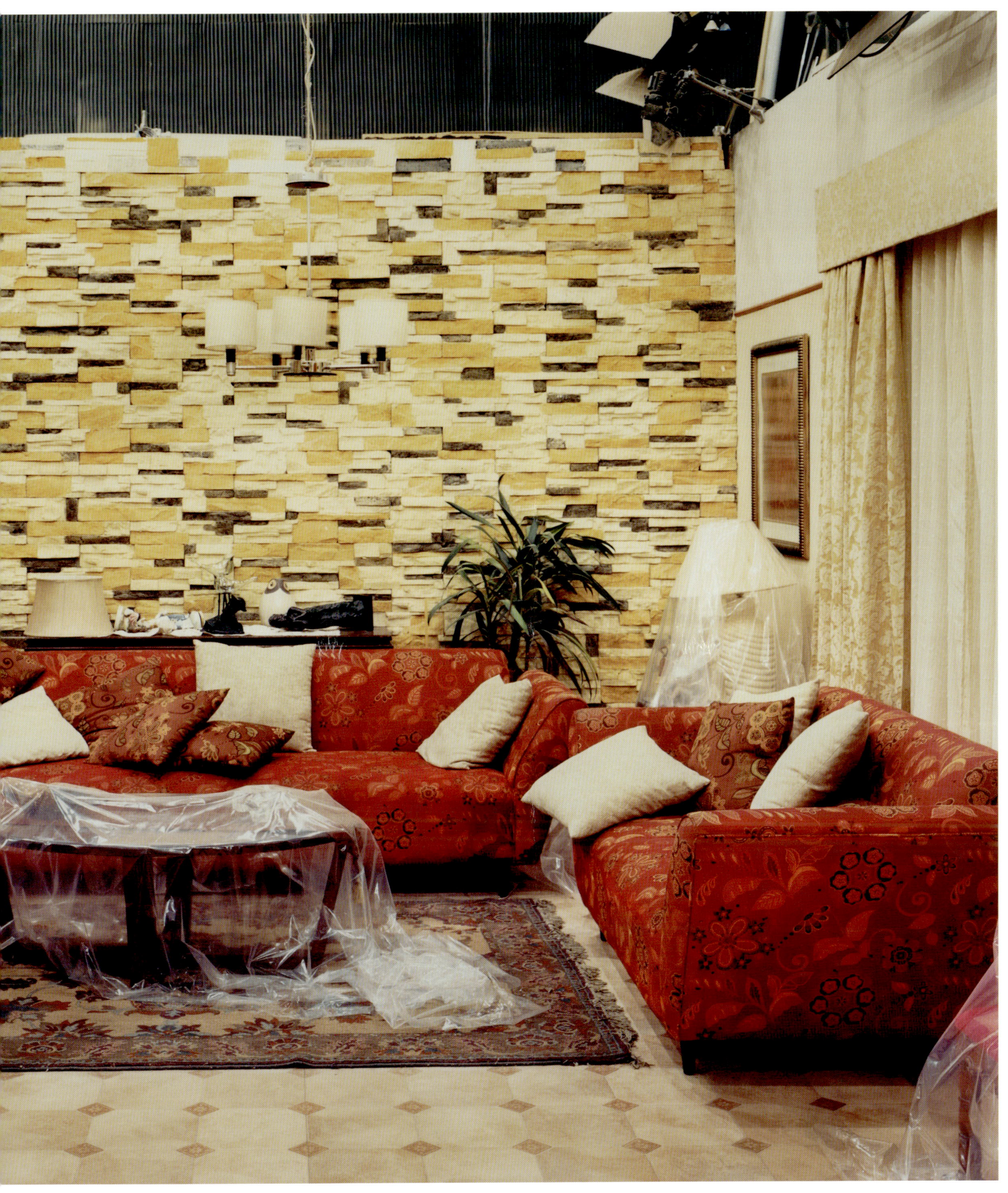

Synopsis of *Un Gancho al Corazón* (A Blow to the Heart)

This is a story of the true love between professional boxer Valentina Lopez (nicknamed "La Monita") and Mauricio Sermeño, former racecar driver and now owner and president of the Sermeño Real Estate Company. An entertaining family melodrama with many interesting locations and exciting adventures, it is full of intrigues and misunderstandings, but above all, seasoned with a great deal of tears, laughter, and love.

The story begins with Valentina in a great fight, which she loses because she injures her hand, forcing her to look for another job while recovering. She does this on the sly, hiding it from her boyfriend and trainer Beto—they've been dating for eight years—and in complicity with his mother, Nieves, who looks on La Monita as a daughter.

Valentina gets a job at Mauricio's company. Mauricio has a big heart and has decided to adopt three orphaned brothers. This doesn't sit well with his girlfriend, Constanza, who detests them. All she cares about is leading Mauricio to the altar, more because of his economic and social status than for Mauricio himself.

In her quest to marry, Constanza counts on the help of Jerónimo and Óscar Cárdenas, Mauricio's cousin and employee, respectively. All they care about is the power and money of the story's protagonist, and also separating him from Valentina and from his three adopted children, who adore La Monita.

But, Constanza, Jerónimo, and Óscar fail to take into account the love that Valentina and Mauricio feel for each other, a love that will triumph again and again despite all efforts to separate them, because from the first moment the boxer and the ex-racecar driver met, they were completely enamored with each other. The intensity and sincerity of their feelings overcomes any obstacle put in their path.

Sebastián Óscar Rulli as Mauricio Sermeño
Un Gancho al Corazón (A Blow to the Heart), 2009

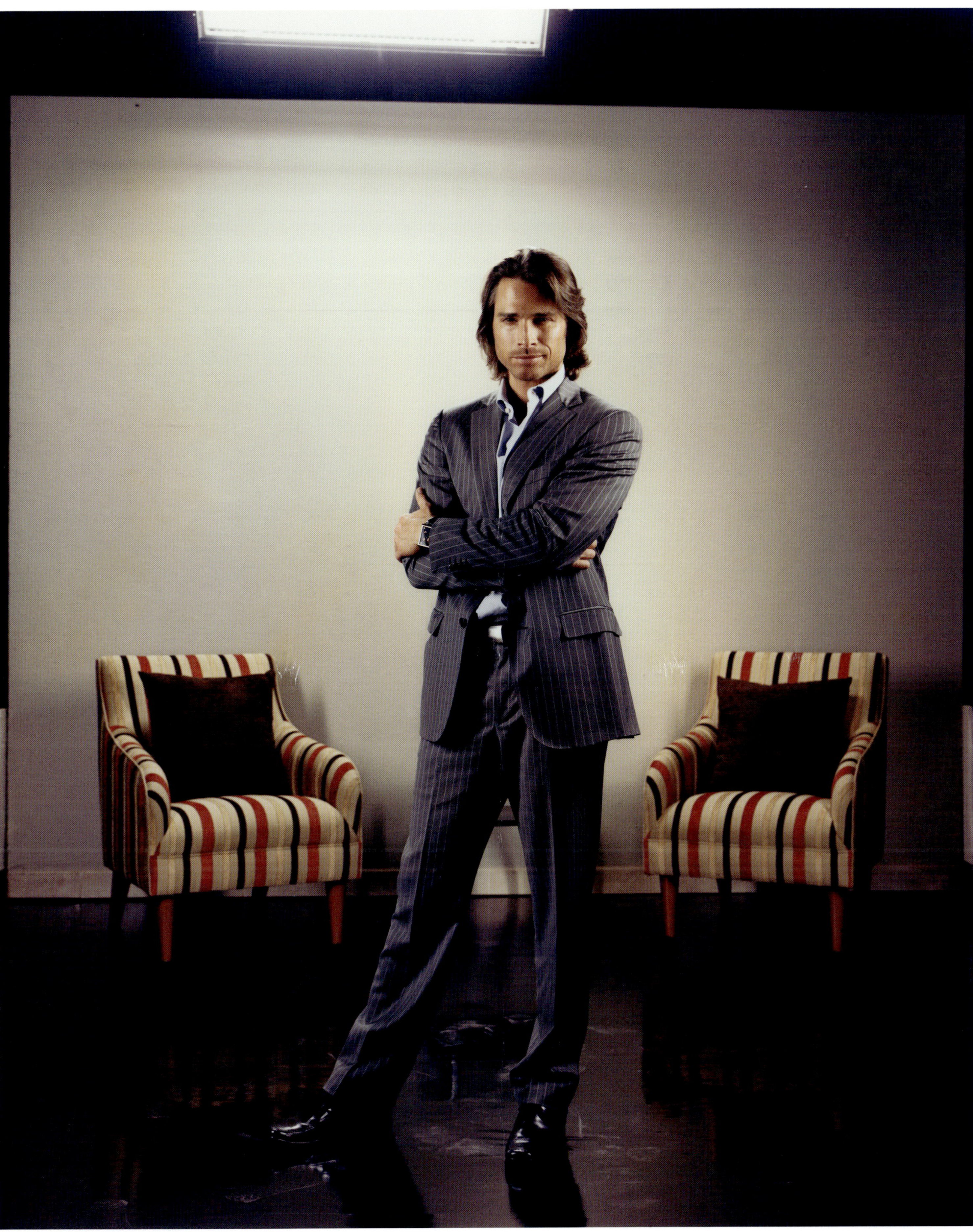

Vanessa Guzmán as Verónica Santillán Vidal
Amar Otra Vez (Loving Again), 2004

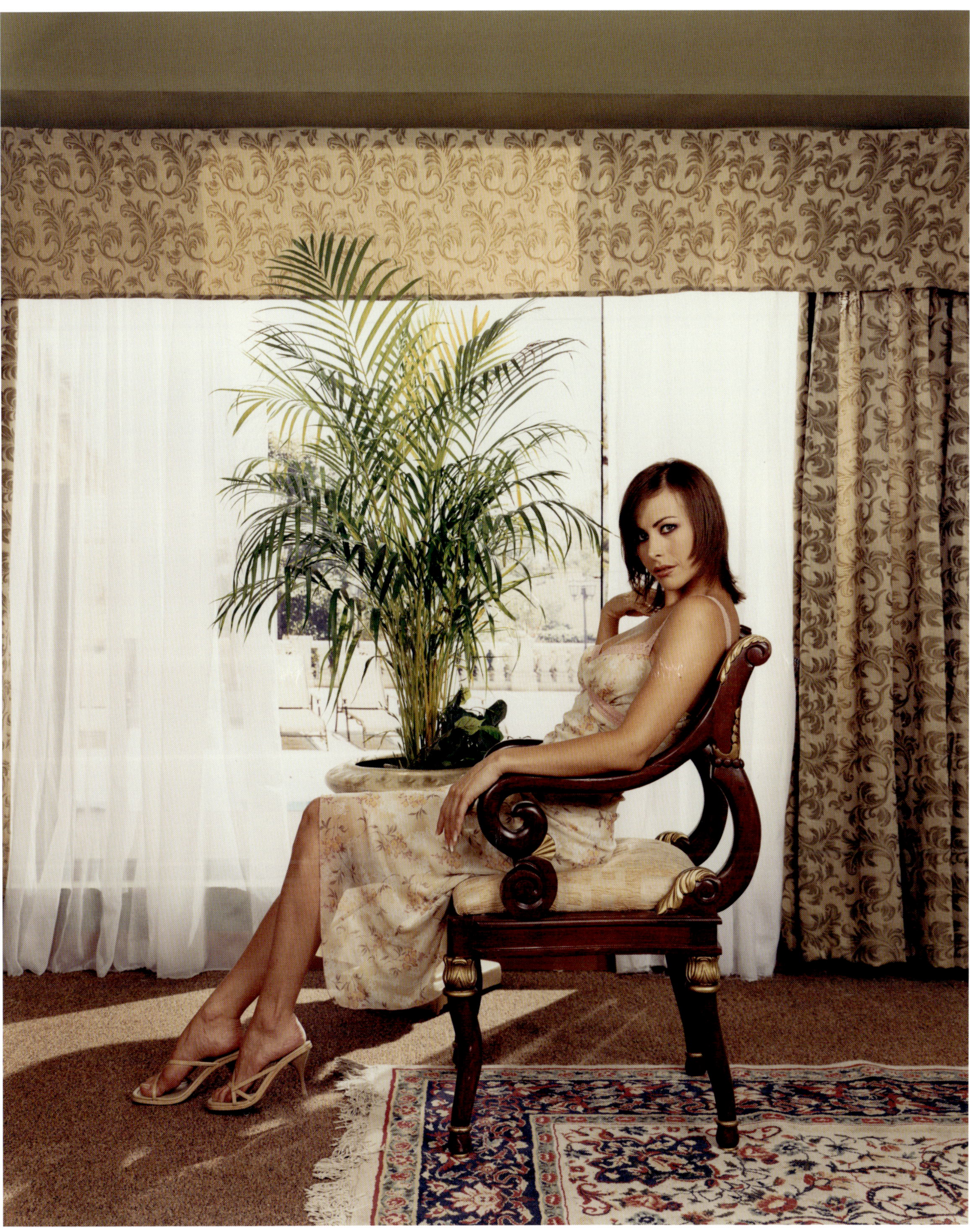

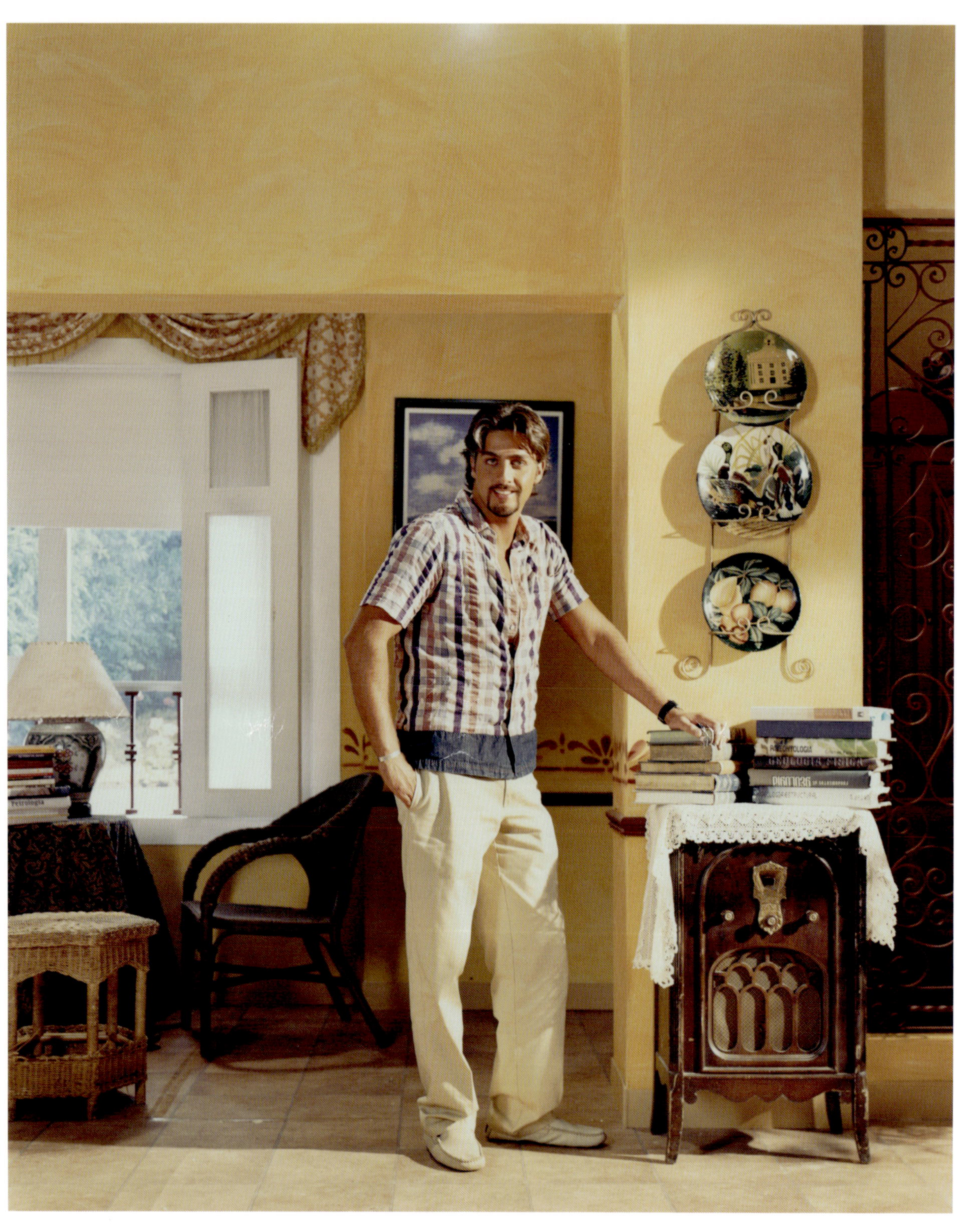

Marco Méndez as Luis Duarte López
Rubí, 2004

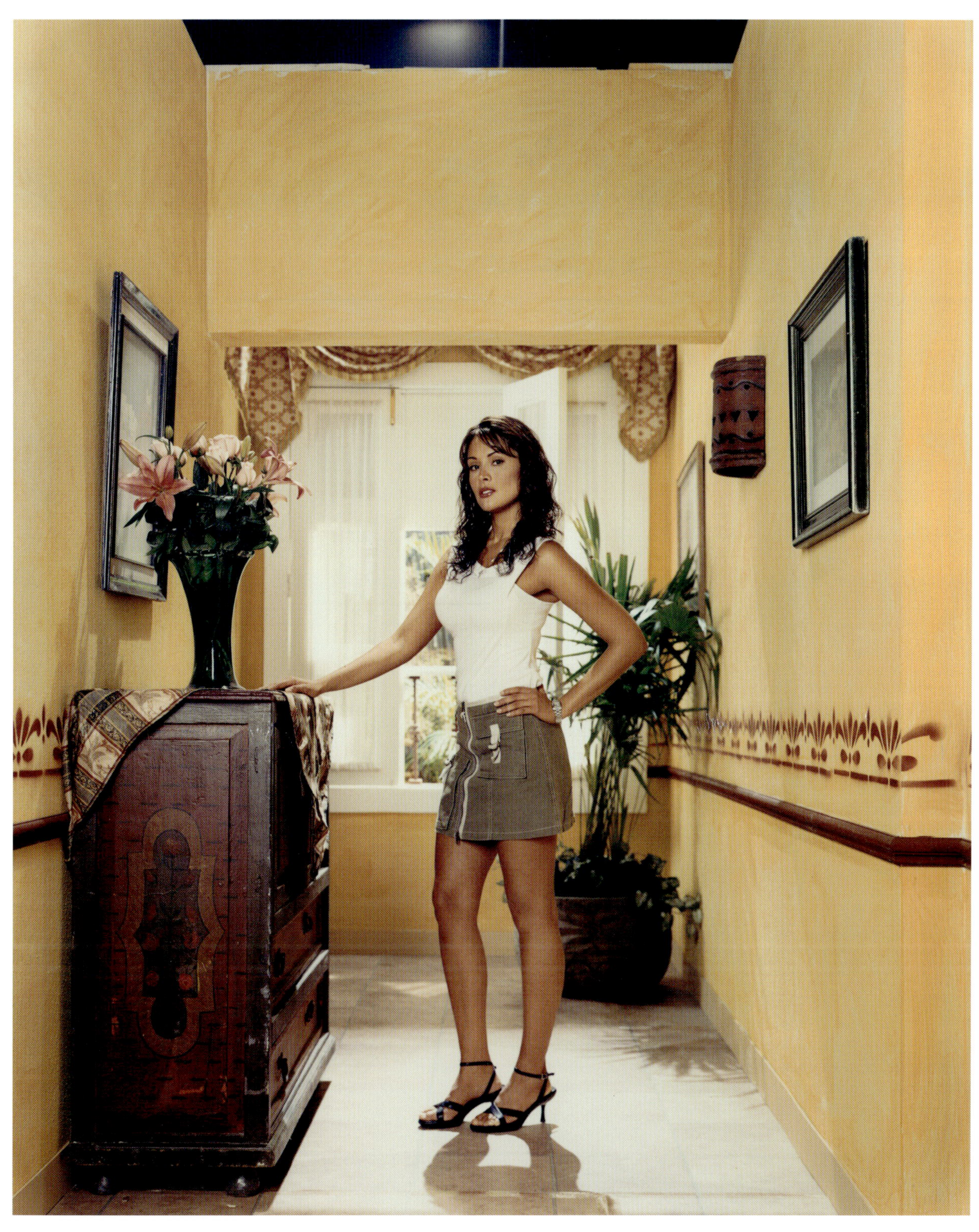

Tania Vázquez as Sofía Cárdenas Ruiz
Rubí, 2004

Susana González as Cinthia Montero Báez

La Que No Podía Amar (The One Who Could Not Love), 2011

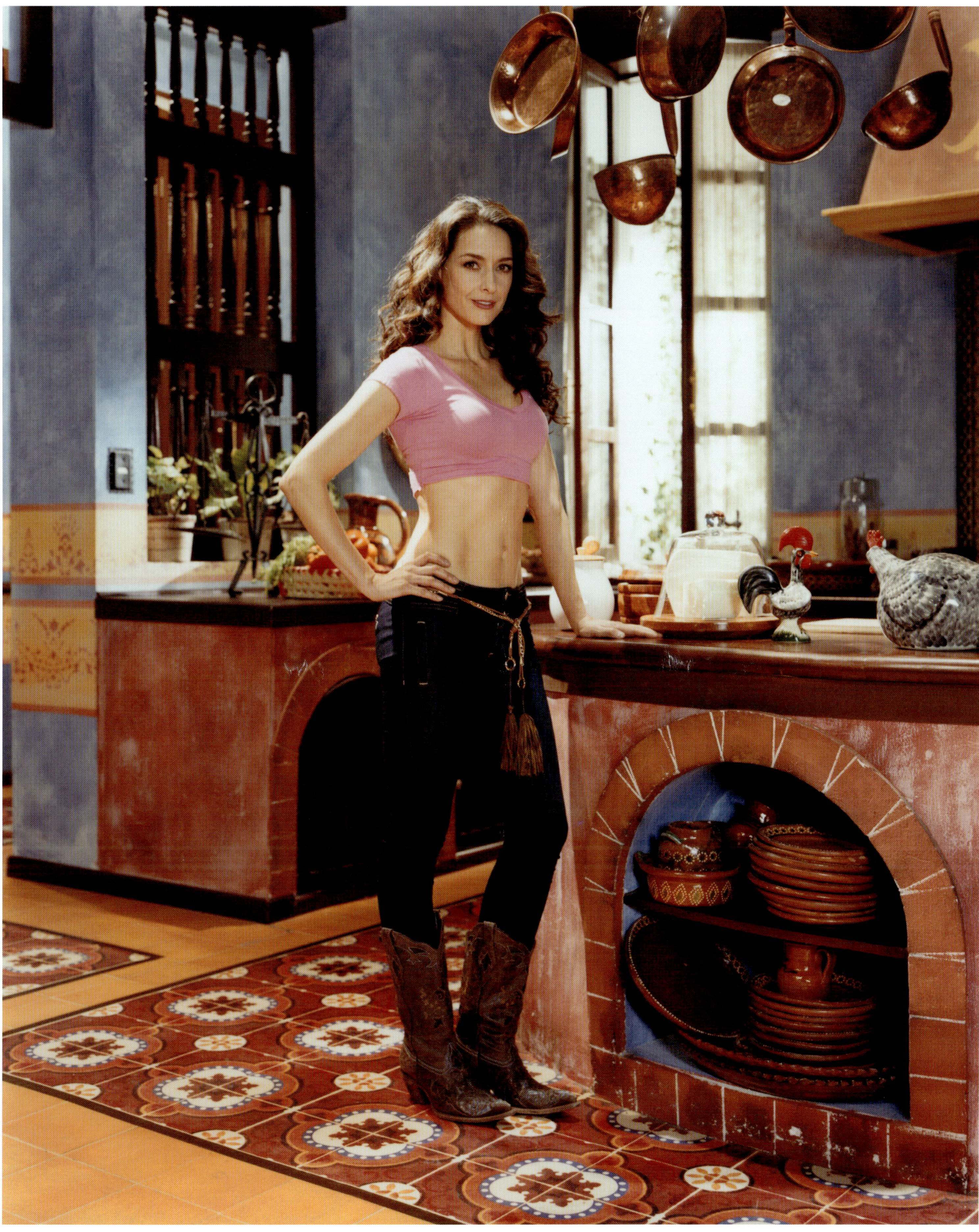

JUAN JIMÉNEZ

Juan has always been a good student. He is about to finish his medical studies, to which he has devoted himself body and soul, because he dreams of getting his parents out of the poor neighborhood where they have always lived. His life is transformed when he falls in love with Renata, a rich girl who despises him. He is twenty-four years old.

Ernesto D'Alessio as Juan Jiménez
Heridas de Amor (Wounds of Love), 2006

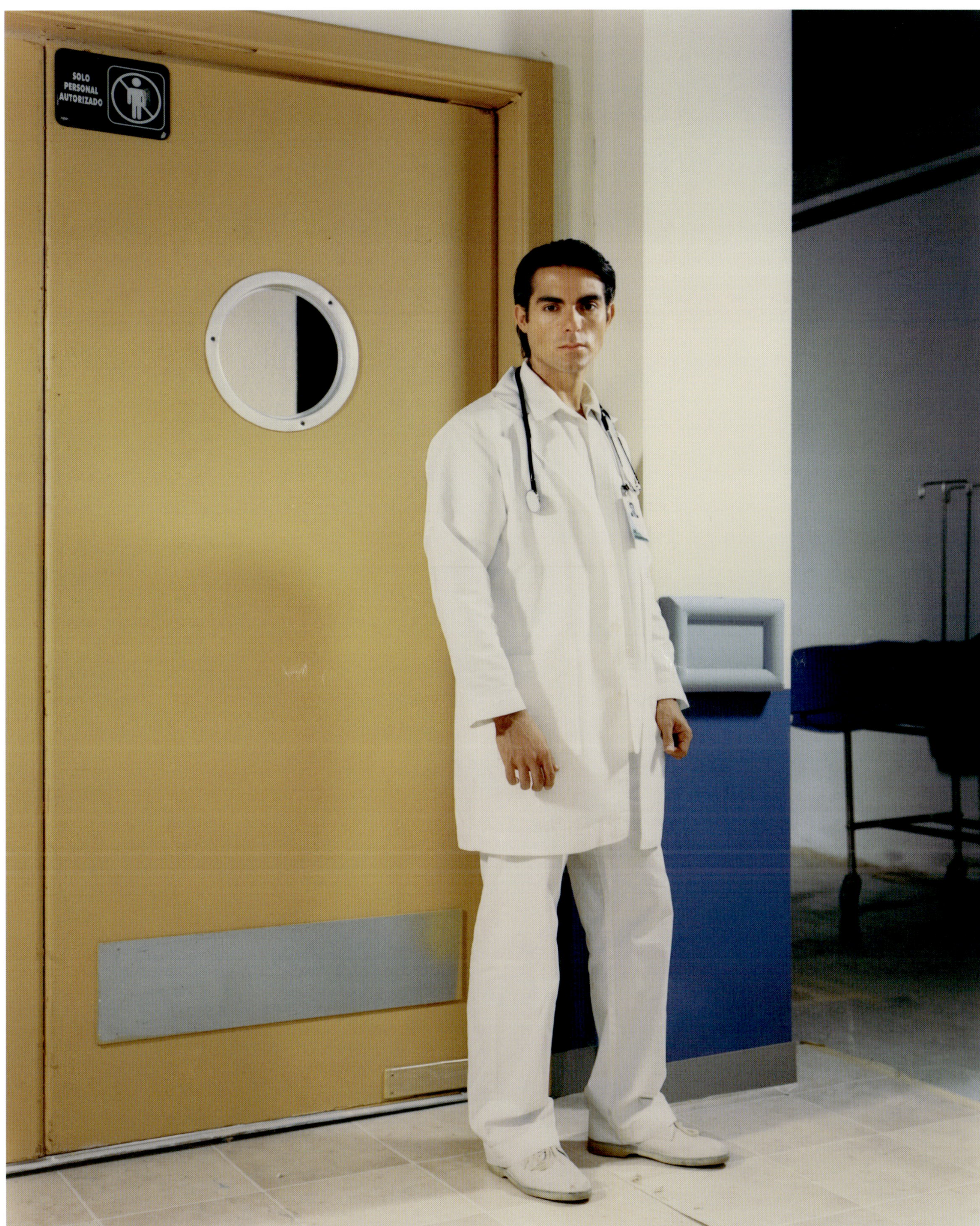
SOLO
PERSONAL
AUTORIZADO

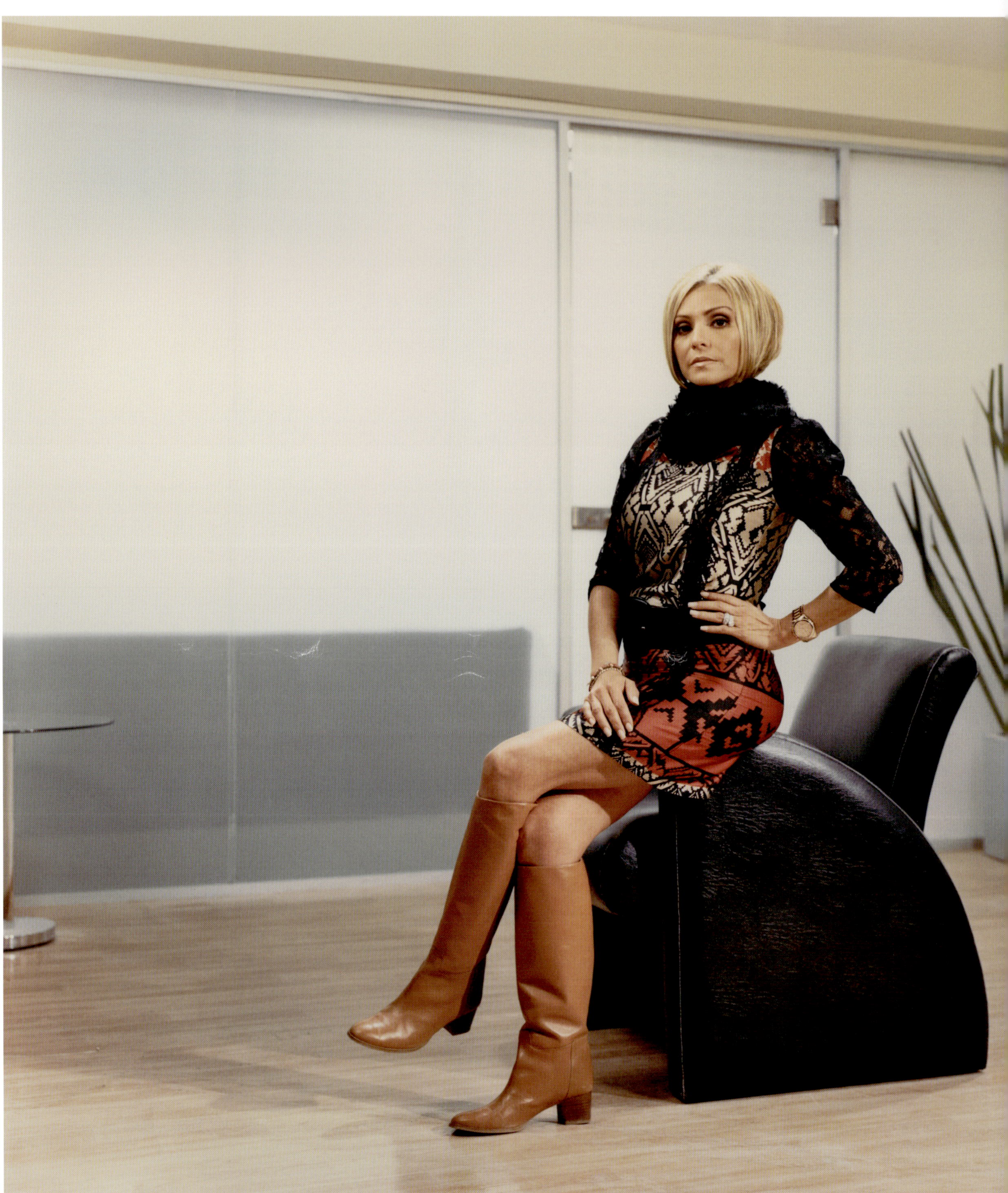

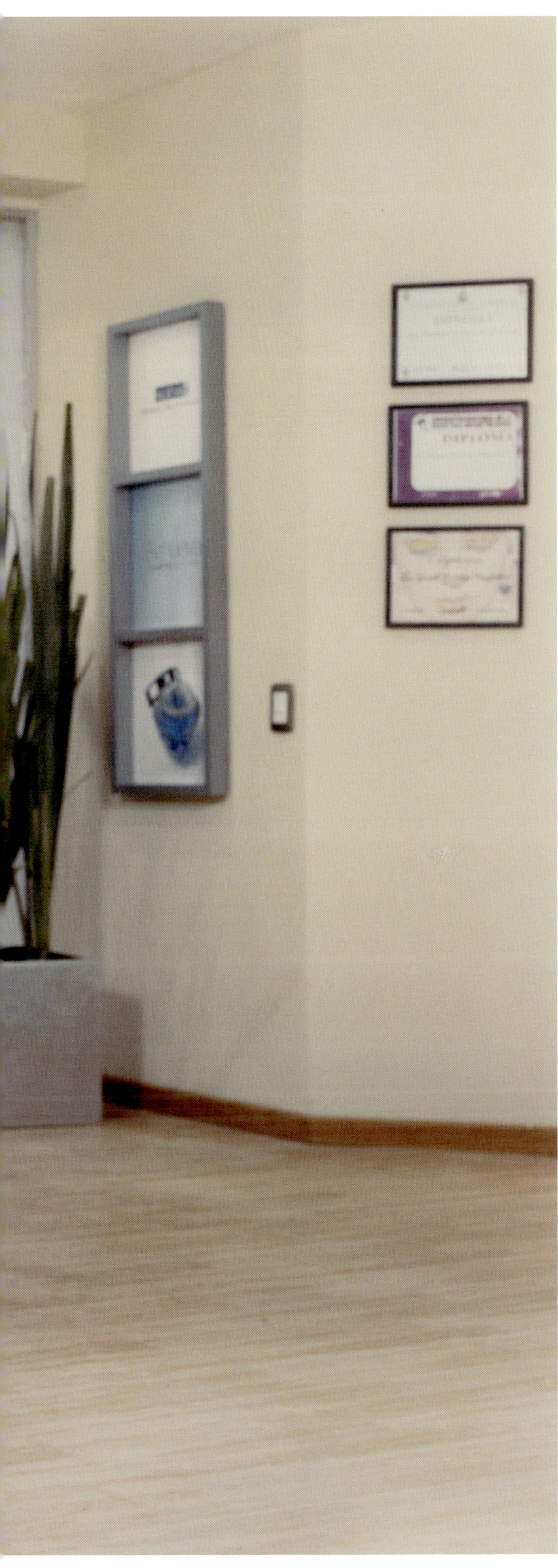

Daniela Castro as Pina Arteaga
Una Familia Con Suerte (One Family with Luck), 2011

87 *Corazones al Límite* (Hearts to the Limit), 2004

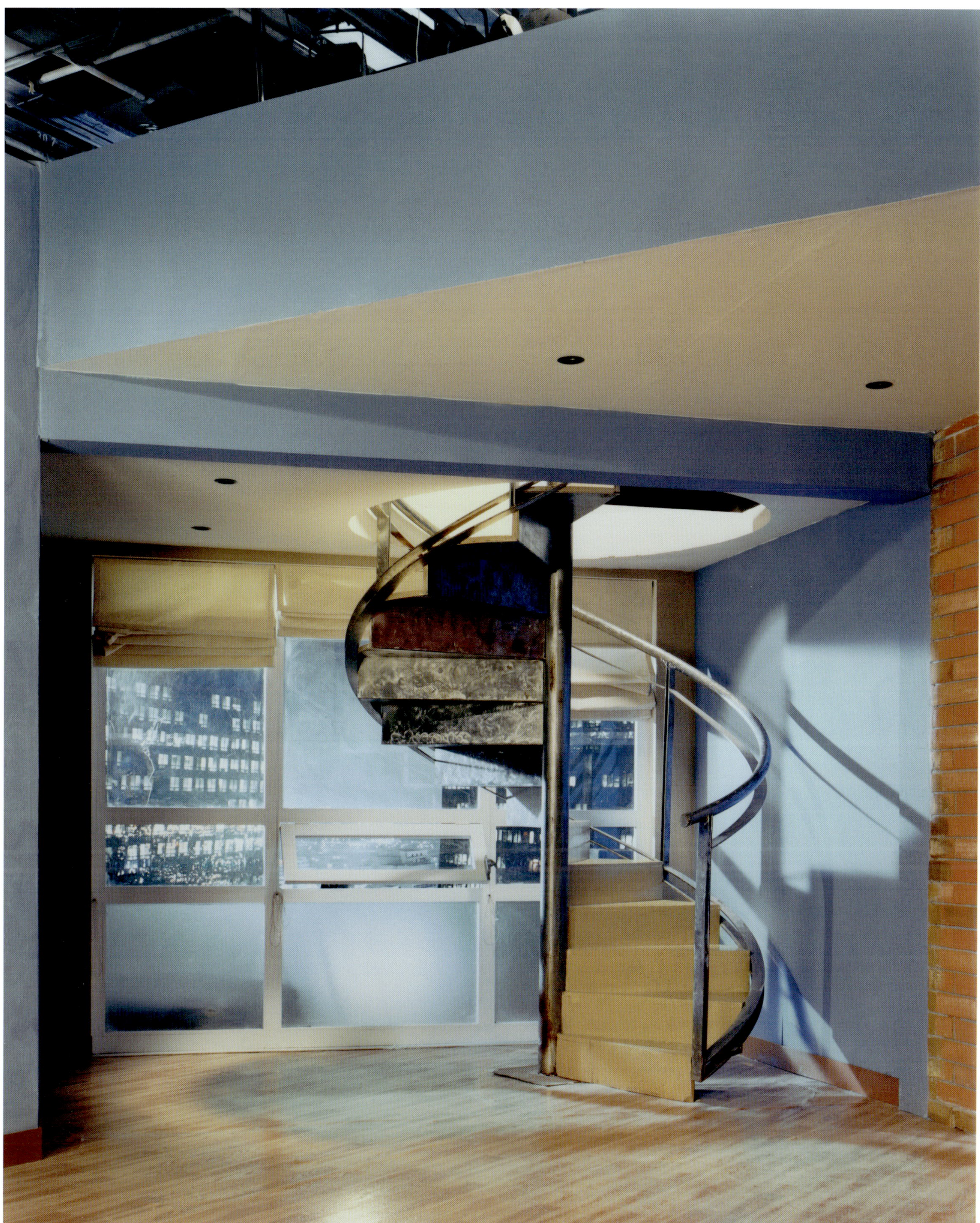

88 *Amor Real* (True Love), 2003

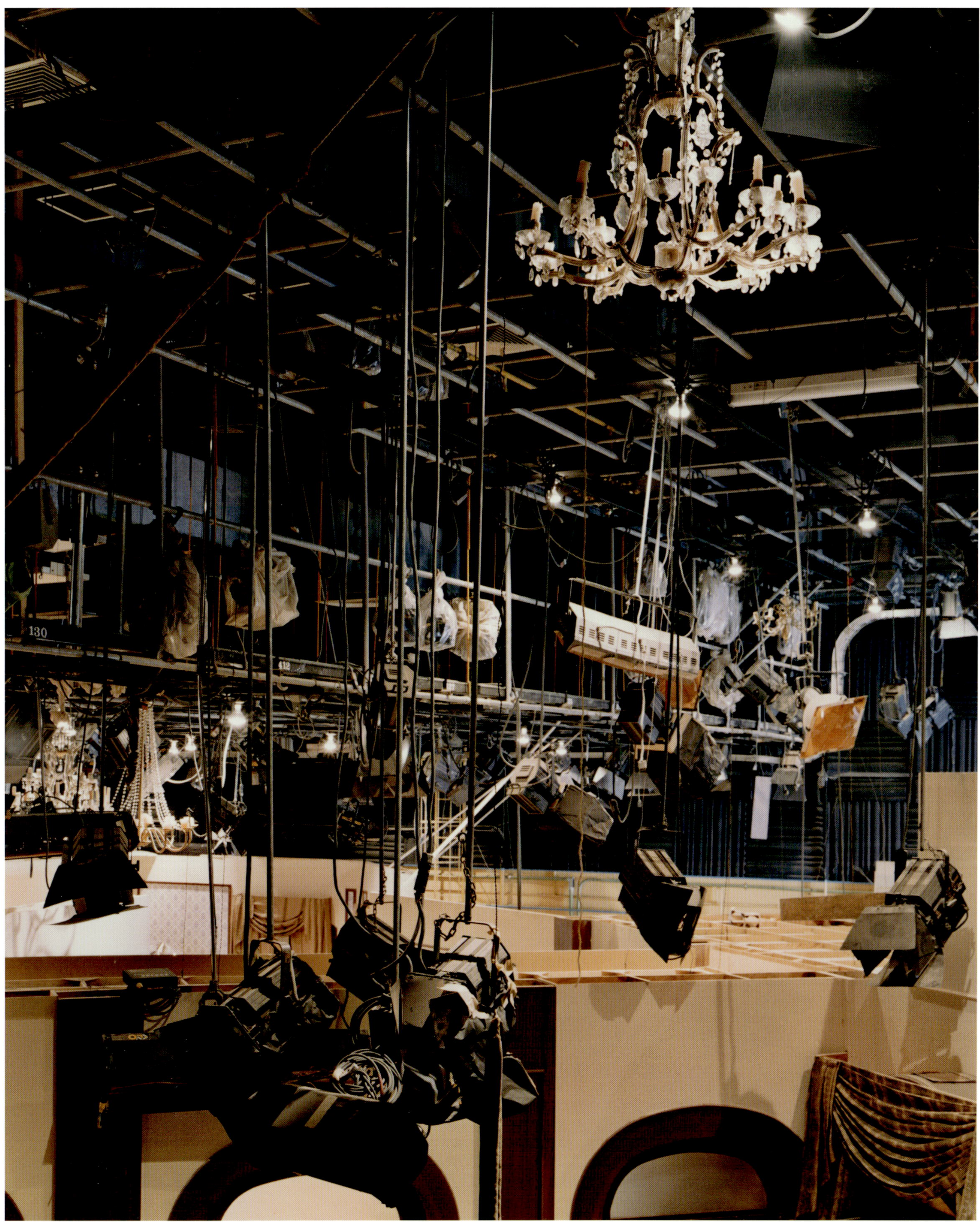
130

89 *Atrévete a Soñar* (Dare to Dream), 2009

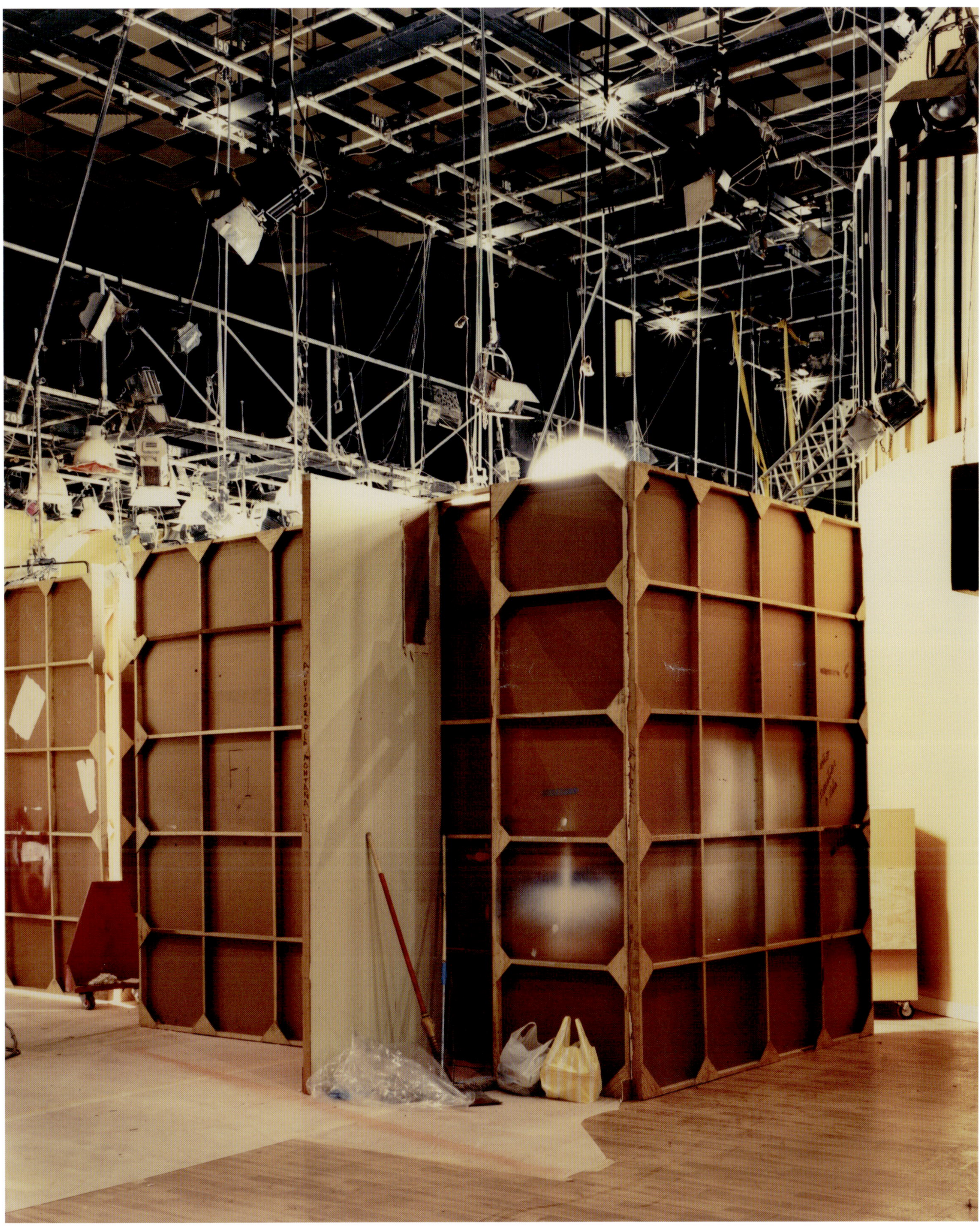

This project started while I was creative director of *COLORS* magazine at Benetton's Fabrica in Treviso, Italy. We needed a subject for a new issue. Earlier, there had been talk about doing something on an acting school as part of the schools issue (#48). That particular school, Televisa's Centro de Educación Artística (CEA), was in Mexico City at Televisa studios. Although the school taught many things, it mainly taught students to be telenovela actors. CEA hadn't made it into the schools issue, but, like many ideas at *COLORS*, it stayed on a list that would get passed around every once in a while. So when it came up again, I thought that it could be interesting to do a whole issue not just on the school, but on telenovelas in general.

With *COLORS*, I had photographed in refugee camps in Tanzania, a mental hospital in Cuba, slums in Latin America, and modern slavery in India. Outside of *COLORS*, I had done a lot of editorial work, which included photographing celebrities. Although the aesthetics of telenovelas were not really the same as my own, and I didn't watch them (except sometimes at the laundromat), the more I thought about it, the more telenovelas seemed like a great vehicle through which to explore many of my interests, and also some of my own history.

With the actors, sets, and lighting, we could look at issues of race, class, and beauty through a very different aesthetic than the more traditional documentary portraiture we were using in *COLORS* at the time. I wanted to make formal, almost painterly portraits of the actors, dressed in character and on set. There was a wide range of actors. I was interested in the various types, and in how the definitions of beauty and class are often defined by race. Generally, the stars look European. The maids do not. And the villains vary.

The idea of fame could also be discussed. It was interesting that many of the telenovela actors were huge stars in much of the world, but virtually unknown in the U.S. and northern Europe. Also, the sets were amazing. Everything was fabricated to represent all levels of Mexican society. There were mansions, offices, and slums. And everything was lit to a hyper-real perfection.

As for my own history: my family, on my father's side, comes from Mexico. They had crossed the border and settled in California. They had worked as farm workers or house cleaners or in canneries and factories. My father was the first in his family to finish high school and university. He became a lawyer. My family had lived the "American Dream." The dreams embodied in telenovelas were interesting to me because they are similar to an immigrant's dreams. Basically, by working hard, being honorable, and with a bit of luck, after a few obstacles, you can find wealth, love, and happiness.

The first time I went to Televisa, it took over a week to gain access to a telenovela set. But in the meantime, CEA had allowed us to shoot in the school's studio. It had the bare essentials of a telenovela studio: the entranceway, the kitchen, the dining room/living room, and the bedroom. It also had plenty of young aspiring actors, who were eager to participate. When we came in, the class was practicing kissing. The students had to pair up and learn how to make it look good for the camera. After we watched this for a while, the professor told us that we could use the bedroom for portraits. So I decided to use the bed as a type of "casting couch." I let the students choose their poses for the camera. The first volunteers were women. But with a little prompting, the men showed equal interest. This inspired the women to help the men with their poses. Then the lighting crew got involved and helped to make the set look like a proper telenovela. This was my first experience of shooting in the factory of dreams.

Stefan Ruiz

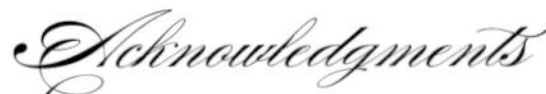

This book is dedicated to Carolina Taveras.

Thanks to the people who were instrumental to this book:
Chris Boot, Denise Wolff, Pablo Helguera,
Fernando Gutiérrez, Gabriella Gomez-Mont, Patrick Lyn,
Renzo di Renzo, Carlos Mustiennes, Santiago Fernández Stelley,
Greg Basdevant, Morgan Sheasby, Michel Mallard,
Raphaëlle Stopin, Richard Buckley.

Thanks to those at Televisa for granting access and making this project possible:
Mauricio Maillé, Adriana Patiño Flores,
Fernanda Monterde Gabilondo, Olivia Flores González,
Jannett Guerrero.

Thanks to those who exhibited the work:
Pippa Oldfield & Anne McNeill at Impressions Gallery, UK;
Leticia Clouthier & Isabel Alvarenga at Instituto Cultural de México, Paris;
Caroll Taveras & Megan Ziegler-Haynes at F.L.O.A.T. Gallery;
Bonnie Rubenstein at CONTACT Photo Festival;
Christina Faesler and Jerónimo Hagerman.

Thanks also to those who helped in the making of the book:
Natalie Espinosa, Maxwell Anderson, Matt Harvey, Ali Esen,
Gregory Dechant, Jessica Palazzo, Phillip Heying;
Brian Dowling at BD Images, London; August Pross, Justin King,
& Bernard Da Silva at LTI NY; LMI Lab, Mexico City.

Thanks to the following for their help and support:
Damian Prado, Diego Perez, Patricia Alpizar Ruiz, Ramiro Chaves,
José Alonso Crespo, Juan Carlos Valdez Dragonne, Pavka Segura,
Erwan Fichou, Bernardo Loyola, Emmanuel Picault, Leila Smara,
Gil Blank, Jason Evans, Shubhankar Ray, James Reid, Nick Griffiths,
Trevor Jackson, Monica Allende, François Renié, Stuart Smith,
Gerardo Montiel Klint, Carlos Alvarez Montero, Dana Lixenberg,
Jacqueline Hassink, Rainbow Blue Nelson, Charles Fréger and
the members of P.O.C., Alain-Paul Mallard, Thomas Bonnouvrier
& Margaux Nelkin at Art and Commerce.

A special thanks to all of the actors and students who allowed me
to photograph them and all of the studio technicians and workers.
Without them this project would not have been possible.

And, of course, thanks to my family.

The Factory of Dreams: Inside Televisa Studios
Photographs by Stefan Ruiz
Essay by Pablo Helguera

Front cover: Daniel Cortés, CEA, Televisa Acting School, 2004

Editor: Denise Wolff
Designer: Studio Fernando Gutiérrez
Production: Matthew Harvey
Copyeditor: Brook Wilensky-Lanford
Work Scholars: Terri Beckles, Andree Gonzalez-Falla, Allison Hall, Samantha Marlow

All plot synopses and character descriptions are from Televisa's promotional materials and website, www.esmas.com.

First edition
Printed in China
10 9 8 7 6 5 4 3 2 1

Library of Congress Control Number: 2011944745
ISBN 978-1-59711-201-7

Aperture Foundation books are available in North America through:

ARTBOOK | D.A.P.
155 Sixth Avenue, 2nd Floor
New York, N.Y. 10013
Phone: (212) 627-1999
Fax: (212) 627-9484
Email: orders@dapinc.com
www.artbook.com

Aperture Foundation books are distributed outside North America by:

Thames & Hudson
181A High Holborn
London WC1V 7QX
United Kingdom
Phone: + 44 20 7845 5000
Fax: + 44 20 7845 5055
Email: sales@thameshudson.co.uk
www.thamesandhudson.com

aperturefoundation
547 West 27th Street
New York, N.Y. 10001
www.aperture.org

Aperture, a not-for-profit foundation, connects the photo community and its audiences with the most inspiring work, the sharpest ideas, and with each other—in print, in person, and online.